Rape, Gender and Class

Ellen Daly

Rape, Gender and Class

Intersections in Courtroom Narratives

Ellen Daly
Policing Institute for the Eastern
Region
Anglia Ruskin University
Chelmsford, UK

ISBN 978-3-030-93924-3   ISBN 978-3-030-93925-0   (eBook)
https://doi.org/10.1007/978-3-030-93925-0

This Palgrave Macmillan imprint is published by the registered company Springer Nature
Switzerland AG
The registered company address is: Gewerbestrasse 11, 6330 Cham, Switzerland

CONTENTS

ABBREVIATIONS

ABE   Achieving Best Evidence [Interview]
CJS   Criminal Justice System
CPS   Crown Prosecution Service
CWJ   Centre for Women's Justice
EVAW   End Violence Against Women Coalition
MoJ   Ministry of Justice
OIC   [Police] Officer in the Case

LIST OF TABLES

CHAPTER 1

Introduction

Abstract This chapter sets out the rationale for the research and how it was done. It also defines some of the key terminology used throughout.

Keywords Rape myths · Court · Rape trials · Court observations

BACKGROUND AND CONTEXT

I write this book at a time when victim-survivors of rape in England and Wales who choose to report to the police have lower than a 2% chance of seeing a charge brought in their case and many of those do not see a conviction (HM Government, 2021). The situation is not dissimilar in other parts of the Westernised world where attrition has long been recognised as a problem (K. Daly & Bouhours, 2010) and prosecution rates have continued to fall through the 2010s, such as in Australia (Schwarz, 2021), Aotearoa New Zealand (RNZ, 2021), Northern Ireland (Harte, 2020), and Scotland (Scottish Government, 2020). Whilst the UK Government, following an end-to-end review of criminal justice responses to rape, has apologised for failing victim-survivors (HM Government, 2021), their recommendations for change have left campaigners dissatisfied and concerned that real change remains a long way off (EVAW, 2021). One of the criticisms levied at the review was its lack of engagement with victim-survivors (Topping, 2021). By consequence of this minimal engagement with victim-survivors, there cannot have been a proper consideration of the structural inequalities that differently impact minoritised and marginalised victim-survivors' ability to access justice. Such considerations are crucial because whilst conviction rates as a whole are inexcusably low, they are even lower for those from minoritised and marginalised groups.

Criminal justice statistics are not routinely collected or broken down in ways that enable proper exploration of underlying complexities and links to social inequalities (Parmar, 2017), but the few studies that have explored this in relation to sexual violence paint a bleak picture. Black and Asian victim-survivors, for example, see lower conviction rates than do white victim-survivors, with Black victim-survivors being the least likely to have their case end in a conviction (Lovett et al., 2007; Munro & Kelly, 2009). Such disparities in conviction rates are reflected in other marginalised groups too. For example, the conviction rate for disabled victim-survivors has been found to be half that of their non-disabled counterparts (Kelly et al., 2005; see also Harris & Grace, 1999), and Hester (2013) found that having a mental health condition significantly lowered the chance of conviction (see also Stanko & Williams, 2009). Similarly, Lovett et al. (2007) found that unemployed victim-survivors saw lower conviction rates, as did victim-survivors who were classed as living in vulnerable housing, both of which are often associated with mental illness (Savage, 2016; Trades Union Congress, 2017) and could also be indicators of low socioeconomic positioning.

Whilst rape myths are commonly used as an explanatory model for low conviction rates (Dinos et al. 2015; Temkin & Krahé, 2008; Willmott et al., 2017), they alone cannot explain the disparities in conviction rates for minoritised and marginalised groups. Research examining police and CPS decision-making in rape cases shines a light on the role of perceived victim-survivor credibility and the role of various systems of oppression in shaping those decisions. For example, victim-survivors with mental health conditions have repeatedly been found to have a higher chance of their cases being dropped due to police or CPS decision-making (Ellison et al., 2015; Stanko & Williams, 2009). The research by Ellison et al. (2015) strongly indicated that these decisions were influenced by stereotypes and prejudices regarding mental health and misconceptions about credibility. Indeed, Hester (2013) noted that police officers commented on the credibility of victim-survivors with mental health conditions, stating that they perceived them as "difficult to understand, confused or even delusional" (p. 13). Likewise, McMillan (2018) found that police officers in her sample often referenced victim-survivors' mental health when considering whether a complaint was a 'false' allegation. Harris and Grace (1999) similarly found that victim-survivors with a learning disability or mental health condition who had their cases dropped at the police stage did so because they were deemed to have made false allegations or would not make a credible witness. Indeed, disabled victim-survivors in Kelly et al.'s (2005) study were twice as likely as non-disabled victim-survivors to have their report recorded as false. Earlier studies also found similar references to mental ill-health, delusions, and 'unstable females' (Gregory & Lees, 1996; Lea et al., 2003), demonstrating the persistence and pervasiveness of such narratives. This is a deeply embedded notion that has long been reflected across multiple Westernised jurisdictions, often reflected through 'unstable women' narratives (e.g. Aiken, 1993; Ellison & Munro, 2010; Minch & Linden, 1987; Raitt & Zeedyk, 2003).

Court observations from 2012 indicated that such narratives often appear alongside rape myths in sexual offences trials (Smith, 2018). Smith's (2018) analysis delineated individual trial narratives related to social class, disability, race, ethnicity, and nationality stereotyping. The stereotyping interlinked with rape myth narratives to bolster defence counsel's undermining of victim-survivors' credibility (Smith, 2018). Given that we know minoritised and marginalised victim-survivors have a lower chance of seeing a conviction in their case, it is crucial that we develop an understanding of what the mechanisms behind this could be at *all* stages of the CJS. The importance of researching and understanding what goes on within the courtroom has been underlined by women's organisations (EVAW, 2021). A further, more contemporary exploration of the role of oppressive cultural narratives in sexual offences trials was therefore warranted to aid in developing this understanding, and this is what the study set out in this book sought to do.

Given that the vast majority of rape cases do not make it to court, the pertinence of researching rape trials may not seem immediately clear. Jury trials hold a symbolic function in the English and Welsh CJS (Smith, 2018) because trial by jury is considered its fundamental cornerstone (Carrabine, 2014; Harper, 2021). Despite this significance, the courtroom remains under-researched compared to earlier stages of the CJS, especially with regard to sexual violence (Smith, 2020). Even though most criminal cases are resolved outside of the Crown Court (MoJ,

2018), the *possibility* for jury trial shapes the preceding points of the CJS, such as police investigation and the gathering of evidence. Assumptions about what may happen in court can therefore inform earlier decisions in the criminal justice process, such as the decision not to prosecute (Brown et al., 2010; CWJ, 2020; Smith & Daly, 2020). With regard to this project specifically, the courtroom was the best place to observe what overarching narratives were formed around victim-survivors and defendants and how they were being constructed.

A NOTE ON 'VICTIM-SURVIVOR' TERMINOLOGY

Although the term 'complainant' is used within the trial process, throughout this book I use the term 'victim-survivor' to refer to those who have been subjected to sexual violence. I decided against using 'complainant' because it does not reflect the very real prospect of revictimisation in court (Jordan, 2013; Temkin & Kráhe, 2008). There is extensive debate among feminist scholars and activists about what terminology is preferable, often positioning the terms 'victim' and 'survivor' as binary. The term 'victim' is often thought to hold negative connotations and position women as passive and powerless, whereas the term 'survivor' is considered to acknowledge victimisation and the agency required to cope with and resist violent oppression (Barry, 1979; Kelly, 1988; Profitt, 1996). Research with those who have been subjected to male violence reveals, however, that this dichotomy is problematic because it does not acknowledge the complexities in navigating the victim and survivor identities, which are not necessarily static nor are they mutually exclusive (Dunn, 2005; Dunn & Creek, 2015; Leisenring, 2006; Papendick & Bohner, 2017). I have therefore chosen to use 'victim-survivor' because it captures that people who have been victimised do not uniformly choose 'victim' or 'survivor'.

Using the term 'victim-survivor' incorporates the advantages of Boyle's (2018) continuum thinking, which unlike a linear journey from 'victim' to 'survivor' recognises that "an individual's movement across this continuum is not uni-directional or strictly chronological" (p. 8). That is, as with Kelly's (1988) original concept of the continuum of sexual violence, women can be positioned at any point along the continuum at any point in time regardless of the points they have been at previously. The concept of a continuum captures the interconnectedness and fluidity of women's self in relation to their experiences, that the victim and survivor identities cannot necessarily be easily distinguished from one another. This conceptualisation recognises that women can identify as a victim or as a survivor or both simultaneously at any time in her life during or after victimisation; she can feel like a survivor one minute and like a victim the next; she can feel like both at the same time.

There remain limitations to using the 'victim-survivor' term to categorise the collective of women who have been subjected to male violence; it cannot, for example, easily capture those who reject both terms or those who feel they have transcended survivorship (Young & Maguire, 2003). Nevertheless, the victim-survivor continuum is flexible and can encapsulate a diverse range of lived experiences and thus seems least likely to impose unwanted labels onto the individuals I observed.

THE STUDY

The research I present in this book comes from court observations that aimed to explore whether rape myths were still common in rape trial narratives, how they were being used, and what role cultural assumptions and stereotypes played in the overarching trial narratives. Court observations are an underused research method, likely due to their time and resource intensive nature, but they are an incredibly useful and important tool for understanding what actually happens inside the courtroom (Smith, 2020). Using court observations as opposed to interviews or surveys was especially advantageous for this research because observing trials in full provided essential context that enabled overarching and subtle narratives to be identified. Whilst useful for triangulation, using survey or interview methods in this case would not have elicited the same depth and nuance as observations because interview and survey participants would not have been able to remember the necessary level of detail and may have been unwilling to describe potentially controversial behaviour (Robson & McCartan, 2016).

The *Contempt of Court Act 1981* prohibits the use of recording equipment in court; therefore, data must be recorded by hand. I recorded my data using speedwriting code to increase efficiency and ability to record verbatim quotes from participants as much as possible. I predetermined the focus for verbatim notes, for example focusing on barristers' questions, and data collection proforma were used to ensure consistent recording of important data (Burman et al., 2007; Smith, 2020).

There are complex ethical considerations with court observations, which are thoughtfully engaged with by Smith (2020). To summarise, court trials fall within the public domain (Baldwin, 2008), and as such, it is not deemed necessary to gain informed consent from those involved in the trial. This does not mean, however, that there is no ethical dilemma here because, as Smith (2018) points out, private matters are being discussed in the courtroom. Furthermore, even if a researcher were to attempt to gain informed consent from all participants, it would be practically impossible because of the public nature of the courtroom—members of the public are generally able to enter and leave the public gallery at any time (Smith, 2020). Following Smith (2020), I therefore sought permission from the judge, via court staff, to take notes in the public gallery and had an information sheet available for any participants who requested further information (though none did).

I observed six trials in 2019 across three courts in the East of England. The key attributes of each case are set out below and in Table 1.1. Whilst other rape trial observation studies have had larger samples, my observations were taking place at a time where the number of rape prosecutions was dramatically falling (CWJ et al., 2020) which made a larger sample difficult to achieve. That said, all six of my observed trials were 'full trials'; that is, they went all the way through to jury deliberations and verdicts, which was not always the case in other observation studies (Smith, 2020). The trials lasted between three and seven days (excluding jury deliberations). This created a large amount of rich data, with an average of 112 pages of typed data per trial. The trials observed were not limited to rape charges, nor were they limited to adult or child offences only. Whilst it has been argued that child and adult sexual offences trials are fundamentally different, I wanted to explore any commonalities in the way narratives were formed. Indeed, my observations did demonstrate that there are important overlaps in the narratives constructed at trial.

The Trials

Table 1.1 sets out key attributes of each trial for quick reference; however, it is beneficial to also provide a broader context for each trial to enable better understanding of the narratives highlighted throughout the book. This section therefore outlines the central prosecution and defence arguments of each trial.

Table 1.1 Case characteristics

Trial	Indictments	Victim-survivor and defendant relationship at time of incident	Victim-survivor demographics[a] at time of trial	Defendant demographics at time of trial	Special measures	Defendant gave live evidence	Verdict
T1	2 × rape	Long-time friends	Female, early 20s, white	Male, early 20s, white	ABE, screens	Yes	Not guilty on both counts
T2	1 × rape	Co-habiting relationship	Female, early 20s, white	Male, early 30s, white	None	Yes	Not guilty
T3	2 × sexual assault	Online acquaintances	Female, 30s, white	Male, 40s, white	Screens	Yes	Guilty (by majority) on both counts
T4	6 × rape 1 × kidnap 1 × assault	Ex-partners	Female, 40s, white, learning disability	Male, 40s, white, learning disability suggested by judge/defence	Screens, intermediary	No	Guilty on 2 × rape. Guilty on assault. Crown offered no evidence on kidnap 4 × assault/criminal damage guilty pleas at outset of trial related to domestic violence against victim-survivor
T5	3 × sexual assault of child U13 1 × causing or inciting sexual activity with child U13	Defendant was the victim-survivor's mother's long-term partner	Male, under 10, white	Male, 40s, white	Live link, removal of wigs and gowns, intermediary	Yes	Not guilty on all counts

(continued)

Table 1.1 (continued)

Trial	Indictments	Victim-survivor and defendant relationship at time of incident	Victim-survivor demographics[a] at time of trial	Defendant demographics at time of trial	Special measures	Defendant gave live evidence	Verdict
T6	2 × indecent assault 5 × sexual assault 6 × sexual activity with a child	Victim-survivors were 2 sisters. Defendant was a friend/partner of their mother. Defendant was later victim-survivorl's partner	Females, late 20s and early 30s, white	Male, 50s, white	Live link, removal of wigs and gowns, intermediary	Yes	Not guilty on all counts

[a]Precise ages are not given to help protect identities; ethnicity was not explicitly stated; only explicitly mentioned disabilities were noted and no visible physical disabilities were observed

Trial 1

Prosecution: The prosecution case was that on two separate occasions the defendant initiated penetrative sex with the victim-survivor whilst she slept after they had been out drinking heavily together. The prosecution argued that because the victim-survivor was asleep she could not have consented, nor could the defendant have reasonably believed she was consenting, and therefore, it was rape. The victim-survivor resisted when she was roused from sleep and the defendant stopped on one occasion and continued on the latter occasion. The victim-survivor did not fully rouse from sleep because she was tired and drunk.

Defence: The defence case was that the sex happened but that it was consensual. Their arguments centred on 'regretted drunken sex'.

Trial 2

Prosecution: The prosecution case was that the defendant initiated penetrative sex with the victim-survivor and despite her verbal and physical resistance he continued; therefore, it was rape. There was digital evidence that the prosecution argued amounted to the defendant admitting and apologising for rape.

Defence: The defence case was that the defendant did not remember the specific incident but had never had non-consensual sex with the victim-survivor. They focused on undermining the digital evidence and providing a motive for lying.

Trial 3

Prosecution: The defendant 'catfished' the victim-survivor, creating two false identities for himself: (a) the 'catfish' identity he presented online and (b) a masseur sent on behalf of the first identity. The prosecution case was that under the pretence of a massage the defendant sexually assaulted the victim-survivor by touching her breasts and by digitally penetrating her vagina. The victim-survivor acquiesced to the breast touching because she thought it was part of a professional massage but did not consent to digital penetration. Because the defendant had entered her home under false pretences as a 'masseur', the breast touching amounted to sexual assault because the victim-survivor's consent had been vitiated by that deception.

Defence: The defendant admitted deceiving the victim-survivor and agreed that the massage occurred. The defence case was that no sexual touching occurred during the massage.

Trial 4
Prosecution: The prosecution case was that the victim-survivor had sex (oral and vaginal) with the defendant over the course of two days, but that none of it was consensual because she was scared of the defendant due to the domestic abuse he had subjected her to.
Defence: The defence argued that the victim-survivor consented, and that the defendant could reasonably believe that the victim-survivor was consenting because she acted like a willing participant.

Trial 5
Prosecution: The prosecution case was that on several occasions the defendant had sexually assaulted the victim-survivor (a pre-pubescent child) whilst in the child's home.
Defence: The defence case was that none of the touching happened and the victim-survivor was lying.

Trial 6
Prosecution: This was a historic case. The prosecution case was that the defendant had raped and sexually assaulted both victim-survivors multiple times throughout their teenage years whilst under the age of consent.
Defence: The defence case was that the allegations relating to victim-survivor2 were entirely false. In relation to victim-survivor1, the defendant's case was that he had engaged in sexual activity with her, but that it only happened after she reached the legal age of consent.

STRUCTURE OF THE BOOK

The remaining chapters in the book set out the main findings of the study and discuss some of the key implications of the research. Chapter 2 presents my observations specifically relating to rape myths, demonstrating that they continue to permeate courtroom narratives in sexual offences trials. This sets the foundation for Chapters 3 and 4 which outline the broader cultural narratives that helped re/produce and thus reinforce rape myths. These narratives were mainly formed from problematic gendered and classed assumptions and centred around notions of respectability (Chapter 3) and trustworthiness (Chapter 4). Finally, Chapter 5 explores some of the implications for policy, practice, and future research, ultimately arguing that a nuanced understanding and appreciation of broader cultural narratives is crucial in understanding the mechanisms that work to differently undermine victim-survivors at trial and thus act as a barrier to justice.

REFERENCES

Aiken, M. M. (1993). False allegation: A concept in the context of rape. *Journal of Psychosocial Nursing and Mental Health Services, 31*(11), 15–20.

Baldwin, J. (2008). Research on the criminal courts. In R. D. King & E. Wincup (Eds.), *Doing research on crime and justice* (2nd ed., pp. 375–398). Oxford University Press.

Barry, K. (1979). *Female sexual slavery*. Prentice-Hall.

Boyle, K. (2018). What's in a name? Theorising the inter-relationships of gender and violence. *Feminist Theory, 20*(1), 19–36.

Brown, J., Horvath, M., Kelly, L., & Westmarland, N. (2010). *Connections and disconnections: Assessing evidence, knowledge and practice in responses to rape* (Project Report). Government Equalities Office.

Burman, M., Jamieson, L., Nicholson, J., & Brooks, O. (2007). *Impact of aspects of the law of evidence in sexual offence trials: An evaluation study*. Scottish Government.

Carrabine, E. (2014). *Criminology: A sociological introduction* (3rd ed.). Routledge.

Centre for Women's Justice. (2020). *Evidence of CPS failure on rape*. https://www.centreforwomensjustice.org.uk/news/2020/6/29/1pti6p5e19unqgl o7wd9mm68d621b7. Accessed 12 April 2021.

Centre for Women's Justice, End Violence Against Women Coalition, Imkaan, & Rape Crisis England & Wales. (2020). *The decriminalisation of rape*. https://rapecrisis.org.uk/media/2396/c-decriminalisation-of-rape-report-cwj-evaw-imkaan-rcew-nov-2020.pdf. Accessed 12 April 2021.

Daly, K., & Bouhours, B. (2010). Rape and attrition in the legal process: A comparative analysis of five countries. *Crime and Justice, 39*(1), 565–650.

Dinos, S., Burrowes, N., Hammond, K., & Cunliffe, C. (2015). A systematic review of juries' assessment of rape victims: Do rape myths impact on juror decision-making? *International Journal of Law, Crime and Justice, 43*(1), 36–49.

Dunn, J. L. (2005). Victims' and 'survivors': Emerging vocabularies of motive for 'battered women who stay'. *Sociological Inquiry, 75*(1), 1–30.

Dunn, J. L., & Creek, S. J. (2015). Identity dilemmas: Toward a more situated understanding. *Symbolic Interaction, 38*(2), 261–284.

Ellison, L., & Munro, V. (2010). A stranger in the bushes, or an elephant in the room? Critical reflections upon received rape myth wisdom in the context of a Mock Jury study. *New Criminal Law Review, 13*(4), 781–801.

Ellison, L., Munro, V., Hohl, K., & Wallang, P. (2015). Challenging criminal justice? Psychosocial disability and rape victimization. *Criminology & Criminal Justice, 15*(2), 225–244.

End Violence Against Women Coalition. (2021). *Leading women's groups deeply disappointed with lack of ambition in government's rape review*. https://

www.endviolenceagainstwomen.org.uk/leading-womens-groups-deeply-dis
appointed-with-lack-of-ambition-in-governments-rape-review-2/. Accessed 1
October 2021.

Gregory, J., & Lees, S. (1996). Attrition in rape and sexual assault cases. *British Journal of Criminology, 36*(1), 1–17.

Harper, J. (2021). Jury trials: A cornerstone of the rule of law? *New Law Journal,* 7924.

Harris, J., & Grace, S. (1999). *A question of evidence? Investigating and prosecuting rape in the 1990s* (No. 196). Home Office.

Harte, L. (2020). PPS report 'shows rape victims are being let down' by justice system in Northern Ireland. *Belfast Telegraph.* https://www.belfasttelegraph.co.uk/news/northern-ireland/pps-report-shows-rape-victims-are-being-let-down-by-justice-system-in-northern-ireland-39712516.html. Accessed 22 July 2021.

Hester, M. (2013). *From report to court: Rape cases and the criminal justice system in the Northeast.* University of Bristol in association with the Northern Rock Foundation.

HM Government. (2021). *The end-to-end rape review report on findings and actions.* https://assets.publishing.service.gov.uk/government/uploads/system/uploads/attachment_data/file/1001417/end-to-end-rape-review-report-with-correction-slip.pdf. Accessed 1 October 2021.

Jordan, J. (2013). From victim to survivor—And from survivor to victim: Reconceptualising the survivor journey. *Sexual Abuse in Australia and New Zealand, 5*(2), 48–56.

Kelly, L. (1988). *Surviving sexual violence.* Polity Press.

Kelly, L., Lovett, J., & Regan, L. (2005). *A gap or a chasm? Attrition in reported rape cases.* Home Office.

Lea, S. J., Lanvers, U., & Shaw, S. (2003). Attrition in rape cases. Developing a profile and identifying relevant factors. *The British Journal of Criminology, 43*(3), 583–599.

Leisenring, A. (2006). Confronting 'victim' discourses: The identity work of battered women. *Symbolic Interaction, 29*(3), 307–330.

Lovett, J., Uzelac, G., Horvath, M., & Kelly, L. (2007). *Rape in the 21st Century: Old behaviours, new contexts and emerging patterns.* Economic and Social Research Council.

McMillan, L. (2018). Police officers' perceptions of false allegations of rape. *Journal of Gender Studies, 27*(1), 9–21.

Minch, C., & Linden, R. (1987). Attrition in the processing of rape cases. *Canadian Journal of Criminology, 29*(4), 389.

Ministry of Justice. (2018). *Criminal court statistics quarterly, England and Wales,* January to March 2018 (annual 2017). https://assets.publishing.

service.gov.uk/government/uploads/system/uploads/attachment_data/file/ 720026/ccsq-bulletin-jan-mar-2018.pdf. Accessed 16 March 2019.

Munro, V., & Kelly, L. (2009). A vicious cycle? Attrition and conviction patterns in contemporary rape cases in England and Wales. In M. Horvath & J. Brown (Eds.), *Rape: Challenging contemporary thinking* (pp. 281–300). Willan.

Papendick, M., & Bohner, G. (2017). 'Passive victim—Strong survivor'? Perceived meaning of labels applied to women who were raped. *PLoS One, 12*(5), e0177550.

Parmar, A. (2017). Intersectionality, British criminology and race: Are we there yet? *Theoretical Criminology, 21*(1), 35–45.

Profitt, N. J. (1996). 'Battered women' as 'victims' and 'survivors': Creating space for resistance. *Canadian Social Work Review, 13*(1), 23–38.

Raitt, F. E., & Zeedyk, M. S. (2003). False memory syndrome: Undermining the credibility of complainants in sexual offences. *International Journal of Law and Psychiatry, 26*(5), 453–471.

RNZ. (2021). Low rape conviction rate shows system is failing—Women's Refuge. *RNZ.* https://www.rnz.co.nz/news/national/439802/low-rape-conviction-rate-shows-system-is-failing-women-s-refuge. Accessed 22 July 2021.

Robson, C., & McCartan, K. (2016). *Real world research: A resource for users of social research methods in applied settings* (4th ed.). Wiley.

Savage, J. (2016). *Mental health and housing.* Mental Health Foundation.

Schwarz, K. (2021). Barriers to justice: 'We are still governed by the idea that women lie about sexual assault'. *The Guardian.* https://www.theguardian.com/society/2021/mar/20/barriers-to-justice-we-are-still-governed-by-the-idea-that-women-lie-about-sexual-assault. Accessed 22 July 2021.

Scottish Government. (2020). *Criminal proceedings in Scotland: 2018–2019.* Scottish Government. https://www.gov.scot/publications/criminal-proceedings-scotland-2018-19/pages/4/. Accessed 22 July 2021.

Smith, O. (2018). *Rape trials in England and Wales: Observing justice and rethinking rape myths.* Palgrave Macmillan.

Smith, O. (2020). *Researching English sexual violence trials using court observation methods: Research methods cases Part 1.* Sage.

Smith, O., & Daly, E. (2020). *Evaluation of the sexual violence complainants' advocate scheme.* Loughborough University.

Stanko, B., & Williams, E. (2009). Reviewing rape and rape allegations in London: What are the vulnerabilities of the victims who report to the police? In M. Horvath & J. Brown (Eds.), *Rape: Challenging contemporary thinking* (pp. 207–225). Willan.

Temkin, J., & Krahé, B. (2008). *Sexual assault and the justice gap.* Hart.

Topping, A. (2021). Rape prosecution review failed to engage with victims, say survivor groups. *The Guardian.* https://www.theguardian.com/society/

2021/may/27/rape-prosecution-review-failed-to-engage-with-victims-say-sur vivor-groups. Accessed 23 September 2021.

Trades Union Congress. (2017). *Mental health and employment.* Trades Union Congress.

Willmott, D., Boduszek, D., & Booth, N. (2017). The English Jury on trial. *Custodial Review, 82,* 12–14.

Young, S. L., & Maguire, K. C. (2003). Talking about sexual violence. *Women and Language, 26*(2), 40.

CHAPTER 2

Rape Myths in the Courtroom

Abstract I use observations of English sexual offences trials from 2019 to show that rape myths remain prevalent in courtroom narratives and are often deployed with subtlety. Problematic ideas reflected in the trial narratives related to: the expectation of victim-survivor resistance; pre- and post-assault relationships between victim-survivors and defendants; the expectation of prompt reporting of assaults; and the expectation that victim-survivors provide consistent and detailed accounts. The chapter also outlines the role of digital evidence as a tool for reinforcing rape myth narratives.

Keywords Rape myths · Court · Rape trials · Digital evidence

An Introduction to Rape Myths

Rape myths are "descriptive or prescriptive beliefs about rape...that serve to deny, downplay or justify sexual violence that men commit against women" (Bohner, 1998 cited in Gerger et al., 2007, p. 423). The recognition of the function of rape myths in this definition is key; it views their function as to blame the victim-survivor for the rape, express disbelief that rape has occurred, and exonerate the perpetrator (Eyssel & Bohner, 2008; Lonsway & Fitzgerald, 1994). Rape myths therefore legitimise sexual violence against women and in doing so reinforce patriarchal ideologies that position women as subordinate to men (Edwards et al., 2011). The ways in which rape myths are expressed have changed over time as society has begun to take sexual violence more seriously; however, the functions have not changed. Contemporary rape myths therefore tend to be expressed more subtly than in the past in order for them to appear more socially acceptable (Eyssel & Bohner, 2008; McMahon & Farmer, 2011). Indeed, this change to subtlety over time has also been observed with sexism more generally, as well as racism (Akrami et al., 2000; Ellemers & Barreto, 2009; Swim et al., 1995). The subtlety of contemporary prejudicial attitudes makes them harder to recognise, which by consequence makes the underlying systems of oppression more resistant to change (Ellemers & Barreto, 2009). The significance of such subtleties and their relationship to rape myths will be explored throughout Chapters 3 and 4; this chapter therefore first establishes how rape myths were deployed in practice in the trials I observed.

Whilst rape myths are numerous and cannot easily be captured as an exhaustive and definitive list, some common examples are set out in Table 2.1 to provide context. The majority of the rape myths in Table 2.1 fit the 'real rape' and 'ideal victim' stereotypes. In the late-1980s, Estrich (1987) outlined the 'real rape' stereotype as a rape perpetrated by a stranger in an outdoor or public place using physical force and violence that the victim-survivor actively attempts to resist. Estrich (1987) argued that this scenario was not the usual reality of rape, and indeed, contemporary research shows that most perpetrators of rape are known to the victim-survivor (Feist et al., 2007; Kelly et al., 2005; MoJ, Home Office and Office for National Statistics, 2013). As there is a stereotype of what a 'real rape' looks like, there is also a stereotype of what an 'ideal victim' looks like. Christie (1986) surmised that the 'ideal victim' is virtuous, blameless, and weak in relation to the perpetrator. This can lead to victim-blaming attitudes when a case involves, for example, a victim-survivor who wore revealing clothing, had consumed alcohol, or had mental health problems (Burt, 1980; Grubb & Turner, 2012; Horvath & Brown, 2006; Kelly et al., 2005; Koss & Harvey, 1987; Lonsway & Fitzgerald, 1994; Sims et al., 2007). Some of Christie's (1986) picture of the ideal victim overlaps with Estrich's (1987) 'real rape' in that the perpetrator is a stranger and is physically strong or intimidating. Further beliefs about the 'ideal victim' include that they report to the police immediately and that

Table 2.1 Common examples of rape myths and their functions. Adapted from Temkin (2010), Eyssel and Bohner (2008), and Burrowes (2013)

Function of myth	Common examples
Blames the victim	Someone who is drunk or has taken drugs has put themselves in a dangerous situation and is at least partly to blame for being raped
	Women are asking to be raped by the way they dress or act
	People working in prostitution cannot be raped
Exonerates the perpetrator	If someone has consented to sex previously or has consented to other sexual acts, it was not rape
	Women expect men to take the lead in sexual interactions so they say 'no' when they really mean 'yes'
	If a woman invites a man over to her house, it means she wants sex
	Putting pressure on a partner for sex isn't rape
	Rape happens because men cannot help themselves once they are sexually aroused
Expresses disbelief	Rape is rare and is usually committed by strangers outside or in public places. It involves physical force and violence, or threats thereof
	It cannot be rape if someone does not scream and attempt to fight back or if they do not have physical injuries as a result of the rape
	Only deviant men are rapists. Men from certain backgrounds are more likely to be rapists (e.g. Black men or working-class men)
	False allegations of rape are common. Women often lie because they regret having sex or they want revenge or attention
	People who have been raped report it immediately. They always give a consistent and thorough account and will be visibly upset

they remember the event clearly and can therefore recount the experience with perfect consistency each time (Burt, 1980; Gerger et al., 2007; Lees, 2002; Lonsway & Fitzgerald, 1994). In fact, evidence shows that victim-survivors often delay reporting to the police (Temkin, 2010), if they choose to report at all, and that traumatic experiences tend to impair memory (Hohl & Conway, 2017).

Although the evidence base relating to rape myths is vast and widely accepted, it is not without its detractors. Reece (2013) extensively critiqued the concept of rape myths, arguing that their prevalence and effect had been overstated. She reasoned that some of the commonly discussed rape myths are in fact not myths because they cannot be proven to be false or can in some instances be true (see also Gurnham, 2016). As Conaghan and Russell (2014) pointed out in their robust appraisal of Reece's arguments, this ignored the more contemporary conceptualisations of rape myths, such as the definition provided at the outset of this chapter, which departed from declaring rape myths 'false beliefs'. Indeed, that was precisely why Lonsway and Fitzgerald (1994, pp. 134–135) added the qualifier "generally" false to their definition, contending that "the truth value of any of these statements in a particular situation is not as significant as the fact that they tend to be universally applied".

There is a wealth of research that suggests rape myth acceptance is relatively high within the general population (see, for example, Bohner et al., 2009; EVAW, 2018; Gerger et al., 2007), and rape myths have long been pointed to as an explanation for poor criminal justice responses to rape (Harris & Grace, 1999; Hohl & Stanko, 2015; Kelly et al., 2005; Temkin & Krahé, 2008). Indeed, court observation studies have, over decades, consistently found that rape myths are deployed with frequency by barristers in sexual violence trials (Adler, 1987; Burman et al., 2007; Durham et al., 2017; Lees, 2002; Smith & Skinner, 2017; Temkin et al., 2018). A large amount of mock jury research has, therefore, explored the idea that jurors may hold prejudicial views that influence their deliberations. Overwhelmingly, that research concludes that juror decision-making *is* influenced by rape myths (see Leverick, 2020 for a review). This is, however, contested by some scholars, who claim that mock jury methodologies cannot be assumed to be reflective of 'real' jurors (Thomas, 2020).

Notably, Thomas (2020) was permitted to conduct research with real jurors in England and Wales (access to juries for research purposes has very rarely been allowed). Thomas' research involved asking people who had just finished serving on a jury whether they agreed with rape myth statements. Most of the jurors overwhelmingly said they did not 'Agree' with the rape myth statements. Thomas therefore asserted that claims that jurors believe rape myths are unfounded. Whilst this research is important and significant, the methodology used cannot justify the sweeping claim that jurors do not believe rape myths, nor can it undermine the decades of research that came before it. Robust critiques detailing why this is have been made elsewhere (Daly et al., 2021; Chalmers et al., 2021). Of particular pertinence for my argument in this chapter is that the statements the jurors in Thomas' (2020) study were asked about were overt examples of rape myths, such as: "If a person doesn't physically fight back, you can't really say it was a rape" and "If a woman sends seriously explicit texts or messages to a man she should not accuse him of rape later on". As has been shown in previous court observation studies, rape myths are rarely deployed so overtly by barristers in court (Smith & Skinner, 2017; Temkin et al., 2018). The observations I set out in this chapter demonstrate that this remained the case in 2019, which is when Thomas' (2020) research was conducted. This means that the jurors in Thomas' (2020) study were not asked about rape myths in a way that reflects how they have been consistently shown to be deployed at trial, including up to the time of Thomas' research (see Daly et al., 2021).

Finally, it has also been argued that juror acceptance of rape myths is irrelevant because most cases do not reach trial (Wolchover & Heaton-Armstrong, 2008). This assertion, however, overlooks the wider cultural implications of rape myth acceptance because it ignores, for example, a victim-survivor's capacity to know that rape myths may impact trial outcomes and thus decide not to seek criminal justice (Daly & Smith, forthcoming). It also ignores that decisions at earlier stages of the criminal justice process can be influenced by predictions of how jurors may view a case (Brown et al. 2010; Smith & Daly, 2020). Studies have repeatedly found that police and prosecutors make decisions on this basis, although a recent judicial review in England and Wales brought by the CWJ found that the CPS had not returned to a 'bookmakers approach' (*EVAWC v DPP* [2021] EWCA Civ 350). Crucially though, whilst the evidence presented by the CWJ fell short of satisfying the Court of Appeal that there had been a change in policy, their evidence clearly indicates that decisions *have* been made by prosecutors on the basis of jury predictions (see also evidence in Smith & Daly, 2020).

How Are Rape Myths Deployed in Practice in Contemporary Trials?

Trial observations are a helpful way to determine how rape myths are deployed in practice at trial. Not only do observations avoid some of the limitations of survey and interview methods, such as social desirability response bias (Fisher, 1993), but they also enable the researcher to consider the overarching trial narratives as a whole. As will become clear throughout this book, a holistic view of trial narratives is important because rape myths are not deployed in simplistic or overt terms; rather they, and the broader narratives that re/produce them, are subtly (though not always so) interwoven throughout and may not always be immediately obvious until viewed as part of the whole.

Rape myths featured in every trial I observed, and the remainder of this chapter sets out some of the ways they were deployed by barristers. In line with previous observation studies in England and Wales (Lees, 2002; Smith, 2018; Temkin et al., 2018), the trials I observed were permeated by problematic ideas relating to: the expectation of victim-survivor resistance; pre- and post-assault relationships between victim-survivors and defendants; the expectation of prompt reporting of assaults; and the expectation that victim-survivors provide consistent and detailed accounts.

The Expectation of Victim-Survivor Resistance

The expectation of victim-survivor resistance stems from the 'real rape' stereotype that says women who are raped call out for help, try to fight off their attacker, and sustain injury as a result. Rape laws in England and Wales were historically constructed based on this assumption (Munro, 2010). Whilst there has been a growing awareness among the public that the 'real rape' stereotype does not accurately reflect the most common experiences of rape, these narratives remain persistent. In England and Wales, there is no longer a requirement for a woman to be subjected to force and to verbally or physically resist in order to demonstrate non-consent; however, this does not preclude barristers from raising the issue at trial. Indeed, research from multiple jurisdictions frequently points to the existence of resistance narratives at rape trials and that both prosecution and defence counsel deploy them (see, for example, Burgin, 2019; Ehrlich, 2001; Smith, 2018).

Smith and Skinner (2017) argued that prosecuting barristers' reliance on resistance narratives draws on the 'real rape' stereotype and as a result legitimates the defence's use of it; Burgin (2019) made a similar argument in an Australian context. Hovdestad and Renner (2021), however, argued that the prosecution bringing evidence of a victim-survivor's resistance does not constitute a rape myth and should therefore not be seen as problematic. This is because consensual sexual encounters do not usually involve one party resisting it. The absence of resistance, however, cannot be said to indicate consent because it is known that victim-survivors often do not resist. Therefore, when defence barristers point to lack of resistance as justifying a reasonable belief in consent, they are drawing on a rape myth (Hovdestad & Renner, 2021). Hovdestad and Renner further argue that the prosecution bringing evidence of resistance does not legitimate defence arguments that are based on the 'real rape' myth. Prosecutors can therefore correctly argue that acts of resistance are *consistent* with rape and support the allegations, but defence counsel cannot correctly argue that a lack of resistance is consistent with consensual sex and therefore undermines the allegations (Hovdestad & Renner, 2021). It would be right for the defence to rebut the evidence brought by the prosecution, but if they simply point to a lack of resistance as an indicator of consent or reasonable belief then it has no relevance. That said, even when it is used in rebuttal to prosecution, the narratives relied upon may still draw on the idea that no resistance indicates consent. In T2, this was achieved by the defence barrister drawing on the problematic notion of 'token resistance'.

Drawing on the Notion of 'Token Resistance'
The resistance narrative in T2 drew on the problematic belief that women often offer 'token resistance' to sex (Edwards et al., 2011); that is, 'when women say no they really mean yes'. The idea of 'token resistance' leads to the notion of victim-survivors not having resisted *enough* for sexual activity to be non-consensual. In this trial, the victim-survivor's evidence was that she made physical and verbal resistance when the defendant (her long-term boyfriend) instigated sex. This was laid out in minute detail through the victim-survivor's evidence-in-chief and in the statement she had given to the police. The defence barrister cross-examined extensively about the exact timing of when the victim-survivor verbally resisted in relation to when the defendant penetrated her:

Defence: [You say you told him 'no get off me', it appears to me that you said it before he had actually penetrated you]
Victim-survivor: I told him to get off me.
Defence: Look at your statement, all the words that you say you said happen before he penetrated you.
Victim-survivor: No.
Judge: <Re-worded defence's question>
Victim-survivor: It says I *kept* telling him (T2).

In an attempt to further demonstrate her point, the defence barrister read out the part of the victim-survivor's police statement that detailed what had happened, and then continued her argument:

Defence: So in your statement, all the words are before.
Victim-survivor: It says I kept telling him.
Defence: But that was before.
Victim-survivor: [It says I kept telling him].
Defence: Then he replied.
Victim-survivor: Yeah and I kept telling him throughout.
Defence: Well that is a matter for the jury.
Judge: [You have to put it in the whole context].
Defence: <Reads the whole section of the statement>. [You felt him get on top, then he tried to put his penis in your vagina.] All of your words in your statement come before that part where you say he put his penis in your vagina.
Victim-survivor: Yes.
Defence: I say it was consensual. Do you agree or disagree?
Victim-survivor: Disagree (T2).

Here the defence was arguing that saying 'no' *before* the penetration took place was not an indication of non-consent. Through this questioning, the defence implied that the defendant could have reasonably believed the victim-survivor was consenting because she did not say 'no' *after* he penetrated her, which is plainly wrong and a worrying assertion. Accordingly, the judge made clear in his summing-up that the timing of the verbal resistance does not need to be after penetration. That said, it is unclear why such a line of questioning was allowed to continue when it was arguably misleading.

Burgin (2019) linked the notion of 'token resistance' to socio-sexual scripts that form a narrative of 'seduction', whereby upon hearing a woman's 'no' it becomes the man's role to persuade her to have sex, and that this constitutes a romantic interaction. In framing the victim-survivor's 'no' as being before penetration and arguing that this meant it was not rape, the defence therefore implied that the defendant had 'successfully convinced' her to consent; that is, the victim-survivor had been offering 'token resistance'. Ehrlich (1998) also noted the influence of 'token resistance' in rape trials, where she identified ways in which defendants attempted to redefine consent to fit their own narrative. Again, this is precisely what the defence in this example attempted to do in her interrogation of the timing of penetration. Also of note in this trial was that the victim-survivor had confronted the defendant about the alleged rape via digital messaging. Whilst I discuss the significance of the digital communications in this trial extensively elsewhere (Daly, 2021), I give a brief summary here to demonstrate how the messages were built into the narrative. The victim-survivor specifically questioned why the defendant had ignored her resistance, using the phrase "you climbed on top of me when I said no" (T2). The defendant did not reply to that message. The prosecution posited that because the defendant did not reply with a denial, he had effectively admitted that the victim-survivor's characterisation was accurate. The defendant therefore claimed that he thought the victim-survivor was talking about "the way I'd argue with her and stand over her" (T2), which the prosecution went on to frame as an explanation that "insults [the jury's] intelligence" (T2). In offering this alternative meaning to the victim-survivor's words, the defendant undermined the corroborative value the messages had for the prosecution case. Digital communications evidence offers an accurate record of conversations that are unaffected by the effects of time and bias on memory; however, this does not mean that it offers objective knowledge (Dodge, 2018). It is malleable and open to interpretation, which means the manner in which it is deployed and the framing that is used can make it corroborative of two conflicting stories (Hlavka & Mulla, 2018). In this case, the jury acquitted the defendant, and whilst it is not possible to know the reasoning behind the jury's decision, it is notable that the resistance narrative and the defendant's reinterpretation of the digital messaging evidence were central to the arguments throughout. Even if the jury did accept the prosecution's argument with regard to the meaning of "you climbed on top me when I said no", the not guilty verdict would mean that the verbal resistance of saying 'no' was not considered *enough* to count as non-consent, which goes back to the problematic notion of 'token resistance'.

The Role of Agency in the Construction of Resistance Narratives
The narratives employed by defence counsel in T1, T3, and T4 when drawing on the expectation of victim-survivor resistance were steeped in linguistic constructions that drew focus to the agency of the victim-survivors. This enabled barristers to make the argument that the defendants had reasonable belief in consent. The linguistic constructions of

agency and non-agency in rape trial narratives have been noted previously by other scholars. For example, Ehrlich's (2001) concept of a grammar of non-agency identifies ways in which defendants use a "variety of linguistic resources that all work to represent him as innocent of unlawful sexual acts of aggression" (p. 38). The use of particular grammatical constructions helps defendants mitigate, diffuse, and obscure their agency, as well as relocate agentive acts to the victim-survivors (Coates et al., 1994; Ehrlich, 2001). Put another way, the linguistic choices of defendants and their barristers wholly or partially remove agency from the defendant and place it with the victim-survivor, thus implying a reasonable belief in consent. The following example from T1 exemplifies this:

> *Defence*: You put a film on, then what happens?
> *Defendant*: We lay on the bed, flirting, full on kissing.
> *Defence*: Were you both fully clothed?
> *Defendant*: Yeah.
> *Defence*: Then what?
> *Defendant*: She was touching me and I was touching her back.
> *Defence*: Over or under clothes?
> *Defendant* Over at first.
> *Defence* How did it progress?
>
> …
>
> *Defendant*: More kissing, then we took our clothes off.
> *Judge*: Who took whose clothes off?
> *Defendant*: We took our own clothes off.
> *Defence*: Did you talk at all?
> *Defendant* We were talking, yes (T1).

In this exchange, the defendant framed all actions as mutual and the only time he said "I" was as a response to the victim-survivor's actions: "She was touching me and I was touching her back". Through this exchange, he placed more agency with the victim-survivor's actions, thus distancing himself from the instigation of sexual activity. This shifted the focus onto the victim-survivor's behaviour. The next example from the same part of the trial illustrates how agentless passive constructions were used by the defence barrister to form a grammar of non-agency for the defendant:

Defence: Clothing came off, her underwear was removed but she kept her
    bra on?
Defendant: Yeah (T1).

The only agency attribution in this example was placed with the
victim-survivor. Agency was placed with the defendant only where it bene-
fited his overall narrative of reasonable belief in consent, the rest of the
time a grammar of non-agency was employed. Thus, as the questioning
continued, the defendant did accept agency where it strengthened his
claim to innocence:

Defence: Did you put your penis in her vagina?
Defendant: Yes.
Defence: How long did it last?
Defendant: Not that long.
Defence: Why did it stop?
Defendant: She said she didn't want to do it.
Defence: So you stopped?
Defendant: Yes (T1).

Here the defendant acknowledged verbal resistance from the victim-
survivor (although the prosecution's case was that the victim-survivor was
asleep so could not have consented) and accepted agency (at least in part)
in stopping. By accepting his agency at this point, the defendant distanced
himself from 'rape' and 'rapist'. This was in contrast to the prosecution's
representation:

Prosecution: You said she said, 'No not now', were you having sex when
    she said that?
Defendant: Yeah.
Prosecution: I suggest you entered her while she was asleep, so you did not
    get her consent.
Defendant No, never.
Prosecution: She woke up after you had penetrated her and that's when she
    said, 'No not now'.
Defendant: No (T1).

Here the prosecution presented the victim-survivor as passive through
sleep and making the verbal resistance when she woke. The victim-
survivor was not questioned about this verbal resistance as she had not

remembered saying it and so it was not in her evidence. This extract related to the first of two alleged rapes, whereas the victim-survivor did recall making resistance in the second alleged rape, which she detailed in her ABE[1]:

> *Police*: Did you make any verbal resistance?
> *Victim-survivor* I said 'Get off' when he kept pulling my hand to him...I don't remember him saying anything.
>
> ...
>
> *Police*: So you said stop 3 times?
> *Victim-survivor*: Yeah (ABE, T1).

There was no cross-examination on this because the victim-survivor said she could no longer remember. The prosecution could have raised this part of her ABE in re-examination in order to clarify; however, whilst he did ask about the defendant pulling her hand towards him, he fell short of asking about her pulling it away. Although it was arguably implied in the victim-survivor saying "I didn't want it to happen" and it happened "several times", it was not made clear at this point that she had actively resisted by repeatedly pulling her hand away.

In contrast to the more implicit arguments in T1, the cross-examination of the victim-survivors in T3 and T4 drew directly on the misconception that women should and do always actively resist. As in T1, the defence in T3 used a grammar of agency to bring scrutiny to the victim-survivor's actions through saying that she "let" it continue, again the connotation being that it was her responsibility to stop it through active resistance:

> *Defence*: [...] then you let the massage continue.
> *Victim-survivor*: Yes, like I said, I wasn't sure [about what had happened ...] (T3).

This framing reflected the 'inferred consent' narrative Ehrlich (2015) found in a Canadian context, where the victim-survivor's passivity was taken to imply consent. This stance completely ignores that it is common

---

[1] In England and Wales, a victim-survivor's video-recorded interview is referred to as an ABE.

for victim-survivors to freeze during a sexual assault (Galliano et al., 1993; Heidt et al., 2005; Nurius et al., 2004; Rothschild, 2000). Indeed, this is precisely how the victim-survivor had described it in her ABE and reiterated during cross-examination:

> It was almost like I sort of froze, thinking, 'Is this normal? No. What should I do?' so I just stayed there and let him finish. (ABE, T3)

The defence explicitly framed the victim-survivor's response as abnormal in his closing speech:

> [Her Honour has directed you about not making assumptions about reactions, but in this case...] you may find it somewhat surprising as to why she took no action at all. (Defence, T3)

Whilst the defence acknowledged the judge's 'myth-busting' direction, he went on to explain to the jury that this case was an exception—a tactic also noted by Smith (2018). He bolstered this claim through also framing the victim-survivor's post-assault behaviour as suspicious, such as not asking the defendant to leave immediately. The defence's assertions drew on rational ideals (see Smith, 2018) that suggest there is a 'normal' way to respond to rape, when in fact it is well established that there is no such thing (Lodrick, 2007; Rothschild, 2000). Furthermore, by placing agency with the victim-survivors, defence barristers were able to frame a lack of resistance as an indicator of consent. The implicit argument being that if a victim-survivor did not resist, it would be reasonable for a defendant to believe she was consenting. Indeed, that argument was explicitly made by defence counsel in T4, as is shown in the later excerpt from the defence's closing speech. Similarly to T3, defence counsel in T4 pointed out opportunities where the victim-survivor could have made resistance and additionally drew on the absence of force to bolster his narrative:

> *Defence*: You didn't say that you didn't want to?
> *Victim-survivor*: No.
> *Defence*: He didn't force you?
> *Victim-survivor*: No.
> *Defence*: To be clear, he undid his trousers, not you?
> *Victim-survivor*: Yeah.
> *Defence*: [You pulled into the layby... Why didn't you just get out of the car then?]
> *Victim-survivor*: Where would I go? In a field?

Defence: [There was a lorry in the layby...].
Victim-survivor: Yeah.
Defence: [Did you get out of the car, scream, bang on the door of the
    lorry?]
Victim-survivor: No, I didn't (T4).

The defendant in T4 had multiple convictions related to domestic
abuse against the victim-survivor, including some that he pleaded guilty
to at the outset of the trial. The prosecution's case was that the victim-
survivor did not freely consent, and the defendant did not reasonably
believe that she was consenting; therefore, the consent narratives in this
trial centred on coercion, compliance, and resistance. Later in the cross-
examination the defence barrister used the victim-survivor's agentive acts
and the absence of verbal resistance to suggest consent:

Defence: You were on top.
Victim-survivor: Yeah.
Defence: How did you get in that position?
Victim-survivor: Just rolling about.
Judge: You got on top of him?
Victim-survivor: Yeah.
Defence: [Knees either side?].
Victim-survivor: Yeah.
Defence: Was it something that just happened?
Victim-survivor: Yeah.
Defence: [A follow on from touching each other sexually?].
Victim-survivor: Yeah.
Defence: [You didn't tell [defendant] at any time you didn't want to do
    that?]
Victim-survivor: No, I didn't (T4).

The implicit suggestion here was that rape can only happen in certain
sexual positions, that 'woman on top' cannot be rape, and was summed
up clearly in defence counsel's closing speech:

[there was no indication from her of a lack of willingness on her part.
He didn't have to repeat what he said, he didn't have to lean over...'It
just happened', she says, 'We touched each other sexually, I took my own
clothes off, had sex without any discussion, I just went on top, rolling
around and I ended up on top'. She did that unprompted, without being
asked, no force or threat.] Dare I say, that woman on top during sex may

not be what you imagine when the word rape is mentioned...you may think that suggests an element of control for the woman...wouldn't it be entirely reasonable for [defendant] to presume consent? (Defence, T4)

This assertion completely obscured the power dynamics involved in intimate partner violence. Men who are violent towards their partners often do not need to resort to violence or threat in order to obtain sex because the underlying pattern of abuse works as an effective tool of coercion (Hamby & Koss, 2003; Kelly, 1987). Becoming an active participant in this context offers women a way to manage risk (Dowds, 2020). That women can be raped even as an active participant demonstrates the problematic nature of defence assertions that a victim-survivor's limited resistance can be taken to prove a defendant's reasonable belief in consent. In this case, the jury appeared to recognise this because they found the defendant guilty, thereby rejecting the defence's apparent assertion that rape can only happen in 'submissive' sex positions. That is, however, not to say that the law in this area is easily applied by jurors or even clearly explained by judges (see Dowds, 2020 for a discussion).

Scrutinising the Sexual Behaviour of Women

Women's sexuality and sexual behaviour have a long history of being scrutinised, including within legal contexts (Bourke, 2007; Clark, 1987; Edwards, 1981). Victim-survivors' sexual behaviour has frequently been used to undermine their credibility at trial through drawing on rape myths that position sexually active women as more likely to have consented and as lacking in moral character, therefore making them untrustworthy (Temkin, 1984); this is sometimes referred to as the 'twin myths' (McGlynn, 2017). In England and Wales, much like most other adversarial jurisdictions, there exists legislation which strictly prohibits the use of evidence relating to a victim-survivor's sexual behaviour, with specific exceptions. This is set out under section 41 of the *Youth Justice and Criminal Evidence Act 1999*. Applications to adduce sexual history evidence should be made in advance of trial so it is not usually possible to tell from court observations whether or not an application has been made unless a s.41 ruling is specifically mentioned during trial. In my observations, s.41 was explicitly mentioned in T1 and T6.

In T6, there was clear reference to a s.41 ruling and how to adhere to its parameters. In this case, defence counsel wished to bring evidence of a third-party relationship of one of the victim-survivors. The ruling had prohibited it, but the defence wanted to ask about the relationship without referencing anything sexual. The judge did not allow this because of the risk it could easily unintentionally adduce sexual history evidence. After a discussion of 'what-ifs', the judge conceded that the defence could in one specific circumstance ask about the relationship in a global way but must run the exact wording by him beforehand *if* that circumstance arose. The line of questioning was ultimately not pursued by the defence so there was not an opportunity to see how this might have played out in practice, but nevertheless it remains an example of good practice.

In T1, s.41 was mentioned in passing, but it was not clear whether an application had been made. There were, however, clear examples of good practice in relation to sexual history evidence in this trial. For example, the judge questioned the defence when she thought he had raised sexual history evidence from a previous sexual encounter between the victim-survivor and the defendant:

> *Judge*: [[Defence], Section 41, did a previous judge make a ruling on that?].
> *Defence*: [No, but I don't think I crossed into that.]
> *Judge*: [Oh yes, you're right, there's no suggestion that anything sexual happened on the night the photos were taken.]
> *Defence*: No (T1).

This demonstrates a judge actively seeking to identify areas of questioning that could need s.41 rulings. On another occasion, the judge intervened to prevent a similar line of questioning by the prosecution:

> *Prosecution*: ...You said you remember him pulling your hand towards him?
> *Victim-survivor*: Yes, several times.
> *Prosecution*: And you remember that?
> *Victim-survivor*: Yes. I didn't want it to happen.
> *Prosecution*: Have you ever touched him-
> *Judge*: Not relevant.
> *Prosecution*: Ok. I am prepared to leave it (T1).

Although s.41 does not apply to the prosecution, anything raised by them is open for explanation or rebuttal by the defence under subsection 5. This means that by stopping prosecution counsel, the judge prevented defence counsel from being able to discuss irrelevant sexual history (see Smith,

2018, on the prevalence of s.41(5) as justification for the introduction of sexual history).

Alongside these examples of good practice, however, there was another line of questioning in the same trial that, even if allowed by a s.41 ruling, seemed entirely irrelevant. The defence questioned the victim-survivor about whether she would usually keep her bra on during consensual sex:

> *Defence*: Your knickers were removed but you kept your bra on.
> *Victim-survivor*: I don't remember.
> *Defence*: Now, please don't think I'm being rude because I'm not. Did you have a complex about your nipples? <pause> You look confused.
> *Victim-survivor*: Yeah.
> *Defence*: Would you keep your bra on because you felt self-conscious about your nipples?
> *Victim-survivor*: Yes.
> *Defence*: But would you keep the bra on if you were having consensual sex?
> *Victim-survivor*: Not necessarily.
> *Defence*: But you might?
> *Victim-survivor*: Yes.
> *Defence*: I suggest that you had consensual sex... (T1).

This questioning was referring generally to the victim-survivor's sexual encounters and was therefore asking about third-parties. The defence's implication was that the victim-survivor might keep her bra on during consensual sex and so that it remained on during the alleged rape could be taken to indicate that she consented. As McGlynn (2017) argued, sexual encounters with third-parties have no bearing on the consideration of consent with someone else, unless it is "so similar...that the similarity cannot reasonably be explained as a coincidence" (*YJCEA* 1999s.41 (3)(c)). However, the ruling in *R v Evans* [2016] EWCA Crim 452 took commonplace sexual activities, namely 'doggy style' and a woman saying 'fuck me harder', as sufficiently unusual and similar to allow inclusion (McGlynn, 2017).

There was no direction to the jury as to how they were permitted to use this evidence and it was not referenced directly in either of the closing speeches. It is therefore unclear what the relevance of this evidence was or why it was adduced. Whether a s.41 ruling was made or not, it remains a line of questioning that is more prejudicial than probative and therefore adds to the existing evidence base showing the inefficacy of the s.41 provisions (Kelly et al., 2006; McGlynn, 2017; Smith, 2018;

Temkin et al., 2018). A woman keeping her bra on during sex should not constitute something so sufficiently out of the ordinary as to qualify as an exception under the s.41 (3)(c) provision, particularly when related to third-parties. It is a standard depiction of sex in television and film. Not only this, but the questioning here was needlessly intrusive. The defence could establish the same facts without resorting to asking intimate details about the victim-survivor's body image. Arguably, it may be beneficial for the defence to make such remarks because it highlights an insecurity in the victim-survivor. Smith (2018) found that defence barristers asked questions about victim-survivors' emotional vulnerabilities and linked these to narratives about mental health and women as pathological in order to portray them as 'damaged goods'. Drawing on this victim-survivor's insecurity could therefore have bolstered the defence's narrative about this victim-survivor as "hysterical" and the defendant's characterisation of her as "crazy" and "psycho", which are discussed in Chapter 4. This example from T1 is problematic because if a s.41 ruling was made, either the evidence adduced was deemed relevant and allowed or the evidence was not deemed relevant but was adduced without challenge anyway, both of which show the inefficacy of s.41. If the evidence was not the subject of a s.41 application, that too signifies inefficacy.

Women's sexual behaviour was also scrutinised far more generally and without reference to s.41. The wording of s.41 vaguely refers to 'sexual behaviour' and 'sexual experience' without further definition, which has led to various Court of Appeal hearings regarding the interpretation of those terms (see Brewis & Stockdale, 2014). There are therefore questions about where the line should be drawn as to what *counts* as sexual history evidence, because evidence about victim-survivors' sexual character aside from physical sexual encounters is often used to the detriment of victim-survivors with no clear probative value other than to encourage the jury to make negative moral judgements about the victim-survivor's character (Burman, 2009; Kelly et al., 2006; McGlynn, 2017). Indeed, I observed narratives that positioned victim-survivors' perceived flirtations as sexual provocation, which serves to simultaneously blame the victim-survivor whilst excusing the defendant and thus provide an avenue to establish 'reasonable' belief in consent. For instance, the victim-survivor in T1 was frequently accused of leading the defendant on, both implicitly and explicitly, because she was perceived to have been flirting with him:

Defence: …You would spend a lot of time together. You would argue a lot. In fact, some people would say that you were like a married couple.
Victim-survivor: No.

...

Defence: You would cuddle. You would ask him for a cuddle.
Victim-survivor Yeah like you cuddle your friends, like you cuddle girl friends.
Defence: [Okay. You would cuddle, you would ask him for a cuddle. He had told you that he was in love with you, you were well aware of his feelings and you were desperate not to lose him as a friend].
Victim-survivor: Yes.
Defence: There came a time when he said he didn't want to carry on the friendship.
Victim-survivor Yes.
Defence: In fact, there was no talk or contact for a time.
Victim-survivor: Yes (T1).

In this excerpt, the defence highlighted the closeness between the victim-survivor and the defendant. The defence put it to the victim-survivor that "you would ask him for a cuddle", positioning her as the instigator of close contact. When her reply clarified it as platonic contact, the defence counsel repeated the statement "you would ask him for a cuddle" before directly referencing her awareness of the defendant's feelings towards her. This also draws on victim-blaming narratives that position women who 'tease' men as more culpable for their own rape (i.e. they were 'asking for it') and defendant's as less culpable (Abrams et al., 2003; Fraser, 2015; Krahé et al., 2007).

As the following extract shows, the defence immediately went on to frame the victim-survivor's actions as selfish:

Defence: [But you didn't want to lose him, so you initiated contact, knowing that it would hurt him. You contacted him to rekindle the relationship].
Victim-survivor: Friendship.
Defence: [I'm not suggesting it was a sexual relationship. You were at the club, happy to see each other. Is it true that you asked him to go on a date?]
Victim-survivor: No, he asked me.
Defence: But you used the term date when you were speaking about it.
Victim-survivor: Best friends day out.
Defence: Did you use that term?
Victim-survivor: I said it's a day out just for us.

Defence: He was pleased, he used the term date.
Victim-survivor: He did (T1).

These examples illustrate part of the defence's overarching narrative that the victim-survivor knew the defendant had feelings for her, selfishly lead him on, had sex with him then regretted it, and so lied about rape. The idea that women lie about rape has been embedded in the legal system for hundreds of years (Smith, 2021) and is reflected in the persistently common misconception that false allegations of rape are common. The narrative in T1 also drew on the problematic notion that flirting signals consent, which positions women as gatekeepers to sex. It suggests that had the victim-survivor not encouraged the defendant then the incidents would not have occurred, thereby simultaneously blaming the victim-survivor and excusing the defendant's alleged actions. The idea that women lie about rape after regretful sex is deeply entrenched in our society, and I discuss this further in Chapter 4. For now, the discussion will focus on the notion of perceived sexual provocation as establishing a reasonable belief in consent. As with the resistance narratives outlined in the previous section, the defence barrister in the above extract utilised Ehrlich's (2001) grammar of agency when speaking about the victim-survivor's actions, thereby placing her actions and behaviour at the forefront rather than the defendant's.

The defence also drew on the defendant's unrequited feelings for the victim-survivor to garner sympathy (see Chapter 4). Defence counsel positioned the victim-survivor as having power over the defendant, which is in stark contrast to the power dynamics of rape. This narrative drew on the sexist idea that women often lead men on for attention or valida-tion, with some even going so far as to argue that women 'leading men on' constitutes sexual abuse (e.g. Mantyla, 2018). Indeed, studies have found increased blame attribution when perceived sexual provocation was involved (see Gravelin et al., 2019, for an overview). In partic-ular, research has shown that women who initiate contact or dates are viewed as more culpable if they are raped and that some men view being 'led on' as a justification for rape (Muehlenhard, 1988; Muehlenhard & Linton, 1987; Muehlenhard & MacNaughton, 1988). These public atti-tudes remain prevalent (e.g. EVAW, 2018; ICM, 2005), and therefore, it can be assumed that some jurors may subscribe to these views. This gives sway to defence narratives that frame victim-survivors as sexual provoca-teurs. Indeed, McGlynn (2017) pointed out how these vague references

to victim-survivors' sexual character serve to undermine their 'moral credibility', thus positioning them as undeserving of sympathy and minimising
the defendant's actions. This narrative was used by the defendant in T1,
who gave a conflicting account of who had suggested a date and placed
the victim-survivor as the agentive party in flirting and instigating intimate
contact:

> *Defence*: And there was talk of going on a date?
> *Defendant*: Yeah, she said to me 'If you wouldn't mind, I'd love for you
> to take me on a date' and I said I'd love to.
> *Defence*: [So you bought her drinks all evening?].
> *Defendant*: Yes.
> *Defence*: [How was she acting towards you in the club?].
> *Defendant*: [Different, she was flirty, always wanting to cuddle me, always
> wanting to kiss me. Full on kissing like snogging.] (T1)

This drew on the problematic idea that if a woman flirts with a man she
must want to have sex with him, and that flirting implies consent for
later sexual activity (Burgin & Flynn, 2019; McGlynn, 2017). Pointing
to victim-survivors' perceived flirtations in order to demonstrate consent
or reasonable belief in consent is a tactic noted by defence barristers in
Carline and Gunby's research (2011). In T1, this tactic was made clear in
the defence's closing remarks:

> [You know that they frequently shared a bed together. She knew that he
> was in love with her, that he was infatuated. You know she knew he broke
> it off because she couldn't feel the same. You know she got desperate to be
> back with him, you know she said that she wanted to see if she had sexual
> feelings for him. You know she was snogging him. You know they were
> like a couple that night, no flirting with others. You know that.] (Defence,
> T1)

This narrative worked together with the resistance narratives in this trial
and both narratives relied on the grammar of agency and non-agency
to shift focus and blame onto the victim-survivor's actions. The framing
of women's everyday behaviour as indicating consent is referred to by
Ehrlich (2015) as 'inferred consent' and by Burgin and Flynn (2019) as
'implied consent' (see also Cossins, 2020). In the context of Australian
rape trials, Burgin and Flynn (2019) argued that narratives of implied
consent function at trial to provide defendants an 'objective' claim to

reasonable belief in consent and therefore constitute legally sanctioned victim-blaming.

Scrutiny of victim-survivors' sexual behaviour was not only seen in the adult sexual offences cases outlined thus far, it was also seen in T6 which related to historic child sexual abuse. In T6, the defendant admitted to a sexual relationship with one of the victim-survivors but claimed that it began only after the victim-survivor's 16th birthday, whereas she claimed it began when she was 15 (the age of consent in England and Wales is 16). In the following example, the defence highlighted the victim-survivor's consent whilst ignoring the broader context of age of consent violations:

> *Defence*: ... I'm going to suggest that your evidence is that you wanted to kiss and have sex with [defendant].
> *Victim-survivor1*: Yes.
> *Defence*: [So what you told the police is you consented to everything sexual with [defendant].
> *Victim-survivor1*: Yes (T6).

This narrative served to excuse or minimise the defendant's behaviour by highlighting the victim-survivor's agency. The historical context of age of consent laws and surrounding discourses shows how this may be a valuable narrative for a defence barrister to draw on. For instance, historically men were often excused for statutory rape if they claimed the victim-survivor was promiscuous (Bourke, 2007). By highlighting the sexual agency of this victim-survivor, then, the defence distanced her from the 'innocence' often attributed to children and ignored that contemporary discourses around age of consent focus on protecting against exploitation (Benedet, 2010; Waites, 2005) rather than protecting 'virginity' (Bourke, 2007). Some research has, however, indicated that this type of narrative, that which aims to highlight victim-survivor 'promiscuity' in age of consent cases, does not necessarily work in favour of the defendant and may in fact work against them (Horvath & Giner-Sorolla, 2007).

Moreover, throughout this trial the defence sought to downplay the defendant's relationship with the victim-survivors' mother:

> *Defence*: Before he was kicked out, you were not partners, it was just sexual?
> *Mother*: Yeah.
> *Defence*: He wasn't a stepfather?
> *Mother*: He was a stepfather figure (T6).

This arguably attempted to distance the defendant from cultural narratives of 'incest' and child sexual abuse, ignoring that the defendant had been in a relationship with the mother through both victim-survivors' early teenage years. Narratives of child sexual abuse position the younger party as lacking in agency (Waites, 2005); therefore, highlighting the victim-survivor's agency can distance the defendant from that narrative. The narrative in this trial obscured the power dynamics whilst positioning the victim-survivor as a willing participant, and thus minimised the defendant's actions. The above extract also provides an example of victim-survivors' mothers' sexual behaviour being used in trial to undermine the claims and credibility of victim-survivors. This was not an isolated example and so I now turn to a brief exploration of other such examples within T6 as well as examples in T5.

Scrutinising the Sexual Behaviour of Victim-Survivors' Mothers
Unlike for victim-survivors, the sexual behaviour of other witnesses in rape trials is not protected by s.41 of the *YJCEA*. Interestingly, my observations in the two trials involving child sex offences (one with a child victim-survivor, one a historic case with two adult victim-survivors) indicated that the sexual history of the mothers can be used to undermine the credibility of the family as a whole, and as such undermine the victim-survivors.

In T5, the mother of the child victim-survivor was subjected to intrusive questioning about her lifestyle and parenting skills, seemingly to undermine her credibility and bolster the narrative of her as vindictive (this is discussed further in Chapter 4). In addition, there was a question regarding her sexual history with the defendant, where the question was worded in such a way as to suggest casual sex, drawing on middle-class ideals of respectability which suggest women who have sex outside of relationships are 'promiscuous' (see Chapter 3 for classed narratives of respectability).

> *Defence*: You broke up, then some time later he came round, you end up
>   in bed together and that's when [youngest son] was created.
> *Mother*: I don't remember, maybe (T5).

Whilst on its own this question may not seem inflammatory, it was set within a context of questions that suggested the witness had involvement with social services and portrayed her as a 'benefit cheat', drawing on classed 'single mothers' narratives (see Chapter 3). Therefore, the use of this mother's sexual history, which had no relevance as to whether or not the defendant abused her child, was used to help undermine her credibility and, by proxy, the credibility of her son.

Similarly, classed narratives positioned the family in T6 as not conforming to ideals of respectability. The mother's sexual relationship with the defendant was referred to on multiple occasions. The defence insinuated that the daughters were aware of their mother's sexual habits with the defendant and had used that to bolster their 'invented' allegations. For example, the defence drew attention to the sexual relationship between the mother and the defendant:

> *Defence*: [Did you do sexual acts on the bus?].
> *Mother*: Yes.
> *Defence*: Where were your daughters when that happened?
> *Mother*: 9 out of 10 times it was a double decker so we would be upstairs.
>
> …
>
> *Defence*: Would it be sexual intercourse?
> *Mother*: Yes (T6).

The defence later raised this in relation to the victim-survivors:

> *Defence*: They were young teenagers at the time?
> *Mother*: I can't remember.
> *Defence*: Would you agree you'd talk to them about the affair?
> *Mother*: Now and again, not very often.
> *Defence*: Did you tell them about sexual things?
> *Mother*: No.
> *Defence*: I suggest you told them you had sex on the bus.
> *Mother*: No.
> *Defence*: Were they aware you had sex on the bus?
> *Mother*: I don't know if they were or not.
> *Defence*: No more questions (T6).

Whilst the line of argument in T6 can be legitimate, these examples nevertheless show that with regard to child sexual offences, victim-survivors' credibility can not only be undermined through adducing evidence relating to their own sexual history, but also by that of their mothers. This is because women have historically been positioned as untrustworthy, particularly with regard to their sexual behaviour (Bourke, 2007; Clark, 1987). The gendered cultural narratives regarding the untrustworthiness of women are discussed further in Chapter 4. The use of mothers' sexual history in child sexual offences trials does not appear to be an area previously explored in scholarship and is certainly an area that warrants further investigation.

The Expectation of Immediate Escape and No Further Contact

A range of rape myths set out expectations for what a 'true' victim-survivor would do in the aftermath of sexual violence. Barristers at trial can cast victim-survivors' behaviour against these expectations and any deviation from them can therefore be framed as irrational and suspicious (Smith, 2018). In all trials where victim-survivors were adults at the time of the alleged assaults (T1, T2, T3, and T4), their immediate responses were scrutinised and held up against ideas about what a 'rational' person might do. For example, the idea that victim-survivors immediately escape and seek assistance was drawn upon in T3 and T4. In T4, the victim-survivor's post-assault behaviour was scrutinised and framed as 'choice':

> the fact that [victim-survivor] chose to stay with [defendant], [you know from your own common sense that she could have left at any point …]. (Defence, T4)

By framing the victim-survivor's response as a choice, the defence placed agency with the victim-survivor and presented it as "fact". By urging the jury to draw on their "common sense" when considering the victim-survivor's actions, the defence implied that her behaviour did not match with what a rational person would do in that situation. The victim-survivor was also criticised for remaining in the defendant's car when he had left her alone whilst he went inside a friend's house. This narrative was bolstered by evidence elicited from defence witnesses who encountered her and the defendant together in the aftermath of the rapes, who described the victim-survivor's demeanour as "fine" and "normal" (T4).

This was a case where the defendant had multiple convictions relating to domestic abuse against the victim-survivor. The 'why didn't she leave' narrative so commonly associated with domestic abuse (see Duggan, 2018) permeated questioning about this victim-survivor's behaviour and her reaction to the various acts of aggression and sexual violence. It was drawn together in the closing remarks:

> [there were more opportunities for her to have got away than I could possibly even begin to suggest]…[There is one single thing that I say against [victim-survivor] saying she was so fearful], when she gave her evidence to police in her video, she said that she lay in his bed with him, [waiting for him to go to sleep, but she dozed off first]. I make no apologies for perhaps sounding harsh, [prosecution say she was kidnapped, raped 4 times, petrified, desperate to escape], but she just dozed off? I don't know what sort of things keep you awake at night, […work, an argument…there are some things you just can't switch off from and go to sleep]. (Defence, T4)

The defence minimised the victim-survivor's trauma by comparing it to work stresses or an argument. Counsel's argument also positioned the only 'rational' response as to leave as soon as possible. Whilst this victim-survivor's post-assault behaviour might not seem rational to some, it is well established that victim-survivors of intimate partner violence often form strong attachments to the perpetrator through trauma bonding (Reid et al., 2013). Similarly, another common response to trauma is to befriend the perpetrator. This is what Lodrick (2007) refers to as the 'friend' response to trauma. The 'friend' response is the use of social engagement as a way of minimising further harm (Lodrick, 2007). This response was also seen in the victim-survivors in T1, T2, T3, and T6 to varying degrees and was presented by the defence in each trial as something that undermined the victim-survivors' accounts. To illustrate, the victim-survivor in T3 described what could be considered a 'friend' response:

> *Victim-survivor*: …Can I just say something else?
> *Defence*: <looks taken aback, looks to Judge>
> *Judge*: If it's in answer to the question.
> *Victim-survivor*: It's related. [I didn't know what to do, I got dressed and we went downstairs] <says the rest whilst crying> [I just wanted to feel normal and so I played this piano piece to him cos I'd said that I would.] Cos that's what you're gonna ask me next, 'Why did you do that?'
>
> …
>
> *Defence*: He asked you to play piano.

Victim-survivor: Yes.
Defence: [You played three songs].
Victim-survivor: [No, I played one. I can tell you what it was: [music artist]] (T3)

In pre-empting the defence's question, the victim-survivor was able to explain her response to the jury, positioning it as a way of regaining some sense of normalcy. Her acquiescence to the defendant's request of her to play piano for him can be seen as a reaction to fear of further harm. Furthermore, it demonstrates that the 'friend' response is not only a subconscious reaction, but that it can be an actively chosen form of passivity. Similarly, in T4, the prosecution's closing speech focused heavily on the difference between consent and compliance and the role of fear in compliance. In doing this, the prosecution had rationalised the victim-survivor's post-assault responses for the jury. The defendants in these two trials (T3 and T4) were both found guilty, so arguably the counter-narratives employed by victim-survivors and prosecution barristers did enough to broaden the narrow confines of what was presented as reasonable by the defence.

In T1, T2, and T6, the 'friend' responses and associated scrutiny from the defence barristers tended to manifest in relation to the 'continued contact' myth, which says that the 'rational' response to rape is to cut off all contact with the perpetrator. That the victim-survivors in T1, T2, and T6 had maintained contact with the defendants after alleged incidents of rape was treated with suspicion by the defence barristers, which reflects previous findings from rape trial observations (Smith & Skinner, 2017). In T1, the defence directly referred to continued contact between the victim-survivor and defendant after the first alleged rape and used it to suggest that the victim-survivor had consented:

Defence: I submit that you do remember it all and you had consensual sex [with the defendant].
Victim-survivor: No.
Defence: [He is suggesting that you weren't that drunk, he checks with you whether you still want to go on a date. You say, 'Now I've done that I've really fucked you around'. You still want to go on a date with him to see how you feel, and this is after you've had sex.]
Victim-survivor: Yes.
Defence: The events of that night don't stop you from seeing each other and spending time together.
Victim-survivor: No (T1).

Here the defence presented the victim-survivor's continued contact with the defendant and agreement to a 'date' as incompatible with an absence of consent. Similarly, in T2, the defence used continued contact as a tool to undermine the victim-survivor's narrative of non-consent:

> *Defence*: [That summer you went to festivals, spent time with his family...]
> *Victim-survivor*: Yes.
> *Defence*: So not all bad then?
> *Victim-survivor*: Yeah (T2).

In this case, the victim-survivor and defendant were in a long-term relationship when the alleged rape occurred, and they remained in a relationship for approximately six months afterwards. The victim-survivor reported to the police two months after the end of the relationship. In both excerpts above, the defence implied consent or untruthfulness by pointing to continued contact, which ignores the complexities women face in labelling their experiences as rape. The 'real rape' myth positions the rapist as a deviant 'other', which makes it difficult for victim-survivors who are raped by someone close to them, be it a friend, family member, or intimate partner, to reconcile this image with the person who has harmed them (Kahn et al., 2003; Peterson & Muehlenhard, 2011). This means it often takes time for women to recognise or accept what has happened to them as rape. This is also true of acquaintance rape. Indeed, the victim-survivor in T1 stated "I didn't want to believe it" when cross-examined about why she had not immediately identified the experience as rape. In the above extract from T2, the defence's characterisation of the relationship not being "all bad" after the alleged rape seemed to present a false dichotomy of relationships as either wholly good or wholly bad (Smith & Skinner, 2017), which is an oversimplification that serves to undermine the victim-survivor's story. The prosecution attempted to resist this narrative through reference to youth and immaturity:

> [Victim-survivor] was very young girl and what happened in [month] was clearly very distressing for her and continued to be beyond then. (Prosecution, T2)

> [Victim-survivor] was young, she stayed. You heard that she stopped giving blowjobs to [defendant], and you may think that is an indication, that someone might stop doing that because of being raped. (Prosecution, T2)

In these examples, the prosecutor implied that the victim-survivor stayed in the relationship after the alleged rape because she was "young" and "immature", and these were words she used throughout her closing speech. This narrative served to infantilise the victim-survivor, which presumably aimed to position her as 'victim' in the eyes of the jury. The narrative was patronising, which is particularly important in this case because the victim-survivor was observing the trial from the public gallery and was therefore listening to what was being said. What this narrative also implied was that older women would have left, which is by no means necessarily the case—women of all ages stay with violent and abusive men for many complex reasons (Duggan, 2018). The prosecution therefore reinforced the problematic and pervasive cultural narrative that asks, 'why didn't she leave?'. Whether or not this may have been a damaging narrative in this trial, it served to reinforce the narrative for those hearing it, including the victim-survivor, which could have wider social implications. The prosecutor could have instead addressed the defence's assertions by challenging the broader structural mechanisms that impact these decisions for women, rather than by pointing to individual characteristics of the victim-survivor and ultimately reinforcing victim-blaming narratives.

In T2, not only was the victim-survivor's behaviour questioned because she had continued the relationship but also because she had continued sexual contact with the defendant after the end of the relationship:

Defence: In some of that time he had tried to get back together with you.
Victim-survivor: Yeah.
Defence: I'm going to say that there were times between when you were intimate together.
Victim-survivor: Yeah (T2).

Defence counsel also attempted to get a prosecution witness, the victim-survivor's friend, to confirm post-relationship sexual encounters between the victim-survivor and the defendant, through asking him to interpret social media messages he had received from her:

Defence: Look at page 4 please, the message that starts 'I try and I try…', please read that in your head then I will ask you about it. <pause> If I was to suggest that [victim-survivor] and [defendant] were still having sex-
Judge: How can he answer that?
Prosecution: Yes, he can't answer that.

It is reassuring that both the judge and prosecution immediately took issue with this line of questioning and intervened; however, the judge then accepted the defence's reasoning:

> *Defence*: I just want his understanding of the relationship.
> *Judge*: Okay.
> *Defence*: Was that your impression?
> *Friend*: I wouldn't know.
> *Defence*: Was your understanding that it had ended?
> *Friend*: Yeah that was my impression.

Defence counsel also questioned the OIC about it:

> *Defence*: It remains her stance that she had ended communication with [defendant].
> *OIC*: No, she said the relationship ended, not that she stopped all contact.
> *Defence*: Did she tell you or anyone else that she had continued to have sex with [defendant] through [month after break-up]?
> *OIC*: I never asked that question and I wouldn't want to assume.
> *Defence*: Was it your impression that [defendant's] sexual advances were unwanted?
> *OIC*: Yes.
> *Defence*: [When did you become aware that [victim-survivor] had had sexual relations with [defendant] in that time?]
> *OIC*: I can't recall.
> *Defence*: [That is not something she puts in any police statement].
> *OIC*: I can't recall (T2).

Here the defence seemed to be implying that the victim-survivor had deliberately omitted the information, which feeds into portrayals of women as calculating liars (see Chapter 4). Again, this line of questioning ignored what is known about trauma responses. The implied reasoning is that a woman would not continue to have sex with her rapist; however, it is known that women often stay in relationships with men who have assaulted them, be that physically or sexually, for myriad complex reasons (Duggan, 2018; Payne & Wermeling, 2009; Rhodes & McKenzie, 1998). The defence therefore oversimplified an extremely complex issue in order to imply that the victim-survivor either must have consented or must be lying. The prosecution in T2 anticipated the defence's reliance on misunderstandings about continued contact and addressed it in her closing remarks:

> As I said to you at the start of this case, there are many ways victims react to rape. It is easy to say 'why didn't she leave?' and think 'I wouldn't have put up with that'. [Value judgements are easy to make but they have no place here]. (Prosecution, T2)

Whilst it is not possible to say whether or to what degree the jury might have considered this aspect of the trial narrative in their decision to acquit the defendant, it may be fair to assume it had some bearing given that the defence relied heavily on it as a tool for undermining the victim-survivor in her closing remarks:

> What you do know about [victim-survivor's] credibility is that she also reported to the police that [defendant] was pestering her, sending unwanted messages to her asking for sex, [and she tells the police that is not something she is interested in because they split for good in [month] and she wants nothing to do with him, she signs that statement, she produces messages, and then what we can see is that there is a wealth of communication both ways, she gives a number of statements,] does she say in any of them that she carried on sleeping with him? Now that doesn't help you with the rape, but it does help you with credibility, doesn't it? (Defence, T2)

Here the defence explicitly suggested that the victim-survivor was not credible because she had not included the continued sexual relationship in her statements. The defence also referred to the "wealth of communication both ways", drawing on the misconception that victim-survivors never communicate with their rapists. This narrative also demonstrates how evidence about a victim-survivor's sexual behaviour can be adduced and used to undermine her. It should be noted that it was not possible to determine whether an application to adduce the above evidence had been made under s.41 of the *YJCEA* as no such application was observed in this trial (nor in any of the others). This is not surprising because s.41 applications should be made before trial begins. Whilst I do not go into depth within this book with regard to s.41, I will be writing about it elsewhere (Daly and Herriott, forthcoming).

The above extracts from T1 and T2 showed that defence barristers were able to use digital communications between victim-survivors and defendants to cast doubt on the prosecution cases by evidencing continued contact between the parties. In contrast, the defence in T6 used a single piece of digital communication to do this:

> *Defence*: ...Did you send [defendant] a happy birthday message on Facebook in [10 years after alleged rapes]?
> *Victim-survivor2*: Yeah (T6)

That was the final question in the cross-examination of that victim-survivor and was completely unrelated to the previous questions about whether she had discussed allegations with her sister. Again, the suggestion that a 'happy birthday' message from victim-survivor to defendant a decade after the alleged incidents could be relevant to credibility completely ignored the potential for trauma bonding and the 'friend response' discussed earlier, particularly because this victim-survivor had viewed the defendant as a stepfather figure. Furthermore, there was no digital evidence bundle in this case, which suggests that a 'fishing expedition' may have been carried out in an attempt to find evidence of communication that might be used to undermine credibility, which is a well-known tactic used by defence teams in Westernised adversarial jurisdictions (Browning, 2011; Carimico et al., 2016; Diss, 2013; Smith & Daly, 2020). That this tactic is so widely used is indicative of its value and demonstrates how pervasive rape myths, in this case myths about continued contact, can be used as tools to undermine victim-survivors' credibility. Indeed, analysis by Howell and Heberlig (2007) demonstrated that even before the ubiquity of smart phones, digital evidence had long been recognised as a useful tool for undermining the claims of victim-survivors in court.

Victim-Survivors Delaying Disclosures and Reporting

Another common rape myth reflected in my observations related to the timeframes within which victim-survivors chose to make their reports to police or to third-parties; that is, it is suspicious if a victim-survivor does not report a rape to the police immediately. Despite it being recognised that delayed reporting of rape is not uncommon, it has often been used as a tool for undermining victim-survivors in court (Adler, 1987; Brereton,

1997; Bronitt, 1998; Raitt, 2004; Smith, 2018). Mock jury research has shown that jurors do reference this myth in deliberation (Ellison & Munro, 2009; Taylor & Joudo, 2005; Temkin, 2010). Arguably, this is because the delayed reporting myth remains commonly held in wider society (Ellison & Munro, 2009; Raitt, 2004; Rose et al., 2006).

In T2, T5, and T6, the victim-survivors did not make police reports straightaway; however, this was not treated with suspicion in all cases. Both T5 and T6 related to child sex offences, and in T5, the victim-survivor was still a child at the time of the trial. This victim-survivor's delayed reporting was not treated as suspicious, which may have been because he was a young child and because his mother gave evidence that he had tried to disclose the alleged abuse to her earlier, but she had not taken it seriously. In contrast, the victim-survivors in T6 were adults when they made historic allegations against the defendant. The delay in their reporting to police was met with suspicion, though not due to the delay in reporting as such, but rather the delay in the full allegations being made to police. Victim-survivor2 had begun to make a complaint five years after the alleged rape and sexual assaults but then declined to give a statement. Five years later, the allegations were made again, and victim-survivor1 added her complaint a few months on. The defence used these delays and staggered disclosures to help build a gendered narrative of collusion, which is explored further in Chapter 4.

The victim-survivor in T2 disclosed to a friend around six months after the alleged rape, via social media messaging, before reporting to the police two months later. The defence used the fact that her disclosure was digital to suggest that she could have told her friend sooner because the digital means by which she disclosed were available to her from the time of the alleged rape:

> *Defence*: So, [if she wanted to, she could have spoken to you at that time, you weren't working abroad, your phone wasn't broken?]
> *Friend*: No, [there was nothing to stop her, but I do feel that it was easier for her to speak more freely about these issues post-relationship]
> *Defence*: Obviously you just have [victim-survivor's] side of events, because you've never spoken to [defendant] (T2)

The victim-survivor's friend gave reasoning for why she may have delayed reporting; however, the defence dismissed it as biased, using minimising language to do so. The reasoning articulated by the victim-survivor's friend was in line with what is known about disclosures of sexual violence, thus the defence's dismissal aimed to downplay the fact that delayed reporting is common and rational. Similarly to T6, the defence in T2 used the delay in reporting to bolster her gendered narrative of women as vengeful liars (see Chapter 4).

Victim-Survivors Reporting to Police Within 24 Hours

In both T1 and T3, the victim-survivors disclosed within 24 hours of the incidents (in T1 it was the second incident). Both women confided in their friends (in T1 this was after the report to police; in T3 it was before), and these disclosures were treated as suspicious by the defence barristers. For example, the defence in T1 employed a gendered narrative of women as scheming, calculating liars:

> In the time between her report and ABE she messaged people to tell them something really bad had happened that was so difficult for her to talk about, yet she keeps telling people. This, we submit, is a way for her to garner support and sympathy to keep up her charade. (Defence, T1)

The defence was not able to undermine the prosecution's case by arguing that the victim-survivor had delayed reporting to the police and had therefore behaved suspiciously, but by reframing it as an act of manipulation he was able to undermine what might otherwise be framed as the victim-survivor's 'rational' behaviour as problematic. This was also a tactic used in T3 where the defence implied the victim-survivor had colluded with her friend. These findings from T1 and T3, as well as the preceding finding from T2, suggest that it could be *who* the victim-survivors tell, rather than *when*, that has more of a bearing for the narratives of suspicion deployed by defence barristers. Whilst judges usually give judicial directions explaining that there is no typical response to rape and that a delayed report does not mean a false report, the direction does not go so far as to explain that victim-survivors often speak to third-parties (e.g. friends and family) before deciding whether to make a report to police (Brooks-Hay, 2019). It should therefore be considered a normal and rational response to trauma, rather than treated with suspicion.

As well as being treated with suspicion for telling her friends about the sexual assaults, the victim-survivor in T3 was criticised for not calling someone immediately (and whilst the defendant was still in her home), even though she did call someone within hours of the assaults and went to the police in under 24 hours:

> *Defence*: You didn't think at that stage it was-
> *Victim-survivor*: I thought it was odd [I've never had a full body massage before, I didn't know if that was included] [...]
> *Defence*: You could have called [friend].
> *Victim-survivor*: My phone wasn't near me.
> *Defence*: [Q&A about [friend] having been at her house earlier that afternoon and saying she could call him if she felt uncomfortable with the massage]. Why didn't you call [friend]?
> *Victim-survivor*: [I called him as soon as [defendant] left].
> *Defence*: You didn't call the police?
> *Victim-survivor*: No (T3).

This example from T3 also calls into question what is regarded as *soon enough*. The defence argued that the victim-survivor could have called her friend as soon as she felt uncomfortable with the way the massage was going. This is significant because the defence was then by implication suggesting that what the victim-survivor *should* have done was to call her friend not even in the immediate aftermath of the assaults, but whilst the defendant still had his hands on her.

> We know that her good friend [name] has been with her that day, he told her how the massage might happen, she asked about how a professional massage happens. So we have there a clear indication that he said she could ring him, and he told her he would come round if she called (Defence, T3)

Delayed reporting has long been held against victim-survivors, with prompt reporting therefore lauded as a way to help towards being believed and viewed as credible. Yet these examples show that the power of the 'women lie about rape' myth can be used by defence barristers to undermine victim-survivors 'doing the right thing' by reporting promptly. This produces an alarming 'damned if they do, damned if they don't' predicament for victim-survivors. The significance of the 'women lie about rape' myth and the salience of classed and gendered cultural narratives in reinforcing it are explored in Chapter 4.

Myths About (In)Consistent Accounts of Rape and Sexual Assault

Prosecution and defence counsel in all trials pointed to consistencies and inconsistencies, respectively, in the victim-survivors' accounts. Barristers usually recognised that accounts will inevitably bear some inconsistencies and so they focused on the *levels* of consistency. For example, in T3, the prosecution characterised the victim-survivor's accounts as having "no meaningful inconsistencies":

> She immediately told three friends and all accounts are consistent with what she told the police, there are no *meaningful* inconsistencies, and I stress the word meaningful, there of course are some, but you are sensible people, you understand why some of these exist. (Prosecution, T3)

However, the defence asked the jury to consider whether those same accounts were "internally consistent":

> Consistency, is her account consistent? [You can't say you're sure], is it *internally* consistent?...[I'm sure you will give very careful consideration. Consider the evidence very, very carefully]. Single unsupported, inconsistent word [is not enough to make you sure enough to return a guilty verdict]. (Defence, T3)

Despite asking whether it was "internally consistent" and thereby implicitly conceding that some inconsistencies with other witnesses are inevitable, the defence went on to say that the victim-survivor's "unsupported, inconsistent word" was not enough to make them sure beyond a reasonable doubt that she was being truthful. This ignores modern understandings of memory (see Hohl & Conway, 2017) and extensive neuropsychological evidence about the impact of trauma on memory coding (see Lodrick, 2007), with the implication being that the victim-survivor's story will be consistent if truthful, when this is not the case. Such arguments hark back to the corroboration warning that judges used to be required to give to juries in sexual offences trials, warning them of the dangers of convicting based on the unsupported word of a victim-survivor. The mandatory warning was based on historic gendered narratives that positioned women as untrustworthy and the belief that false allegations of rape were common (Leahy, 2014). Indeed, it is perfectly possible in English law to make a conviction based on the testimony of a single witness. The defence barrister's words, then, were

rooted in those same gendered narratives. Though it is no longer mandatory, judges may at their own discretion give a corroboration warning;
however, the judge in T3 did not deem it necessary to do so.

Similarly to T3, consistency in T5 was qualified as 'fundamentally' true
by the prosecution:

> Detail is important, but not the be all and end all, [each individual expe-
> rience of it will be remembered differently, the Learned Judge has given
> you a number of warnings, be careful, then stand back and consider where
> we are. Although details differ, the *fundamental* story is not untrue. I'm
> sure you have heard people tell stories of something you've witnessed, and
> you've thought 'hang on, that's not how he told it last time', but you
> know the story to be true]. (Prosecution, T5)

However, again the defence seemed to call for nothing but 100%
accuracy:

> Accuracy, reliability, truthfulness. That's what this case is about… because
> it stands and falls on the word of one little boy…It is a fact that children
> lie, it is a fact that adults lie. Children make things up…[his] evidence is
> peppered with inconsistencies [and worryingly this is a child who has also
> been found to say a host of different things… He may not have set out
> deliberately doing this, it takes courage to say you were lying, imagine how
> hard it is for a child to admit to mum, school, grandmother, aunts, that it
> wasn't true.] (Defence, T5)

These suggestions from the defence barristers in T3 and T5 that only
complete accuracy was sufficient to make the jury sure enough to convict
reflect the false dichotomy observed by Smith and Skinner (2017) that
presented victim-survivors' accounts as either wholly truthful or wholly
untruthful. It is also interesting considering that Munro and Kelly (2009)
found that being too consistent may work against victim-survivors. This
suggests there is a very narrow margin in which victim-survivors will be
deemed honest and credible (Smith, 2018).

The focus on consistency in T2 presented slightly differently to the
examples above. Whilst both the defence and prosecution pointed the jury
to consider the consistency of the victim-survivor's accounts, the focus
was on different aspects of her accounts:

> She decides to tell her friend about it and she later tells the police the same account as she gave to her friend.] She gives a very simple, utterly truthful account. The defence's case is that she made it up [...]. But she never wavers, never embellishes, she simply says it how it is. (Prosecution, T2)

Here the prosecution pointed to the consistency between the victim-survivor's account of the alleged rape given to her friend, the police, and in her live testimony. The level of consistency in these accounts left the defence without opportunity to point the jury towards inconsistencies in how she described what had happened. The tactic taken by the defence was instead to point to inconsistencies in peripheral areas:

> You can see whether things have a ring of truth to them..., [she says she only mentioned it via text, but then she has said in interview that she had said it in arguments]. These are not conversations about who forgot to buy the milk, you would think she would remember talking about it, [... she would] have flashbacks, she would have it clear in her mind. [She says she can't remember what was said], does that ring true to you? Can you be satisfied? (Defence, T2).

The defence highlighted inconsistencies in the victim-survivor's recollection of how and when she had confronted the defendant about the alleged rape. Defence counsel drew on ideas of what a rational person might remember and treated the victim-survivor's poor recollection of conversations from two and a half years prior with suspicion. By making the comparison with conversations about mundane everyday conversation, the defence implied that a 'normal' person would remember every conversation about a traumatic event. This completely misrepresented and obscured what is known about the effects of trauma on memory (Hohl & Conway, 2017; Lodrick, 2007) and that men's aggression can become a mundane feature of life for many women (Stanko, 2013). It also ignored the complexities women face in recognising rape, especially in romantic relationships (Kahn et al., 2003; Peterson & Muehlenhard, 2011). To argue that the victim-survivor should remember all conversations she had with the defendant relating to the alleged rape merely because rape is traumatic assumes that the victim-survivor had *at the time* fully recognised that trauma.

Furthermore, the defence argued that the victim-survivor would have had flashbacks to the conversations because of the trauma. Whilst it is true that flashbacks are a common trauma response (Duke et al., 2007), it is not a universal response and the defence was not talking about the traumatic event itself but conversations about that event. It therefore seems that the defence was implying that the victim-survivor was lying because she had not said she had flashbacks to *conversations* (not the alleged rape itself). With the final remark in the above extract the defence clearly suggested to the jury that the victim-survivor was not being truthful because she cannot, two and a half years on, remember in detail all of the times she confronted the defendant about the alleged rape. The implication, then, seemed to be that she was lying about the confrontations so she was not trustworthy, and thus, the jury could not be sure she was not lying about the alleged rape. The defendant in this case was acquitted so it seems that the defence's attempts to undermine the victim-survivor's consistent accounts were successful. Although it is not possible to know the basis on which the jury made their decision, it is clear that they did not find the victim-survivor credible enough to convict based on her testimony.

Digital evidence has also provided a new way for barristers to undermine the credibility of both victim-survivors' and defendants' stories, by focusing on inconsistencies in their recollections of conversations which often largely took place via digital platforms. For example, if a victim-survivor stated that she could not remember saying something, and it was subsequently shown in digital evidence, it was used to accuse her of lying. The following excerpt demonstrates this:

> She said she 'wasn't prepared', she said she couldn't remember saying it, but when she was shown the messages it was clear that she had said that. (Defence, T1)

The focus on inconsistencies in victim-survivors' evidence ignores a large established evidence base which shows that truthful accounts are not told in the same way each time, that small details do change, and that human memory and recall is imperfect (McMillan, 2007; Temkin, 2000). To expect a consistent account each time is unreasonable. Nevertheless, defence barristers frequently turn to consistency as an indicator of truth and painstakingly highlight every inconsistency in victim-survivors' accounts and testimonies, whilst prosecution barristers draw on consistencies in victim-survivors' accounts to bolster the victim-survivor's credibility. This ignores that human recall is imperfect and positions victim-survivors' evidence as either wholly accurate or wholly inaccurate (Smith, 2018). This ignores the reality that there will inevitably be both accurate and inaccurate elements of each account because of the limitations to human memory and the added issue of passing time degrading memories.

The effect of the passage of time on memory was particularly pertinent in T6 because the allegations related to historic sexual abuse. The defence relied heavily on inconsistencies in the accounts from both victim-survivors. The prosecution preempted this:

> There are a number of inconsistencies between what you heard, I am not going to go through them, they are there. … insofar as these inconsistencies are concerned, you may think for example that in [victim-survivor2's] first account [there was a discrepancy of 1 year], well we all have difficulty with years don't we? … It is important for you to consider [the inconsistencies] … [Given the effect of people dealing with the passage of time, is it surprising? You may come to the conclusion that actually [both victim-survivors] have been quite consistent about what they say, and when we apply it to known dates it all starts to fit into place]. (Prosecution, T6)

The prosecution attempted to rationalise the inconsistencies for the jury through first pointing out that it is common for people, including rape victim-survivors, to have difficulty accurately placing time in memories (Friedman, 1993; Janssen et al., 2006; London et al., 2008). Second, the barrister pointed to the consistent elements of the testimony, much like the "meaningful" (T3) and "fundamental" (T5) consistencies in T3 and T5. The defence barrister spent a significant portion of her closing speech delineating inconsistencies in the victim-survivors' stories, especially victim-survivor2, and had prefaced this with the following:

> [regarding [victim-survivor2] it means being sure that not only is she trustworthy but is she accurate and reliable, and we say you can't be sure about that. Her evidence is clearly inconsistent and unreliable, and my learned friend says well that's time, that's not a case of getting small things wrong, it's enormous inconsistencies, each account is entirely different]. (Defence, T6)

The defence's assertion that each account was entirely different was at odds with the prosecution's characterisation of consistency. The inconsistencies largely came from the difficulty the victim-survivors had with time and location in their accounts, which has been established as a common issue with memory (Friedman, 1993; Janssen et al., 2006; London et al., 2008). The emphasis on such peripheral details has long been a noted tactic used by defence barristers in rape trials (Ellison, 2002; Temkin, 2000; Wheatcroft et al., 2009). The defence barrister in T6 also sought to undermine victim-survivor2's explanation for some of her inconsistencies, which was that she did not recount her experiences in her ABE in a linear way:

[her account in court was] completely different to her account to [police officer] ... when challenged she said she was just saying things, not in order, but you have it there in the ABE transcript, you have the connecting words ... you would know if it was oral, you would know if it was intercourse ... she's in a safe space in the police station, no-one is giving her a hard time. (Defence, T6)

The defence therefore suggested that stories must be linear in order to be considered true and consistent; however, evidence has shown that victim-survivors are often unable to articulate their stories with linearity in their ABEs (Gilmore, 2001; McMillan & Thomas, 2009).

Not only do victim-survivor's accounts have to be suitably consistent, but their accounts must also be whole and complete with every detail from the first disclosure. The omission of details was used against the victim-survivors in T2 and T6 as a way of portraying them as untrustworthy, thus undermining their credibility. As outlined earlier in this chapter, the victim-survivor in T2 did not tell the police that she had had sexual contact with the defendant after the end of their relationship and this was used by the defence as a tool in the cross-examination of not just the victim-survivor but also the OIC. In her closing remarks, defence counsel pointed to this omission as an indication of dishonesty:

What you do know about [victim-survivor's] credibility is that she also reported to the police that [defendant] was pestering her, sending unwanted messages to her asking for sex, [and she tells the police that is not something she is interested in because they split for good in [month] and she wants nothing to do with him, she signs that statement, she produces messages, and then what we can see is that there is a wealth of communication both ways, she gives a number of statements], does she say in any of them that she carried on sleeping with him? Now that doesn't help you with the rape, but it does help you with credibility, doesn't it? (Defence, T2)

Similarly, in T6 omissions, in both victim-survivors stories were highlighted by the defence in her closing remarks:

[other inconsistencies include at [specific event], there was no mention of oral in the ABE]. (Defence, T6)

[having made up allegations about [defendant] kissing her when she was a child, which none of us had heard before, then when she was challenged she backtracks and says it was when she was 15. She says it happened [in specific place], but you know [defendant] wasn't working [in specific place]. (Defence, T6)

There are many reasons a victim-survivor may (consciously or unconsciously) hold back some details or information when disclosing sexual violence. For instance, McMillan and Thomas (2009) found that victim-survivors were not always able to recall or provide specific details in their police interviews. Furthermore, many victim-survivors have a fear of not being believed (Molina & Poppleton, 2020), and so it stands to reason that they may choose not to give certain details to the police when they make a report. Moreover, victim-survivors are well aware of rape myths and these factor into their decisions about whether to tell, when to tell, who to tell, and what they tell (Molina & Poppleton, 2020; Smith & Daly, 2020).

How Is Digital Evidence Used at Trial?

The use of digital evidence in sexual offences investigations has come under increasing scrutiny, with criticisms centring on excessive requests for access to data contained on victim-survivors' digital devices, such as their phone and social media data. There have been growing concerns that irrelevant digital communications evidence can be used at court to undermine victim-survivors because its malleability can serve to help reinforce culturally embedded rape myths and victim-blaming attitudes (Boux & Daum, 2015; Dodge, 2018; Hlavka & Mulla, 2018; Powell et al., 2015). Indeed, social media has been described as a 'treasure trove' for defence teams (Browning, 2011) and so-called 'fishing expeditions' have long been a noted defence tactic (Boux & Daum, 2015; Carimico et al., 2016; Dodge, 2018; Howell & Heberlig, 2007; Sholl, 2013; Uncel, 2011). Whilst it is of course imperative that relevant material is disclosed to the defence, challenges arise when access to data goes beyond what is relevant or is used in ways that undermine victim-survivors based on myths about sexual violence (Temkin & Krahé, 2008).

It is also worth noting that as well as being a potential tool for undermining victim-survivors, it is of course possible for digital evidence to strengthen the prosecution case (Boux & Daum, 2015; Carimico et al., 2016; Dodge, 2018; Ramirez & Denault, 2019). Two studies in England and Wales have compared the assistive value of digital data for the prosecution and defence, but with contrasting findings. Rumney and McPhee (2020) found that digital data assisted the prosecution in 36% of cases where such data had been accessed, whereas it was considered to be of assistance to the defence in 31% of cases where data was accessed. In contrast, Murphy et al. (2021) found that digital evidence assisted the victim-survivor's case almost half (7%) as often as it did for the accused (12%), but most of the time (47%) it supported neither. Whilst both studies used case file analysis, it is not possible to ascertain whether the same method of analysis was used to determine the assistive value of the digital data because this information is not provided by Murphy et al. (2021). Rumney and McPhee (2020) assessed the evidence against CPS disclosure guidance but did not consult with defence lawyers, which is significant because they could have drawn different conclusions as to the usefulness of the evidence for defence strategies at trial.

The observations outlined throughout this chapter have shown that the concerns about digital evidence were well-founded, because digital evidence was indeed used to support rape myth narratives. Examples from T1, T2, and T6 showed how digital communications evidence played a significant role in defence characterisations of victim-survivors' post-assault behaviour as irrational, especially in relation to continued contact with the defendant and the how, when, and who of disclosing. Digital evidence also played a significant role in defence counsel pointing to inconsistencies to undermine victim-survivors' stories. Defence barristers looked to digital messages to compare to flawed recollections in live testimony to 'prove' that victim-survivors' were at best unreliable or at worst liars. A similar tactic was used by the prosecution in T3 where the defendant denied saying to the victim-survivor immediately after sexually assaulting her that he had been paid to give her a massage with a "happy ending". The term "happy ending" was used in the digital messages where the victim-survivor confronted him, and so he claimed that to him 'happy ending' had a different meaning than the common sexual understanding of the term; he claimed he was referring to an emotional state of feeling happy after a massage. Through pointing to the inconsistency between the defendant's denial of saying it at the scene and the presence of the phrase in the messages, the prosecution strongly argued that the defendant did in fact say it:

> [then we have the [victim-survivor's] evidence he said 'happy ending' [at the scene], that he denied...But significantly, why does he say 'including happy ending, that's what I asked for'? If he didn't say it at the scene, then why did he mention it after?] Well that's easy, he can't hide from electronic messages, but he can deny saying something. So what I want you to draw from that is that this is a feeble denial and attempt to justify what he knows he has done. (Prosecution, T3)

The prosecution barrister demonstrated the view that digital evidence can be useful in strengthening cases against defendants because it cannot be 'hidden from', which reflects the idea that digital evidence can act as a 'model witness' (Dodge, 2018) in supporting victim-survivors' reports of sexual violence. Whilst it seemed the jury in T3 did not accept the defendant's version because they found him guilty, a similar defence tactic in T2 seemed to assist them. As was outlined briefly earlier, the defendant offered an alternative meaning to the phrase "you climbed on top of me when I said no" and the defence were able to further undermine the victim-survivor's version through drawing on the problematic notion of 'token resistance'. As my analysis elsewhere (Daly, 2021) demonstrates in more detail, it is very easy, then, for the defence to create alterative meanings for digital evidence and bolster them through drawing on rape myths and cultural narratives. There are further examples throughout Chapters 3 and 4 that exemplify how gendered cultural narratives were drawn upon by defence counsel to infuse meaning to digital communications evidence in ways that undermined the credibility of victim-survivors, such as bolstering characterisations of them as 'crazy' and 'conniving'.

SUMMARY

The evidence I have presented in this chapter demonstrates that rape myths continue to permeate sexual offences trials. Rape myths often were not referred to in overt terms, rather they subtly infused the overarching trial narratives at various points, helping to build an overall picture of a rape or assault that did not conform to the 'real rape' prototype and a victim-survivor who did not fit with the notion of an 'ideal victim'. Examination of the linguistic choices of barristers revealed that focusing on the agency of victim-survivors (and downplaying or obscuring the agency of defendants) plays a key role in this subtlety. Agency becomes a valuable tool for defence counsel because rape myths primarily focus on victim-survivors' behaviour: what they *did* that made them blameworthy, that invited sexual assault, or made it inevitable; what they *should* have done to avoid it; and how they *should* have acted afterwards. Digital evidence was also a key tool in reinforcing defence deployment of rape myths within the overarching trial narratives and even where digital evidence seemed to support the prosecution case more than the defence case, defence counsel were able to draw on rape myths as a tool for undermining the veracity of the evidence.

Importantly, my observations also uncovered new ways in which some rape myths can be deployed. For example, that even prompt reporting (i.e. within 24 hours of the assault) was constructed as suspicious by defence barristers through drawing on myths about what counts as 'reasonable' post-assault behaviour. The worrying dilemma this presents for victim-survivors, that their behaviour can always be portrayed as suspicious no matter what they do, could have serious implications for their faith in the justice system. The ubiquity of digital communications evidence in social life also provided an avenue for defence counsel to not only criticise *when* victim-survivors told, but also *who* and *how*. Another concerning observation was that the sexual behaviour of victim-survivors' mothers could also be used to undermine victim-survivors in trials relating to child sex offences. Unlike victim-survivors, there is no legal protection for mothers in this regard. It appears, then, that where legal or procedural protections are in place to protect victim-survivors from intrusive cross-examinations, their mothers can become a proxy for character assassinations by the defence (this argument is built further in Chapters 3 and 4).

As well as delineating the deployment of rape myths and the tools used in their deployment, this chapter has begun to untangle some of the cultural narratives that re/produce them. For example, cultural narratives that position women as untrustworthy both produce and are reproduced by the myth that says women routinely lie about rape. The significance of cultural narratives and their relationship with rape myths within trial narratives forms the basis of Chapters 3 and 4.

REFERENCES

Abrams, D., Viki, G. T., Masser, B., & Bohner, G. (2003). Perceptions of stranger and acquaintance rape. *Journal of Personality and Social Psychology, 84*(1), 111–125.

Adler, Z. (1987). *Rape on trial.* Routledge & Paul.

Akrami, N., Ekehammar, B., & Araya, T. (2000). Classical and modern racial prejudice: A study of attitudes toward immigrants in Sweden. *European Journal of Social Psychology, 30*(4), 521–532.

Benedet, J. (2010). The age of innocence: A cautious defense of raising the age of consent in Canadian sexual assault law. *New Criminal Law Review: An International and Interdisciplinary Journal, 13*(4), 665–687.

Bohner, G., Eyssel, F., Pina, A., Siebler, F., & Viki, G. T. (2009). Rape myth acceptance: Cognitive, affective and behavioural effects of beliefs that blame the victim and exonerate the perpetrator. In M. Horvath & J. Brown (Eds.), *Rape: Challenging contemporary thinking* (pp. 17–45). Willan.

Bourke, J. (2007). *Rape: A history from 1860 to the present day.* Virago Press.

Boux, H. J., & Daum, C. W. (2015). At the intersection of social media and rape culture. *University of Illinois Journal of Law, Technology & Policy, 2015*(1), 149–186.

Brereton, D. (1997). How different are rape trials? A comparison of the cross-examination of complainants in rape and assault trial. *British Journal of Criminology, Delinquency and Deviant Social Behaviour, 37,* 242.

Brewis, B., & Stockdale, M. (2014). Interpretation of S.41 of the Youth Justice and Criminal Evidence Act 1999: Meaning of 'Sexual Behaviour of the Complainant': *R v RP* [2013] EWCA Crim 2331. *The Journal of Criminal Law, 78*(2), 106–109.

Bronitt, S. (1998). The rules of recent complaint: Rape myths and the legal construction of the "reasonable" rape victim. In P. Easteal (Ed.), *Balancing the scales: Rape, law reform and Australian culture* (pp. 41–59). Federation Press.

Brooks-Hay, O. (2019). Doing the "right thing"? Understanding why rape victim-survivors report to the police. *Feminist Criminology, 15*(2), 174–195.

Brown, J., Horvath, M., Kelly, L., & Westmarland, N. (2010). *Connections and disconnections: Assessing evidence, knowledge and practice in responses to rape* (Project Report). Government Equalities Office.

Browning, J. G. (2011). Digging for the digital dirt: Discovery and use of evidence from social media sites. *SMU Science and Technology Law Review, 14*(3), 465–496.

Burgin, R. (2019). Persistent narratives of force and resistance: Affirmative consent as law reform. *The British Journal of Criminology, 59*(2), 296–314.

Burgin, R., & Flynn, A. (2019). Women's behavior as implied consent: Male "reasonableness" in Australian rape law. *Criminology & Criminal Justice, 23*(1), 334–352.

Burman, M. (2009). Evidencing sexual assault: Women in the witness box. *Probation Journal, 56*(4), 379–398.

Burman, M., Jamieson, L., Nicholson, J., & Brooks, O. (2007). *Impact of aspects of the law of evidence in sexual offence trials: An evaluation study*. Scottish Government.

Burrowes, N. (2013). *Responding to the challenge of rape myths in court: A guide for prosecutors*. NB Research.

Burt, M. R. (1980). Cultural myths and supports for rape. *Journal of Personality and Social Psychology, 38*(2), 217–230.

Carimico, G., Huynh, T., & Wells, S. (2016). Rape and sexual assault. *The Georgetown Journal of Gender and the Law, 17*(1), 359–410.

Carline, A., & Gunby, C. (2011). "How an ordinary jury makes sense of it is a mystery": Barristers' perspectives on rape, consent and the Sexual Offences Act 2003. *The Liverpool Law Review, 32*(3), 237–250.

Chalmers, J., Leverick, F., & Munro, V. E. (2021). Why the jury is, and should still be, out on rape deliberation. *Criminal Law Review, 2021*(9), 753–771.

Christie, N. (1986). The ideal victim. In E. A. Fattah (Ed.), *From crime policy to victim policy* (pp. 17–30). Palgrave Macmillan.

Clark, A. (1987). *Women's silence, men's violence: Sexual assault in England, 1770–1845*. Pandora.

Coates, L., Bavelas, J. B., & Gibson, J. (1994). Anomalous language in sexual assault trial judgments. *Discourse & Society, 5*(2), 189–206.

Conaghan, J., & Russell, Y. (2014). Rape myths, law, and feminist research: 'Myths about myths'? *Feminist Legal Studies, 22*(1), 48.

Cossins, A. (2020). *Closing the justice gap for adult and child sexual assault*. Palgrave Macmillan.

Daly, E. (2021). Making new meanings: The entextualisation of digital communications evidence in English sexual offences trials. *Crime, Media, Culture* [online first]. https://doi.org/10.1177/17416590211048251

Daly, E., Smith, O., Bows, H., Brown, J., Chalmers, J., Cowan, S., et al. (2021). Myths about myths? A commentary on Thomas (2020) and the question of jury rape myth acceptance. *Journal of Gender-Based Violence* [online first]. https://doi.org/10.1332/239868021X16371459419254

Diss, L. E. (2013). Whether you 'like' it or not: The inclusion of social media evidence in sexual harassment cases and how courts can effectively control it. *Boston College Law Review, 54*(4), 1841.

Dodge, A. (2018). The digital witness: The role of digital evidence in criminal justice responses to sexual violence. *Feminist Theory, 19*(3), 303–321.

Dowds, E. (2020). Towards a contextual definition of rape: Consent, coercion and constructive force. *The Modern Law Review, 83*(1), 35–63.

Duggan, M. (2018). *Revisiting the 'ideal victim': Developments in critical victimology.* Policy Press.

Duke, L. A., Allen, D. N., Rozee, P. D., & Bommaritto, M. (2007). The sensitivity and specificity of flashbacks and nightmares to trauma. *Journal of Anxiety Disorders, 22*(2), 319–327.

Durham, R., Lawson, R., Lord, A., & Baird, V. (2017). *Seeing is believing the Northumbria Court observers panel. Report on 30 rape trials 2015–16.* Vera Baird Police & Crime Commissioner.

Edwards, K., Turchik, J., Dardis, C., Reynolds, N., & Gidycz, C. (2011). Rape myths: History, individual and institutional-level presence, and implications for change. *Sex Roles, 65*(11), 761–773.

Edwards, S. (1981). *Female sexuality and the law: A study of constructs of female sexuality as they inform statute and legal procedure.* M. Robertson.

Ehrlich, S. (1998). The discursive reconstruction of sexual consent. *Discourse & Society, 9*(2), 149–171.

Ehrlich, S. (2001). *Representing rape.* Routledge.

Ehrlich, S. (2015). *'Inferring' consent in the context of rape and sexual assault* (p. 141). Oxford University Press.

Ellemers, N., & Barreto, M. (2009). Collective action in modern times: How modern expressions of prejudice prevent collective action. *Journal of Social Issues, 65*(4), 749–768.

Ellison, L. (2002). *The adversarial process and the vulnerable witness.* Oxford University Press.

Ellison, L., & Munro, V. (2009). Reacting to rape. *The British Journal of Criminology, 49*(2), 202–219.

End Violence Against Women Coalition. (2018). *Attitudes to sexual consent.* https://www.endviolenceagainstwomen.org.uk/wp-content/uploads/1-Attitudes-to-sexual-consent-Research-findings-FINAL.pdf. Accessed 12 November 2020.

Estrich, S. (1987). *Real rape.* Harvard University Press.

Eyssel, F., & Bohner, G. (2008). Modern rape myths: The Acceptance of Modern Myths about Sexual Aggression (AMMSA) Scale. In M. A. Morrison & T.

G. Morrison (Eds.), *The psychology of modern prejudice* (pp. 261–276). Nova Science Publishers.

Feist, A., Ashe, J., Lawrence, J., McPhee, D., & Wilson, R. (2007). *Investigating and detecting recorded offences of rape.* http://webarchive.nationalarchives. gov.uk/20110218140524/http://rds.homeoffice.gov.uk/rds/pdfs07/rdsolr 1807.pdf. Accessed 12 February 2019.

Fisher, R. J. (1993). Social desirability bias and the validity of indirect questioning. *The Journal of Consumer Research, 20*(2), 303–315.

Fraser, C. (2015). From 'ladies first' to 'asking for it': Benevolent sexism in the maintenance of rape culture. *California Law Review, 103*(1), 141–203.

Friedman, W. J. (1993). Memory for the time of past events. *Psychological Bulletin, 113*(1), 44–66.

Galliano, G., Noble, L. M., Travis, L. A., & Puechl, C. (1993). Victim reactions during rape/sexual assault. *Journal of Interpersonal Violence, 8*(1), 109.

Gerger, H., Kley, H., Bohner, G., & Siebler, F. (2007). The acceptance of modern myths about sexual aggression scale: Development and validation in German and English. *Aggressive Behavior, 33*(5), 422–440.

Gilmore, L. (2001). *The limits of autobiography: Trauma and testimony.* Cornell University Press.

Gravelin, C. R., Biernat, M., & Bucher, C. E. (2019). Blaming the victim of acquaintance rape: Individual, situational, and sociocultural factors. *Frontiers in Psychology, 9*, 2422.

Grubb, A., & Turner, E. (2012). Attribution of blame in rape cases: A review of the impact of rape myth acceptance, gender role conformity and substance use on victim blaming. *Aggression and Violent Behavior, 17*(5), 443–452.

Gurnham, D. (2016). A critique of carceral feminist arguments on rape myths and sexual scripts. *New Criminal Law Review, 19*(2), 141–170.

Hamby, S. L., & Koss, M. P. (2003). Shades of gray: A qualitative study of terms used in the measurement of sexual victimization. *Psychology of Women Quarterly, 27*(3), 243–255.

Harris, J., & Grace, S. (1999). *A question of evidence? Investigating and prosecuting rape in the 1990s* (No. 196). Home Office.

Heidt, J. M., Marx, B. P., & Forsyth, J. P. (2005). Tonic immobility and childhood sexual abuse: A preliminary report evaluating the sequela of rape-induced paralysis. *Behaviour Research And Therapy, 43*(9), 1157–1171.

Hlavka, H. R., & Mulla, S. (2018). "That's how she talks": Animating text message evidence in the sexual assault trial. *Law & Society Review, 52*(2), 401–435.

Hohl, K., & Conway, M. A. (2017). Memory as evidence: How normal features of victim memory lead to the attrition of rape complaints. *Criminology & Criminal Justice, 17*(3), 248–265.

Hohl, K., & Stanko, E. A. (2015). Complaints of rape and the criminal justice system: Fresh evidence on the attrition problem in England and Wales. *European Journal of Criminology, 12*(3), 324–341.

Horvath, M., & Brown, J. (2006). The role of drugs and alcohol in rape. *Medicine, Science and the Law, 46*(3), 219–228.

Horvath, M., & Giner-Sorolla, R. (2007). Below the age of consent: Influences on moral and legal judgments of adult-adolescent sexual relationships. *Journal of Applied Social Psychology, 37*(12), 2980–3009.

Hovdestad, W., & Renner, E. (2021). *What does it mean to use a "real rape" myth in a sexual assault trial?* Social & Legal Studies Blog. https://socialandlegalstudies.wordpress.com/2021/02/08/what-does-it-mean-to-use-a-real-rape-myth-in-a-sexual-assault-trial/. Accessed 21 March 2021.

Howell, B. A., & Herberlig, B. M. (2007). The Lamar Owens case: How digital evidence contributed to an acquittal in an explosive rape case. *The Computer & Internet Lawyer, 24*(12), 1–4.

ICM. (2005). *Sexual assault research report.* Prepared for Amnesty International. https://web.archive.org/web/20060207094708/https://www.amnesty.org.uk/images/ul/s/sexual_assault_summary_report_2.doc. Accessed 15 April 2019.

Janssen, S. M. J., Chessa, A. G., & Murre, J. M. J. (2006). Memory for time: How people date events. *Memory & Cognition, 34*(1), 138–147.

Kahn, A. S., Jackson, J., Kully, C., Badger, K., & Halvorsen, J. (2003). Calling it rape: Differences in experiences of women who do or Do not label their sexual assault as rape. *Psychology of Women Quarterly, 27,* 233–242.

Kelly, L. (1987). The continuum of sexual violence. In J. Hanmer & M. Maynard (Eds.), *Women, violence and social control* (pp. 46–60). Macmillan.

Kelly, L., Lovett, J., & Regan, L. (2005). *A gap or a chasm? Attrition in reported rape cases.* Home Office.

Kelly, L., Temkin, J., & Griffiths, S. (2006). *Section 41: An evaluation of new legislation limiting sexual history evidence in rape trials.* Home Office.

Koss, M. P., & Harvey, M. R. (1987). *The rape victim: Clinical and community interventions.* Lexington.

Krahé, B., Temkin, J., & Bieneck, S. (2007). Schema-driven information processing in judgements about rape. *Applied Cognitive Psychology, 21*(5), 601–619.

Leahy, S. (2014). The corroboration warning in sexual offence trials: Final vestige of the historic suspicion of sexual offence complainants or a necessary protection for defendants? *International Journal of Evidence & Proof, 18*(1), 41–64.

Lees, S. (2002). *Carnal knowledge: Rape on trial* (2nd ed.). Women's Press.

Leverick, F. (2020). What do we know about rape myths and juror decision making? *International Journal of Evidence & Proof, 24*(3), 255–279.

Lodrick, Z. (2007). Psychological trauma: What every trauma worker should know. *British Journal of Psychotherapy Integration, 4*(2), 18–29.

London, K., Bruck, M., Wright, D. B., & Ceci, S. J. (2008). Review of the contemporary literature on how children report sexual abuse to others: Findings, methodological issues, and implications for forensic interviewers. *Memory, 16*(1), 29–47.

Lonsway, K. A., & Fitzgerald, L. F. (1994). Rape myths. *Psychology of Women Quarterly, 18*(2), 133–164.

Mantyla, K. (2018). *Dave Daubenmire: It's 'sexual abuse' for women to lead men on.* https://www.rightwingwatch.org/post/dave-daubenmire-its-sexual-abuse-for-women-to-lead-men-on/. Accessed 9 February 2020.

McGlynn, C. (2017). Rape trials and sexual history evidence: Reforming the law on third-party evidence. *The Journal of Criminal Law, 81*(5), 367–392.

McMahon, S., & Farmer, L. G. (2011). An updated measure for assessing subtle rape myths. *Social Work Research, 35*(2), 71–81.

McMillan, L. (2007). *Feminists organising against gendered violence.* Palgrave Macmillan.

McMillan, L., & Thomas, M. (2009). Police interviews of rape victims: Tensions and contradictions. In M. Horvath & J. Brown (Eds.), *Rape: Challenging contemporary thinking* (pp. 255–280). Willan.

Ministry of Justice, Home Office, & Office for National Statistics. (2013). *An overview of sexual offending in England and Wales.* https://www.gov.uk/government/uploads/system/uploads/attachment_data/file/214970/sexual-offending-overview-jan-2013.pdf. Accessed 16 March 2019.

Molina, J., & Poppleton, S. (2020). *Rape survivors and the criminal justice system.* Victims' Commissioner.

Muehlenhard, C. L. (1988). Misinterpreted dating behaviors and the risk of date rape. *Journal of Social and Clinical Psychology, 6*(1), 20–37.

Muehlenhard, C. L., & Linton, M. A. (1987). Date rape and sexual aggression in dating situations. *Journal of Counseling Psychology, 34*(2), 186–196.

Muehlenhard, C. L., & MacNaughton, J. S. (1988). Women's beliefs about women who "lead men on." *Journal of Social and Clinical Psychology, 7*(1), 65–79.

Munro, V. (2010). An unholy trinity? Non-consent, coercion and exploitation in contemporary legal responses to sexual violence in England and Wales. *Current Legal Problems, 63*(1), 45–71.

Munro, V., & Kelly, L. (2009). A vicious cycle? Attrition and conviction patterns in contemporary rape cases in England and Wales. In M. Horvath & J. Brown (Eds.), *Rape: Challenging contemporary thinking* (pp. 281–300). Willan.

Murphy, A., Hine, B., Yesberg, J. A., Wunsch, D., & Charleton, B. (2021). Lessons from London: A contemporary examination of the factors affecting attrition among rape complaints. *Psychology, Crime & Law* [online first].

Nurius, P. S., Norris, J., Macy, R. J., & Huang, B. (2004). Women's situational coping with acquaintance sexual assault. *Violence Against Women, 10*(5), 450–478.

Payne, D., & Wermeling, L. (2009). Domestic violence and the female victim: The real reason women stay! *Journal of Multicultural, Gender and Minority Studies, 3*(1), 1–6.

Peterson, Z. D., & Muehlenhard, C. L. (2011). A match-and-motivation model of how women label their nonconsensual sexual experiences. *Psychology of Women Quarterly, 35*(4), 558–570.

Powell, A, Henry, N., & Flynn, A. (2015). *Rape justice*. Palgrave Macmillan.

Raitt, F. (2004). Expert evidence as context: Historical patterns and contemporary attitudes in the prosecution of sexual offences. *Feminist Legal Studies, 12*(2), 233–244.

Ramirez, F. A., & Denault, V. (2019). *Facebook, female victims, and social media evidence in sexual assault trials*. Presented at the 10th International Conference on Social Media & Society, Toronto, Canada.

Reece, H. (2013). Rape myths: Is elite opinion right and popular opinion wrong? *Oxford Journal of Legal Studies, 33*(3), 445–473.

Reid, J. A., Haskell, R. A., Dillahunt-Aspillaga, C., & Thor, J. A. (2013). Contemporary review of empirical and clinical studies of trauma bonding in violent or exploitative relationships. *International Journal of Psychology Research, 8*(1), 37.

Rhodes, N. R., & McKenzie, E. B. (1998). Why do battered women stay? *Aggression and Violent Behavior, 3*(4), 391–406.

Rose, M., Nadler, J., & Clark, J. (2006). Appropriately upset? Emotion norms and perceptions of crime victims. *Law and Human Behavior, 30*(2), 203–219.

Rothschild, B. (2000). *The body remembers*. Norton.

Rumney, P., & McPhee, D. (2020) The evidential value of electronic communications data in rape and sexual offence cases. *Criminal Law Review*, 1–16.

Sholl, E. W. (2013). Exhibit facebook: The discoverability and admissibility of social media evidence. *Tulane Journal of Technology and Intellectual Property, 16*, 207–230.

Sims, C. M., Noel, N. E., & Maisto, S. A. (2007). Rape blame as a function of alcohol presence and resistance type. *Addictive Behaviors, 32*(12), 2766–2775.

Smith, O. (2018). *Rape trials in England and Wales: Observing justice and rethinking rape myths*. Palgrave Macmillan.

Smith, O. (2021). Cultural scaffolding and the long view of rape trials. In R. Killean, E. Dowds, & A. M. McAlinden (Eds.), *Sexual violence on trial* (pp. 241–253). Routledge.

Smith, O., & Daly, E. (2020). *Evaluation of the sexual violence complainants' advocate scheme.* Loughborough University.

Smith, O., & Skinner, T. (2017). How rape myths are used and challenged in rape and sexual assault trials. *Social & Legal Studies, 26*(4), 441–466.

Stanko, E. (2013). *Intimate intrusions.* Taylor and Francis.

Swim, J. K., Aikin, K. J., Hall, W. S., & Hunter, B. A. (1995). Sexism and racism: Old-fashioned and modern prejudices. *Journal of Personality and Social Psychology, 68*(2), 199–214.

Taylor, N., & Joudo, J. L. (2005). *The impact of pre-recorded video and closed-circuit television testimony by adult sexual assault complainants on jury decision-making: An experimental study.* Australian Institute of Criminology.

Temkin, J. (1984). Regulating sexual history evidence—The limits of discretionary legislation. *International and Comparative Law Quarterly, 33*(4), 942–978.

Temkin, J. (2000). Prosecuting and defending rape: Perspectives from the bar. *Journal of Law and Society, 27*(2), 219–248.

Temkin, J. (2010). 'And always keep a-hold of nurse, for fear of finding something worse': Challenging rape myths in the courtroom. *New Criminal Law Review: An International and Interdisciplinary Journal, 13*(4), 710–734.

Temkin, J., Gray, J. M., & Barrett, J. (2018). Different functions of rape myth use in court: Findings from a trial observation study. *Feminist Criminology, 13*(2), 205–226.

Temkin, J., & Krahé, B. (2008). *Sexual assault and the justice gap.* Hart.

Thomas, C. (2020). The 21st century jury: Contempt, bias and the impact of jury service. *Criminal Law Review, 11,* 987–1011.

Uncel, M. (2011). "Facebook is now friends with the court": Current federal rules and social media evidence. *Jurimetrics, 52,* 43–69.

Waites, M. (2005). *The age of consent.* Palgrave Macmillan.

Wheatcroft, J. M., Wagstaff, G. F., & Moran, A. (2009). Revictimizing the victim? How rape victims experience the UK legal system. *Victims & Offenders, 4*(3), 265–284.

Wolchover, D., & Heaton-Armstrong, A. (2008). Debunking rape myths. *New Law Journal, 158*(7305), 117.

CHAPTER 3

Respectability

Abstract The previous chapter outlined that rape myths remain a prominent feature in courtroom narratives and serve to undermine accounts of rape and sexual assault. The present chapter builds on this by establishing ways in which those myths are scaffolded by and interact with broader cultural narratives and systems of oppression to further disadvantage victim-survivors and benefit defendants. Intersecting gendered and classed cultural narratives worked as mechanisms to further undermine victim-survivors and bolster the credibility of defendants by differently framing them through lenses of what counts as respectable.

Keywords Rape myths · Court · Rape trials · Cultural narratives · Social class · Intersectionality

The previous chapter outlined that rape myths remain a prominent feature in courtroom narratives and serve to undermine accounts of rape and sexual assault. The present chapter builds on this by establishing ways in which those myths are scaffolded by and interact with broader cultural narratives and systems of oppression to further disadvantage victim-survivors and benefit defendants. Intersecting gendered and classed cultural narratives worked as mechanisms to further undermine victim-survivors and bolster the credibility of defendants by differently

E. Daly, *Rape, Gender and Class*,
https://doi.org/10.1007/978-3-030-93925-0_3

framing them through lenses of what counts as respectable. Crucially, the structural inequalities and systems of oppression reflected in the narratives deployed by barristers may not necessarily be congruent with the lived reality of the victim-survivors or defendants. That is, a narrative may draw on working-class stereotypes, but that does not mean the victim-survivor or defendant would describe or identify themselves as such. Characteristics of participants became salient at trial without the choice of the victim-survivor or defendant because their perceived affiliation to a particular group was imposed on them by barristers through the narratives they employed. This is made possible by the combative nature of barrister conduct in the adversarial trial (Smith, 2018) and the controlled question-and-answer format of testimonies, where witnesses are constrained in their ability to provide a free narrative or challenge the content or manner of the questions (Brown et al., 2010; Ainsworth, 2015).

A small body of observational research has begun to go beyond exploring rape myths in the courtroom, taking an intersectional feminist approach to explore how minoritised and marginalised victim-survivors may be differently undermined through defence counsel drawing on a range of stereotypes. Powell et al. (2017) observed child sexual assault trials in the US, identifying courtroom narratives that drew on established gender, race, class, and age stereotypes in order to undermine the credibility of victim-survivors. Their analysis drew attention to the role of structural inequalities and systems of oppression in courtroom narratives. Powell et al. (2017) identified three core cultural narratives in their observations: invisible wounds, rebellious adolescents, and dysfunctional families. Each of these narratives were interwoven with rape myths. For example, when drawing on the notion of rebellious adolescents, which positioned teenagers as defiant and deceitful, defence counsel were relying on the myth that false allegations are common and the associated gendered cultural narrative that women are untrustworthy and lie about rape. In England and Wales, Smith (2018) carried out an intersectional analysis of her trial observations. Like Powell et al. (2017), she found that rape trial narratives were permeated by oppressive cultural narratives. Although Smith's (2018) analysis did not highlight common narrative themes across the sample, it did delineate individual trial narratives related to social class, disability, race, ethnicity, and nationality stereotyping. Again, the stereotyping identified by Smith (2018) interlinked with rape myth narratives to bolster defence counsel's undermining of victim-survivors' credibility.

What Are Cultural Narratives and Why Do They Matter?

According to Fivush (2010), cultural narratives provide a "shared understanding of the shape of a life and how a life is to be understood" (p. 90). They "describe those stories about persons, places, or things that contain consistent storylines and thematic content across individuals and settings" within a culture (Glover, 2003, p. 193). These narratives provide frameworks for understanding how people and places are embedded within a particular culture and enable people to make sense of their lives, interactions, and experiences (McLean et al., 2018; Richardson, 1997). Cultural narratives are also a framework for understanding what it means to be part of a particular social category, such as 'woman' or 'heterosexual' (Hammack & Toolis, 2016; McLean & Syed, 2016), and enable people to make sense of their positioning within the world in relation to others (McKenzie-Mohr & Lafrance, 2011). This is because power and oppression play a crucial role in shaping cultural narratives (McLean et al., 2018).

It is commonly understood that cultural narratives produce and reproduce power structures, thereby helping to maintain the status quo for the powerful (Lafrance & McKenzie-Mohr, 2014; McKenzie-Mohr & Lafrance, 2011; Stanley, 2007). For example, in writing about the trope of the American Dream, Hsu (1996) and Pierre (2004) demonstrate how cultural narratives of ethnicity serve to reinforce the dominant white middle-class ideology through the production and reproduction of 'cultural racism'. Cultural narratives therefore reflect structural inequalities and systems of oppression within our society. Myths and stereotypes permeate cultural narratives and serve to subtly dictate the 'proper' way to behave according to the dominant ideology; that is, cultural narratives are "designed to maintain and buttress the values and interests of the dominant group, and to do so in such a way as to remove all but the most banal signs of the center's rule" (Hsu, 1996, p. 38).

Some scholars have conceptualised cultural narratives as purely hegemonic. For example, for Powell et al. (2017), cultural narratives are the "shared perspectives of dominant groups" (p. 459), which implies there are no cultural narratives available for those not part of a dominant group. In contrast, other scholars understand cultural narratives as made up of master narratives and counter-narratives (Richardson, 1997; Yamamoto et al., 1994), where master narratives are those that frame the dominant understanding of or within a cultural group, and counter-narratives are those that oppose or are not congruent with master narratives. It is the master narratives which are hegemonic because they are created by the powerful to maintain their interests (Richardson, 1997). These master narratives determine what is expected and unexpected in a life experience and what therefore comes to be taken for granted and accepted as truth (Lafrance & McKenzie-Mohr, 2014; McLean et al., 2018). This makes these narratives "both more 'tellable' and 'hearable' than their marginalized alternatives" (Lafrance & McKenzie-Mohr, 2014, p. 3) because those who are marginalised in society are silenced and unheard (Stanley, 2007).

These 'marginalised alternatives', or counter-narratives, are narratives that provide an alternative, or resistant, understanding of the world and of self to those who are oppressed by master narratives (Nelson, 2001). The role of these narratives is to "expose the lies which hold together the ideological armour of privilege, domination and oppression" (Harris et al., 2001, p. 14). This quality of resistance led some to refer to them as 'resistance narratives' (Fivush, 2010). These theoretical perspectives have emancipatory aims; therefore, consideration of resistance narratives is important because these narratives can play an important role in cultural change (McLean et al., 2018). Decades of feminist scholarship and activism have produced resistance narratives, but some "remain heavily individualized and medicalized through the language of trauma and post-traumatic stress disorder" (Lafrance & McKenzie-Mohr, 2014, p. 2). This demonstrates the rigid and persistent nature of master narratives and the difficulty faced in forming effective resistance narratives. To view or produce resistance narratives as a binary counter to a master narrative is simplistic and to construct a resistance narrative as the opposite of a master narrative constrains its ability to counter, which can lead to resistance narratives that both challenge *and* reproduce hegemonic master narratives (Lafrance & McKenzie-Mohr, 2014; McLean et al., 2018).

Cultural narratives, both master and resistance, cannot capture the complexity of how things are experienced. As Brown (2013) puts it,

> no single story can encompass the richness of experience and much goes untold. Women's stories reveal gaps and contradictions in a selective process about what information to include. (p. 7)

Indeed, Loseke (2001) argues that what she calls the 'formula story' of wife abuse glosses over the nuances and complexities of women's lived experience in favour of "lurid accounts of heinous behaviour, depraved perpetrators, and helpless victims" (p. 107). Formula stories are theorised similarly to master narratives in that both "refer to narratives of typical actors engaging in typical behaviors within typical plots leading to expectable moral evaluations" (Loseke, 2007, p. 664). Following Loseke (2001), then, rape myths can be viewed as part of the master narrative for rape in that they reflect the notion of the distinctive actors of 'aggressive man' as perpetrator and 'blameless woman' as victim (DiBennardo, 2018; Nilsson, 2019; O'Hara, 2012; Schwark, 2017). The attitudes and beliefs expressed through rape myths are reflected in the formation of the master narrative and are reproduced by it. This is often conceptualised as 'rape culture', which refers to the multifarious societal attitudes and beliefs that create a conducive context for sexual violence to occur and that normalise and encourage said violence (Buchwald et al., 1993). The concept therefore looks beyond the individual to the underlying cultural practices and narratives that act as cultural scaffolding for rape (Gavey, 2005). Rape culture is a symptom of a patriarchal, heteronormative society (Brownmiller, 1975; Herman, 1984), and cultural narratives that re/produce rape myths serve to perpetuate rape culture and thus reinforce patriarchal and heteronormative ideologies. It is not only sexism and heteronormativity that are reinforced by rape culture, because rape culture also produces and reproduces other oppressions along, for example, ableist and classist lines (Fanghanel, 2020). Indeed, an intersectional feminist perspective recognises that:

> although all women and girls are in some way subject to gender discrimination, all women and girls are not discriminated against in the same way..., hierarchical structures interact and intersect with gender inequality, and [manifest differently] according to other markers of a woman's or a girl's social location. (Vera-Gray, 2017, p. 128)

These 'hierarchical structures' are produced and reproduced in cultural narratives. The concept of cultural narratives is therefore useful in exploring how structures of inequality and oppression, as well as rape myths, are drawn upon to differently undermine victim-survivors in the courtroom.

WHAT COUNTS AS 'RESPECTABLE'?

Narratives of respectability permeated all six trials. These narratives drew on middle-class ideals of respectability whilst also drawing on working-class stereotypes, thereby positioning victim-survivors, and some other prosecution witnesses, as not credible because they did not adhere to middle-class ideals. This section shows how these narratives were formulated at the intersection of gender, class, and age. According to Skeggs (1997), respectability is a significant marker by which class is measured and ascribed. As such, I first establish how barristers highlighted parts of witnesses' personal circumstances that were congruent with wider cultural narratives about working-class people in Britain. Then, the intersections of victim-survivors' gender, class, and age are explored through two prevalent narrative themes—sexuality and motherhood—and contrasted with framings of defendants as respectable men.

Establishing Social Class in Trial Narratives

Social class was often indicated within the trial narratives through 'micro-examinations'. I use the term 'micro-examination' to distinguish smaller chunks of questioning within the sub-genres of trial (i.e. evidence-in-chief, cross-examination, and re-examination). In the context of how social class was signified, the micro-examinations usually consisted of short sets of introductory or scene-setting questions used to characterise the background of the witnesses. The questions were brief and subtly pointed to stigmatising cultural narratives; thus, they could be seen as akin to microaggressions (see Sue et al., 2007). These micro-examinations worked to underpin working-class[1] narratives within the observed trials. The working-class narratives, therefore, were rarely formed through direct reference to working-class stereotypes; rather, they were built through small details throughout the trial narratives that culminated in a working-class backdrop. All victim-survivors, defendants, and other witnesses in the trials were racialised as white and were therefore racially privileged. This

---

[1] There are varying definitions of working-class and the usefulness of the term in the twenty-first century is contested (Harvey, 2005; Payne, 2013); however, for my purposes I am using the term not to define the people in the trials but to reflect a set of stereotypes that exist in our society about people perceived to be from working-class communities or low socioeconomic backgrounds. This is not a comment on whether the participants were or were not working-class or would identify themselves as such.

racialisation did however help form the working-class narratives because whiteness is salient in dominant working-class stereotypes in Britain, with a delineation between respectable and non-respectable working-class whites (Lawler, 2012; Skeggs, 2004; Watt, 2006). The discussions of class throughout this book therefore specifically relate to narratives about white working-class,[2] and specifically white British working-class.[3]

Through micro-examinations of victim-survivors and defendants, small details were presented which when taken together pointed towards being working-class. These details included reference to the towns and villages they resided in, which in all but T3 included areas considered deprived[4] (Department for Communities and Local Government, 2015), and the types of accommodation they lived in, for example social housing (T4) or 'council estates' (T5, T6) or caravans (T6). Haylett (2003) and Skeggs (2004) note the significance of 'place' in representations of the working-classes, and Mannay (2015) further notes that this can become of particular pertinence in formations of working-class motherhood with mothers (and their children) being labelled a 'type' of mother/family based on where they live. All of the trials involved some allegations that took place in domestic settings; therefore, descriptions of those dwellings were relevant, but these 'crumbs' elicited through micro-examinations underpinned the wider narrative.

The types of (un)employment of victim-survivors and defendants were also detailed in each trial. In all trials, victim-survivors and defendants who were employed, or had been around the time of the alleged incidents, were in types of employment[5] and/or working patterns typically considered working-class in contemporary society according to analysis by

[2] I note that race in general and whiteness in particular are not objective truths, rather social constructions shaped by social, political, and historical contexts that have tangible effects on lived experience (e.g. Byrne, 2006; Feagin, 2020; Frankenberg, 1993; Rasmussen et al., 2001).

[3] Nationality is key to both racialisation and class narratives. For example, EU migrants and white Irish are differently stereotyped to white British working-classes. I therefore acknowledge that the use of white British is not unproblematic as it homogenises a diverse group that includes generational descendants of, for example, EU migrants.

[4] Living in an area considered deprived does not mean all the people living there are deprived; however, for the purpose of this analysis, it is the 'reputation' of these areas as deprived that informs the narratives. It is not a comment on whether the individuals in these trials were themselves necessarily deprived.

[5] In order to help protect confidentiality, these jobs cannot be specified.

Roberts (2011), and in some cases, this was characterised by the precarity of their employment (Skeggs, 2011). The victim-survivor and defendant in T2 were in receipt of housing benefit, which was introduced into the narrative through the defendant's police interview transcript which was read into evidence in court. The defendant was explaining to the police officers what he thought had led to the deterioration of his relationship with the victim-survivor since the time of the alleged rape. It is unclear why the reference to social welfare was not edited out of the transcript, as it is difficult to see what relevance this level of detail could have to the case. Simply commenting that there were arguments about finances would have sufficed to make the same point, and there was no suggestion from the defence that these difficulties were a motive for the victim-survivor to stay in the relationship or to lie about rape.

The victim-survivor in T4 and the victim-survivor's mother in T5 were long-term unemployed because of disability (T4) and full-time parenting responsibilities (T5) and were in receipt of social welfare. This was directly raised by the defence in both trials. For example:

> *Defence*: There were texts between you and [friend]?
> *Victim-survivor*: Yeah.
> *Defence*: Talking about your benefits?
> *Victim-survivor*: Yeah.
> *Defence*: Then you text her a few days later to update her after you've been to the police?
> *Victim-survivor*: Yeah. (T4)

In this extract, the defence counsel mentioned social welfare ('benefits') to reference a text message exchange between the victim-survivor and a friend; however, it was irrelevant to the case and because it formed no part of any arguments put forth by either barrister, it did not need to be asked. The defence could have established that the victim-survivor had texted her friend without referencing social welfare; removing the question "Talking about your benefits?" would not have altered the information elicited. By drawing the jury's attention to the victim-survivor being in receipt of social welfare, the defence arguably relied on stereotypes of 'scroungers' and the 'underserving poor' (Hancock & Mooney, 2011; Morrison, 2019; Romano, 2017). Such narratives have long been pervasive in Britain, with 'the poor' being scapegoated for perceived economic and social ills (Morrison, 2019; Welshman, 2013). In particular,

Murray's (1990, 1994, 2001) widely criticised work on 'the underclass', which depicted 'the poor' as 'feckless' and reliant on social welfare, strongly influenced policy and media portrayals throughout the 1990s and into the 2000s, with a resurgence under Coalition and Conservative Governments in the 2010s (MacDonald et al., 2020). This framing ignores structural inequalities, viewing poverty as resultant of individual failure or laziness, and understands 'respectability' as something achieved through participating in the workforce (Patrick, 2016). These political and media discourses are also reflected in popular culture through 'reality' TV shows such as *Benefits Street*, and thus, powerful 'scrounger' narratives have become culturally embedded in Britain (Day et al., 2020; Patrick, 2016). Reflecting these narratives in the courtroom can therefore be beneficial to barristers wishing to portray a witness as objectionable or untrustworthy.

In T5, the defence counsel mentioned social welfare in a more overtly disparaging way, compared with T4, during cross-examination of the child victim-survivor's mother:

> *Defence*: I'm going to suggest that he moved in with you.
> *Mother*: No, my neighbour.
> *Defence*: I know you talked about 'officially', but we don't care about officially, we don't care about what you did to keep benefits. (T5)

Defence counsel later repeated this reference:

> *Defence*: And you struggled at this time with chores around the house?
> *Mother*: Yeah.
> *Defence*: And that is when [defendant] moved in next door, because you didn't want to lose benefits?
> *Mother*: Yeah. (T5)

In both these extracts, there was direct reference to the 'benefits cheat' stereotype commonly associated with working-class women (Gelsthorpe, 2010). The pertinent issue was that the victim-survivor and defendant began co-habiting, which could have been established without needing to explain the reason for any decisions. An analysis of results from the British Social Attitudes survey found that although public beliefs about the prevalence and morality of benefit fraud has decreased in recent years, it remains more harshly judged than the similar offence of tax avoidance (Geiger et al., 2017). This double standard arguably reflects the tendency for poorer people, particularly social welfare claimants, to be judged more negatively than those who are more affluent (Geiger et al., 2017). Media portrayals are often critical of benefits claimants, reinforce stereotypes about working-class people (Button & Tunley, 2015; Jensen, 2014; Nunn & Biressi, 2010), and draw on the idea of the 'underclass' (see Murray, 1990, 2001) and 'underserving poor' willing to obtain social welfare through fraudulent means (Geiger et al., 2017; Lundstrom, 2013). Drawing on these cultural narratives therefore arguably sought to present the mother in T5 as unlikeable to the jury.

Other aspects of trial narratives further fed into the broad working-class narratives, such as framings of alcohol consumption and domestic abuse, which will be discussed in more detail throughout this chapter as they are points with marked salience to other gendered, ageist, and ableist narratives relating to sexual violence.

Working-Class Femininities as 'Unrespectable'

Women's femininity has long been judged and policed in terms of excessiveness, particularly with regard to sex and alcohol (Mackiewicz, 2015) and particularly for women perceived as working-class (Skeggs, 1997). As Skeggs (1997, 2005) notes, 'promiscuity' and excessiveness, including drunkenness, are commonly associated with working-class femininities. This relates to the middle-class ideal of respectability, which "is one of the most ubiquitous signifiers of class" (Skeggs, 1997, p. 1). Traditional heterosexual femininity was constructed based on middle-class ideals and respectability was used as a measure by which to hold certain groups of people as valued and legitimated whilst 'othering' those not deemed respectable (Lawler, 2005; Skeggs, 1997). Robinson (1984) historically situated these narratives in the obscuring and denial of women's sexuality and desire, particularly along classed and racialised lines. Similarly, Clark (1987) delineated the significance of classed narratives in the construction of working women as unchaste and thus unrapeable. Phipps (2009) and Anthias (2014) have articulated similar thoughts on the intersections of gender and class with regard to sexual violence and it has been a noted form of narrative in previous rape trial observation research in England (Lees, 2002; Smith, 2018).

This was reflected in T1 and T4, where alcohol formed an integral part of constructing classed and gendered narratives. Alcohol was a prominent feature in T1 and a peripheral feature in T4, whereas it was not talked about in any of the other trials. In both T1 and T4, the narratives involving alcohol drew on notions of respectability by referencing the victim-survivors' heavy alcohol consumption, which they each stated in evidence adduced to the court. For example, in T4, the victim-survivor referred to her heavy drinking during her ABE:

> I went to my friend's house and had three cans of beer...5% beers, [didn't affect me much cos I used to drink more than that, I've stopped drinking now, it would just have given me a little tingle in me ear nothing more]. (Victim-survivor, ABE, T4)

In this extract, she suggested that she had previously had difficulty with alcohol, but had stopped drinking heavily by the time of the rapes, which was also confirmed by the defendant in his police interview:

> [<*Q&A*>: Asked if victim-survivor has mental health issues, defendant says yes and references the accident she had. Defendant says that she self-harms and that she used to drink a lot of alcohol, he says she struggles to cope with things]. (Defendant, police interview, T4)

The defendant clearly linked the victim-survivor's drinking to her mental health. This was later built upon through the testimony of a mutual friend of the victim-survivor and defendant:

> *Defence*: Regarding volatility, what does [victim-survivor] do to make you think she's volatile?
> *Friend*: Drinking, the ways she acts.
> *Defence*: And how often do you see that behaviour?
> *Friend*: Occasionally. (T4)

The linking of volatility to alcohol consumption drew on classed and gendered notions of respectability. Gendered stereotypes about women as 'hysterical' and 'crazy' interlinked here with ableist narratives (see Chapter 4) and classed notions of excess, where heavy drinking and violence, including intimate partner violence, have been conceived of as a working-class phenomenon (Bourke, 2007; Phipps, 2009). It had particular salience in the context of this relationship, where the defendant had several convictions relating to domestic abuse perpetrated against the victim-survivor. This notion was arguably given congruence by the judge including it in her summing-up of the evidence for the jury:

> He said that [victim-survivor] has previously told him she's scared of [defendant], but that [victim-survivor] gave as good as she got and can be worse when drinking. (Judge, T4)

The wording the judge used, "gave as good as she got", is problematic because it minimised the defendant's known violent behaviour towards the victim-survivor whilst at the same time equating the victim-survivor's 'volatility' with the defendant's domestic abuse. This is reflective of cultural narratives that quickly villainise women but excuse men for violence, as was illustrated in discourses surrounding a court case involving Johnny Depp and Amanda Heard in the latter half of 2020 (see, for example, Peat, 2020). A similar narrative was found by Hlavka and Mulla (2018) in the US, where defence counsel used the term "gave as good as she got" to support their characterisation of a Black woman victim-survivor as aggressive, again in the context of intimate partner violence. Whilst the victim-survivor in T4 was privileged in this regard due to being racialised as white, the 'aggressive woman' narrative for both her and the victim-survivor in Hlavka and Mulla (2018) sought to distance them from the 'ideal victim' (Christie, 1986), thus minimising the male violence whilst shifting blame onto the victim-survivors.

In T1, the victim-survivor's drinking habits were put under far more scrutiny.

> *Defence*: You get drunk quite often, you often can't remember how you got home. What were you drinking that night?
> *Victim-survivor*: I can't remember.
> *Defence*: You can't remember?
> *Victim-survivor*: Alcohol.
> *Defence*: Yes, well I got that. <chuckles> What type?
> *Victim-survivor*: I don't remember.
> *Defence*: I suggest that you weren't drunk. (T1)

Even though the defence barrister goes on to suggest that the victim-survivor was not drunk, he began by pointing out that she gets drunk often, to the point where she is unable to remember getting home. The supposition that the victim-survivor was not as drunk as she claimed was a key element in the defence, so it is unclear what the purpose of pointing to the victim-survivor's drinking habits prior to the alleged rapes could be other than to impeach her credibility. Whilst it could be argued they were establishing that she had a high tolerance for alcohol, doing so by stating that she often cannot remember how she got home seems incongruent with that purpose. Furthermore, by laughing at the victim-survivor's answer and stating "Yes, well I got that", the defence barrister arguably breached rule C7.1 of the Bar Standards Board's (2020) code of conduct for barristers, which states: "you must not make statements or ask questions merely to insult, humiliate or annoy a witness or any other person". Rule C7 is one of the few rules without further guidance attached to it, so it is not clear where the line is, which is problematic in terms of both practice and accountability. This is important because questions with a purpose of insulting and humiliating may not be asked in isolation; rather, there may be a range of 'subtle' questions that culminate as such. Whilst it may be argued that it goes towards credibility, it is difficult to see the probative value of laughing at a victim-survivor. Indeed, defence counsel later took advantage of an opportunity presented by the victim-survivor in a moment of jest to further comment on her drinking habits:

Judge and Defence: [Talking about what [strong liqueur] is, also mentioning vodka. Jokes between them about [strong liqueur]]
    <Laughs from public gallery [defendant's supporters]>
Victim-survivor : <jokingly> What, now?
    <Laughs from the public gallery [defendant's supporters]>
Defence: You developed a taste for it [vodka]?
Victim-survivor: It's alright, yeah.
Defence: Moving on to the second night.... (T1)

To say someone has 'got a taste for something' is a term often used to indicate frequent consumption of or a strong inclination/desire for something. Within the digital evidence in this case, there was a message from the victim-survivor to the defendant that said: "I know I have a drink problem, I get fucked all the time now" (T1). Given that barristers carefully choose their words, it seems reasonable to conclude that the barrister in this case likely saw an opportunity to strengthen the narrative of this victim-survivor as a 'problem drinker', especially given that he then immediately moved on to a new line of questioning. The value in this insinuation comes from drawing on wider cultural narratives that position 'excessive' substance use as an indicator of a person being unreliable and untrustworthy (Selseng, 2017).

The extract below follows on almost immediately from the extract above and demonstrates that the defence were in fact arguing that the victim-survivor was not drunk.

> *Defence*: [You walked over to McDonalds, walked fine]. How high were your heels?
> *Victim-survivor*: High.
> *Defence*: But you were walking fine. [You were aware enough to go to McDonalds. You weren't that drunk were you?]
> *Victim-survivor*: I was quite drunk.
> *Defence*: *Quite* drunk. Okay. (T1)

Here the defence counsel used repetition and emphasis of the victim-survivor's own words to underscore his point, taking advantage of the differing strength of meaning attributed to the adjective 'quite' (it can mean fairly or very). Also of relevance in this excerpt is the question he used to make this point, that is, the question about the height of her heels. Whilst this was asked within the context of establishing her level of drunkenness, arguably giving relevance, the wider context of this trial's gendered and classed narratives creates further meaning. In addition to the remarks regarding the victim-survivor's drinking habits and the height of her heels, evidence was adduced through police questions in the ABE and through witness testimony regarding the length of her dress. For example, the prosecution asked directly about the victim-survivor's clothing, and the reasoning for this is unclear:

> *Friend*: [[Victim-survivor] was sick before we went out, just once for maybe about ten minutes. We waited for about half an hour and she said she felt okay, so we decided to still go out].
> *Prosecution*: What was [victim-survivor] wearing?
> *Friend*: A dress, mini dress. Black or gold I think.
> *Prosecution*: How much had [victim-survivor] drunk?
> *Friend*: A substantial amount, but we were all the same level of drunk. (T1)

The prosecution asking about what the victim-survivor was wearing seems entirely irrelevant to this line of questioning and arguably to their case at all. Referring to victim-survivors' clothing without cause to could lead to the jury unnecessarily deeming it relevant. The defence later discussed the length of the victim-survivor's dress in the context of establishing the 'mechanics' of how the defendant touched her. Whilst the defence's reasoning for asking about clothing can be argued relevant, the prosecution question cannot. This built on the narratives discussed in Chapter 2 regarding this victim-survivor's perceived flirtatious behaviour by drawing on embedded stereotypes at the intersection of gender and class which position female heavy-drinkers as sexually available (Blume, 1991; Cozzarelli et al., 2002). Significantly, then, a study by Spencer (2016) found that rape victim-survivors from low socioeconomic backgrounds were more often rated as 'promiscuous' than victim-survivors from higher socioeconomic backgrounds and that this correlated with higher levels of blame and negative attitudes towards victim-survivors from lower socioeconomic backgrounds. Furthermore, Riemer et al. (2018) found that by merely holding an alcoholic beverage, women were routinely dehumanised and assessed as sexually available.

The age of the victim-survivor was also of relevance in T1 with regard to these gendered and classed narratives of respectability. The victim-survivor and defendant were both in their early twenties at the time of the trial and late-teens at the time of the alleged rapes, which added youth as a factor. The media and popular culture play a significant role in circulating images and representations that govern what is considered desirable and undesirable behaviour (Blackman & Walkerdine, 2001). So-called 'reality' TV forms a significant part of contemporary popular media, and within it, there is an overrepresentation of young, white, working-class men and women from across the UK (Wood & Skeggs, 2008). Portrayals of them are often disparaging and aim to incite moral judgements of their behaviour (Allen & Mendick, 2013; Skeggs & Wood, 2012). The portrayals on these TV shows are heavily gendered, with the young women depicted in forms of excess in relation to alcohol and sexuality (Nunn & Biressi, 2013; Wood, 2017). That these portrayals are of young *white* men and women is significant because within these classed narratives whiteness becomes a marker of excess, positioning the white working-class as lacking in morals and thereby positioned as non-respectable subjects of disgust (Lawler, 2005; Skeggs, 2004). Indeed, as Skeggs (1997, p. 99) argued, both Black and white working-class women have been "coded as the sexual and deviant other against which femininity was defined", but it cannot, however, be assumed that this happens in the same way. Whiteness, therefore, is salient in this narrative in that it distinguishes a particular type of working-class femininity.

Shows such as *Geordie Shore* and *The Only Way Is Essex* contain images of young white working-class women drinking alcohol to excess and engaging in, or talking about, sexual acts, thus portraying them as hypersexualised and sexually available (Griffin et al., 2013; Payne, 2016; Stepney, 2015; Wood 2017). Alcohol is highly prevalent in 'reality' TV (Barker et al., 2019; Lowe et al., 2018), as is highly gendered language which constructs women as irrationally emotional and objectified sexualised beings (Payne, 2016). As Bailey et al. (2015) noted in their analysis of focus groups in South West England, there are clear distinctions between constructions of young middle-class women's drinking and young working-class women's drinking, with the former coded as respectable and controlled and the latter as unrespectable and immoral. Indeed, working-class women drinking to excess were explicitly referred to as "easy" and "just going round sleeping with people" by the middle-class women in Bailey et al.'s (2015) study. When barristers deploy these classed and gendered narratives about young working-class women, the impact of any sexual history evidence that is introduced is arguably compounded (Smith, 2018). That alcohol can play such an easy role in the formation of narratives about the sexual behaviour of victim-survivors is significant because alcohol is a prominent feature in many rape cases (Hester, 2013; Lovett & Horvath, 2009).

The narratives in T1 therefore culminate in an image of a young, 'promiscuous', working-class woman, who binge drinks often and who does not therefore conform to middle-class ideals of respectability, thereby positioning her as untrustworthy and unreliable and drawing on victim-blaming myths about rape. As Brooks (2002) posits, rape trial narratives are often a reflection of cultural narratives about how women are "supposed to behave" (p. 4). It seems, then, that being perceived as a young working-class woman is used as a tool for undermining credibility by casting them against the image of the 'ideal victim' (Christie, 1986). Whilst the trials discussed here took place in the East of England, classed cultural narratives of female intoxication and sexual behaviour are omnipresent throughout the UK (e.g. Bailey et al., 2015; Lennox et al., 2018; Limmer, 2016). Indeed, drinking culture is highly prevalent in many other Westernised jurisdictions and, as in the UK, young working-class women are pejoratively framed within associated cultural narratives as unrespectable and immoral (e.g. Australia: Brown & Gregg, 2012; Canada: Kovac & Trussell, 2015; Aotearoa New Zealand: Hutton et al., 2016). It therefore seems likely that such narratives could permeate rape and sexual assault trials across Westernised adversarial jurisdictions, although the specific articulations of such narratives would of course vary across nations and regions.

Working-Class Motherhood as 'Unrespectable'

Working-class motherhood has long been scrutinised and viewed as inferior in Britain (Gillies, 2007; Skeggs, 1997, 2004). Indeed, Smart (1995) traced classed notions of 'good mother' through legislation dating back to the seventeenth century. What counts as good, 'respectable' parenting (especially motherhood) is characterised by middle-class values and ideals, and those who do not meet those standards are blamed and vilified (Gillies, 2007). In a similar way, as working-class sexualities are framed as 'unrespectable', then, so is working-class motherhood. Narratives about 'unrespectable' motherhood were present in both trials involving sexual offences against children (T5 and T6). The 'unrespectable mothers' narratives drew on classed stereotypes to judge the mothers of the victim-survivors as respectable or not, and this was then used as a marker of credibility.

In T5, the parenting skills of the child victim-survivor's mother were frequently called into question.

> *Defence*: [Did you catch them both playing video games that were too old for them?]
> *Mother*: Yeah.
> *Defence*: For example? Call of Duty?
> *Mother*: Yeah.
> *Defence*: [Did you catch them watching DVDs that were not age appropriate?]
> *Mother*: Not really, Twilight.
> *Defence*: [When you say to police that [victim-survivor] watches things he shouldn't, what things?]
> *Mother*: Call of Duty. (T5)

In the above excerpt, the defence barrister was questioning the mother about an assertion that her young sons had been watching pornography. Whilst asking about DVDs could therefore be relevant, it is unclear why asking about video games, and specifically a violent video game with no sex or nudity, would be relevant. It therefore seems that asking about *Call of Duty* was a way of building the portrayal of her as a 'bad mother' because her young children were accessing age-inappropriate content. The defence later returned to this point after pursuing several other lines of questioning.

> *Defence*: Okay, was there a time you caught [victim-survivor] watching naked men and women?
> *Mother*: No, I caught [eldest son].
> *Defence*: How old was he?
> *Mother*: Nine.
> *Defence*: Was it age appropriate?
> *Mother*: Very *in*appropriate.
> *Defence*: Was it what would be classed adult pornography?
> *Mother*: Yes. (T5)

The questioning about viewing pornography was relevant to the case as it was suggested that this could have informed a false allegation; however, the above extract was all that was needed for the defence to establish this, which further demonstrates that asking about *Call of Duty* was merely a mechanism by which to portray her as a 'bad mother'. The 'bad mother' narrative was bolstered further in other lines of questioning. For example, during cross-examination, the defence asked about the end of the mother's relationship with the father of her eldest two children:

> *Defence*: You told [defendant] that things were tough when you broke up with [the boys'] dad.
> *Mother*: Yeah.
> *Defence*: What did you mean?
> *Mother*: He used to be violent towards me.
> *Defence*: Did the boys see?
> *Mother*: I don't know, maybe. (T5)

It is difficult to see how this line of questioning could be relevant to the case. Eliciting from the mother that her children may have seen their father being violent towards her arguably drew on cultural narratives that position victims of domestic violence as 'failing to protect' their children. The 'failure to protect' narrative pejoratively shifts blame and responsibility from the perpetrator to the mother (Humphreys et al., 2006) and is pervasive in society (Moulding et al., 2015). The line of questioning in the excerpt above therefore appears to be another way to portray the mother as a 'bad' parent. The defence then used this narrative to contrast-ingly portray the defendant as showing protective parenting behaviour, thereby distancing him from the allegations of sexual abuse:

> *Defence*: When you confided in [defendant], did he say maybe they shouldn't see [their father] as much?
> *Mother*: No, he moaned that he didn't have them enough.
> *Defence*: I'm going to suggest that he did say 'don't you think they shouldn't have contact'.
> *Mother*: No. (T5).

As well as the more subtle references to 'poor parenting' outlined above, the defence also made much more explicit insinuations.

> *Defence*: During that time did you ever get angry at your kids?
> *Mother*: All parents lose their temper with their children.
> *Defence*: I'm only asking you.
> *Mother*: Yeah. (T5)

The defence asked a question that almost any parent would be required to answer 'yes' to, and when the mother pointed that out in her response, the defence drilled down further so that only an affirmative answer could be given. Middle-class ideals characterise calmness and congeniality as appropriate emotional behaviour (Wingfield, 2010); therefore, portraying the mother as angry bolstered the classed narrative that already othered her as working-class. That the anger was directed at her children put this in the context of 'bad parenting'. The defence barrister immediately continued to build on this narrative:

> *Defence*: And the school had significant input with you regarding bound-aries and managing behaviour?
> *Mother*: Only for [eldest son].
> *Defence*: And you struggled at this time with chores around the house?
> *Mother*: Yeah. (T5)

Here the defence drew on the school's involvement and phrased it in such a way that it responsibilised the mother. Additionally, raising the point that the mother had struggled with household chores is further reflective of middle-class motherhood ideals, where the middle-class 'home-maker' is construed of as a virtuous, capable housekeeper in contrast to the working-class 'slovenly', welfare-dependant mother (McRobbie, 2013). Indeed, Walkerdine and Lucey (1989) posited that housework is a gendered practice that is differently regulated for middle- and working-class mothers and is inextricably linked to notions of 'good' and 'bad' mothering, respectively.

The above excerpt was immediately followed with questioning that framed the mother as a 'benefits cheat'. Lone parents, in particular lone mothers, are commonly positioned as 'deficient parents' and 'scroungers' (Dermott & Pomati, 2016). Whilst the mother in T5 was in a relationship, questioning about the victim-survivor's attitude towards his mother's previous partners positioned her as having introduced multiple men into her children's lives. Whilst the questioning was arguably relevant, it further fed into the narrative of her as a 'bad mother' by contrasting her against middle-class values of sexual respectability and the nuclear family. Lone mothers are often conceptualised as representing sexual immorality (Carabine, 2001; Smart, 1992), and Lehtonen (2018) has noted that policy documentation linked 'multiple relationship transitions' to poor outcomes for children and thus to 'poor parenting', reflecting the middle-class ideal of the nuclear family as the expected norm. Lone parenthood, especially lone motherhood, has long been stigmatised in Britain (Skeggs, 2005; Smart, 1992), with political and media discourses frequently positioning lone mothers as being economically deprived and reliant on social welfare (Atkinson et al., 1998; Jun, 2019; Morris & Munt, 2019; Salter, 2018). These gendered and classed portrayals draw on Murray's (1990) concept of an 'underclass' and remain embedded in contemporary society (Morris & Munt, 2019; Salter, 2018; Tihelková, 2015). These narratives draw on the notion of 'benefits scroungers' to frame lone mothers as undeserving (Tihelková, 2015) and thus as unrespectable and 'other' (Jun, 2019). Positioning victim-survivors and their mothers as the unrespectable 'others' in this way invites the jury to make moral judgements based on stigmatising cultural narratives formed on middle-class notions of respectability. As with the classed and gendered narratives of sexual respectability discussed in the previous section, notions of 'unrespectable' working-class motherhood are reflected elsewhere in the Westernised world and thus may also be deployed by lawyers in jurisdictions beyond England and Wales. For example, in the US deeply entrenched stereotypes frame poor and welfare-dependent lone mothers as lazy, immoral, and sexually excessive and are differently articulated depending on racialisation, with the 'welfare queen' trope pejoratively framing Black women and the 'teen mom' and 'white trash' tropes pejoratively framing white women (Bullock et al., 2001; Kendall, 2005; Owen, 2016; van Doorn & Bos, 2017). Similar cultural narratives can be found in Australia (Swain & Howe, 1995; Wolfinger, 2014) and Canada (Harrell et al., 2014; Morrison et al., 2008).

In Britain, working-class mothers have long been responsibilised for 'failings' or problems within their families by being made to feel inadequate in their caring skills and abilities and in having to prove themselves against middle-class ideals of motherhood, for example through 'parenting courses' imposed or encouraged by social workers (Gillies, 2007; Moran et al., 2004; Skeggs, 1997). Though these courses are purported to be aimed at *all* families and at mothers *and* fathers, in practice they are "targeted at poor and disadvantaged mothers" (Gillies, 2007, p. 7). Poor parenting (mothering) is conceptualised as an individual issue rather than the result of structural inequalities (Gillies, 2007; Stewart, 2016), and there is a persistent cultural narrative that "poor parents spawn damaged, antisocial children" (Gillies, 2007, p. 8). Thus, framing the child victim-survivor's mother (T5) as an inferior parent through highlighting interventions from social services, the NSPCC, and the school served to reinforce the portrayal of the victim-survivor as an untrustworthy, 'problem child' who tells antisocial lies (see Chapter 4).

At the same time as positioning the mother as inferior and 'other', the defence portrayed the defendant as a respectable father-figure who took on responsibility for another man's children. For example:

Defence: Moving forward, [defendant] had contact with [defendant and mother's son]
Mother: Yeah.
Defence: He took them all out?
Mother: Sometimes yeah. (T5)

Here the defence drew attention to the defendant's continued contact with all three children as opposed to just his own child. This was reinforced through the defendant's evidence-in-chief. These narratives of 'good dad' versus 'bad mum' played out the broader gendered narratives of 'good man' versus 'bad woman' which permeate rape trials through the portrayal of women as untrustworthy liars (see Chapter 4) and cast men against the 'good men don't rape' fallacy (discussed in the following section).

T6 also involved allegations of child sexual abuse, although they were historic accusations so the victim-survivors in the trial were both adults. The motherhood narrative that ran through this trial was to a lesser extent than T5 but was nevertheless a negatively framed narrative about the mother. The narrative drew on classed and gendered cultural narratives that position working-class women as 'promiscuous' through drawing attention to the mother's sexual history with the defendant (see Chapter 2). When asking about the relationship, the defence stated the age of the victim-survivors as 'young teenagers' before asking questions about what the mother had told them about the relationship. In doing this, the defence arguably sought to portray it as an example of 'bad parenting'. Although not explicitly saying that, it seemed to invite the jury to make moral judgements about the family and the type of people they are. Particularly because this was subsequently used to suggest that victim-survivor2 had made up her allegations and had used her knowledge of the sexual relationship as a basis for those allegations. This narrative reflected stigmatising portrayals of working-class, lone mothers as sexually immoral (Carabine, 2001; Skeggs, 2005; Smart, 1992) which was further supported through the defendant's distancing of himself as a step-father figure in his characterisation of the relationship with the mother as a sexual arrangement rather than a committed relationship. This characterisation was contested by the victim-survivors, their mother, and evidence provided by a neighbour who described it as eventually becoming a co-habiting relationship.

'Respectable' Masculinities: The 'Good Men Don't Rape' Fallacy

In contrast to the respectability narratives about victim-survivors and their mothers, narratives that focused on defendants tended to portray them as 'good men' using notions of respectability. For example, the defendant in T5 was portrayed as honest and courageous, because he had presented himself to the police upon hearing the allegations directly from the (child) victim-survivor's mother:

> [He didn't have to give evidence, he chose to give evidence. He presented himself to police because his heart was broken over the allegations. He has nothing to hide]. Doesn't it take courage to go to the police and say, 'Here I am'? (Defence, T5)

Here the defence framed the defendant's actions as commendable and self-sacrificial, thereby positioning him as morally respectable. This defendant had also been cast by the defence as a respectable father-figure who took on responsibility for another man's children:

> *Defence*: Ok, would you spend time with the boys?
> *Defendant*: Yeah.
> *Defence*: What would you do with [eldest child]?
> *Defendant*: Play football, games, computer games.
> *Defence*: And [victim-survivor], how did you get on?
> *Defendant*: Brilliantly, same as with [eldest child]. (T5)

These things combined to frame the defendant as a 'good man' and contrasted with the defence's characterisation of the victim-survivor as a 'problem child' (see Chapter 4) and the child's mother as a 'bad mother'. Although the defendant had spent years in the children's lives as a co-parent, he was not subjected to the same narratives of blame and condemnation as the mother was with regard to the children's 'problem' behaviour. Rather, those narratives, combined with the 'good man' narratives, served to absolve him. Indeed, this is reflective of Gathings and Parrotta's (2013) observations in US courts where they found 'good man', and particularly 'good father', narratives were associated with lenient sentencing.

The narrative presenting the defendant as a 'good man' was far more overt in T3. In this trial, the defence asked the victim-survivor directly about the defendant's character:

> *Defence*: You wouldn't describe what happened to you as good?
> *Victim-survivor*: No.
> *Defence*: [You wouldn't say the person that did it was nice?]
> *Victim-survivor*: He was nice to me. Not aggressive, not angry. (T3)

Here the defence drew on a false dichotomy of people as either wholly good or wholly bad (Nilsson, 2019). He implied that "nice" people do not perpetrate rape, which ignores the complexity of human beings and that everyone is capable of doing both good and bad things. This response and argument, that 'good men don't rape', is what Jozkowski (2016) refers to as a "cultural fallacy" (p. 255) that stems from pervasive rape culture. That is, it is a logically invalid argument. The defence continued with this narrative throughout the trial, with eight character references for the defendant being read into evidence. This was the only trial in which character references were used. The references referred to the defendant consistently as "a family man", as "a kind, caring and gentle man", as a "helpful" and "happy" man. All expressed their absolute shock at the allegations, with one saying that they trusted the defendant "whole-heartedly". The prosecution attempted to combat the portrayal of the defendant as a 'good, family man' by demonstrating that his actions had clear sexual motives:

> He isn't looking for a kindred spirit, someone to get on with, because he squandered his opportunity for that. They have this unusual thing in common, [both have autistic sons, the difficulties that caused, she opens her heart to [defendant] about her son. His response is not to share], of course he doesn't have to tell her, but wouldn't that have been a very good opportunity to say, 'Goodness, I don't believe it, we have this thing in common'. [So if chat and connection was what he wanted then why didn't he do that? The answer, quite simply, is that was not his intent, his intent was sexual.] (Prosecution, T3)

The defence tried to resist the prosecution's portrayal of the defendant by summing up the character references in his closing speech:

> [perhaps he is] not the type of person in fact that the Crown seek to portray him as...let's remind ourselves about the character references, loudly and consistently they say that this is a caring man, kind, <reads extracts picking out the sentences that contain the positive adjectives>. All, you might conclude, sitting very uneasily with [prosecution's] portrayal. (Defence, T3)

The 'good man' portrayal in this trial was at odds with the defendant's admitted acts of deception. The type of deception he committed is collo-quially known as 'catfishing' and has in fact been legislated against in some jurisdictions (e.g. Derzakarian, 2017). The 'good man' narrative drew on the damaging portrayals and stereotypes about rapists which posi-tion them as a deviant 'other' (Jozkowski, 2016). These are portrayals which are persistently reinforced through the media (Haygarth, 2018; Kitzinger, 2009; O'Hara, 2012). Franiuk et al. (2008) have argued that men's endorsement of the 'real rape' myth is a way for them to distance themselves from rapists, thus creating a counter-narrative of 'good men don't rape'. Pascoe and Hollander (2016) argue that the 'good men don't rape' narrative shifts focus away from structural inequalities and problematic actions and attitudes. The narrative thereby attempts to shift the focus onto individual characteristics. In the context of this trial then, the 'good man' narrative attempted to distinguish the defendant from the deviant 'other' of the 'real rape' myth. The othering of rapists reinforces normative masculine hierarchies (Messner 2016; Pascoe & Hollander, 2016) and this othering often takes place along classed lines (Gavey, 2005). The 'good man' is constructed of white middle-class values and ideals of respectability based on gendered and sexual behaviour (Skeggs, 1997). Although men's sexual violence against women occurs across society, it has commonly been positioned as an issue of the working-classes and thereby acts as a means of distinguishing respectable, non-violent masculinity as middle-class (Phipps, 2009).

The term 'family man' is frequently used to describe men who are devoted to their families and who like to spend time with them. The term reflects a shift in values in the late twentieth century to fathers becoming more orientated around family rather than being relatively uninvolved in family life (Coltrane, 1996). Being a family man has become an increasingly valued characteristic in society because it can be viewed as a sign of progress towards gender equality (Meeussen et al., 2019). Characterising the defendant in T3 as a family man, therefore, implied that he was a man who acts in support of gender equality. However, as Pascoe and Hollander (2016) argue, attitudes and actions that appear on the surface to be supportive of equality can actually serve to reinforce gender, race, and class hierarchies. Indeed, it is important to note that the cultural narrative of the 'family man' obscures that there remains a significant imbalance in the time men and women spend on housework and child rearing activities (DeGroot & Vik, 2019; Dush et al., 2018; Vagni, 2019). Furthermore, because rape is constructed as a masculine crime and by definition can only be committed by males, it may be advantageous to portray the defendant using descriptors associated with femininity as a distancing tool (e.g. kind, gentle, caring, helpful). This could also be true for the 'family man' descriptor, given that it somewhat distances men from traditional masculinities. This is significant because, as Martinez et al. (2018) argued:

> It is difficult to hold men who perpetrate sexual violence accountable if guilt is difficult to attribute to men who have good characteristics in other aspects of their lives. (p. 7)

Martinez et al. (2018) also pointed out that positive character references were noted by the judge in the infamous Brock Turner case as a factor in his sentencing decision, which was later acknowledged as too lenient and resulted in the introduction of mandatory minimum sentencing (Associated Press, 2016; Edwards, 2016):

> And, also, I have considered the character letters that have been provided by Mr. Turner's friends, family, which indicate a period of, essentially, good behavior [sic]. (Perksey, 2016, quoted in Levin, 2016)

This indicates that character references can and do influence people's perceptions and decision-making within the CJS. Indeed, that is the purpose of good character evidence because such evidence is adduced in order to boost the jury's presumption of innocence regarding the defendant (Ross, 2004). Research in the US regarding the impact of defendant character evidence on juror decision-making provided conflicting results, with Effron (2012) suggesting that jurors can 'soften' towards a defendant on the basis of such evidence, whereas mock jury has research suggested positive character evidence had little (Maeder & Hunt, 2011) or no impact on jurors (Hunt & Budesheim, 2004). The use of character evidence in the US is somewhat different to England and Wales; in the former, character witnesses give evidence in person and can be cross-examined, whereas in England and Wales it is more common practice for written statements to be read into evidence. There appears to be no research on the use of good character witnesses or testimonials in England and Wales.

The *Turner* case was a high-profile and controversial case, and the judge was subsequently held to account by the public when he was recalled by public vote in his state of California—something which had not happened for over 80 years (Astor, 2018). There is no such check or accountability for juror decision-making in England and Wales.

SUMMARY

This chapter has outlined ways in which rape myths were scaffolded by and interacted with cultural narratives that reflected wider structural inequalities and systems of oppression. These most commonly related to gender and social class, but also intersected with age. The narratives together served to frame victim-survivors as unrespectable. Constructing narratives about the respectability of victim-survivors provided a means of undermining their credibility, whilst simultaneously bolstering defendants' credibility through characterising them as 'good men'. Classed narratives were underpinned by subtle details that cast witnesses against a working-class backdrop. These were elicited through micro-examinations and included, for example, irrelevant reference to social welfare. Sexism, and to a lesser extent age, intersected with classism in narratives of respectability to scaffold rape myths about *who* an 'ideal victim' is and *how* she should behave. These morality judgements drew on middle-class femininity ideals that value chastity, calmness, and 'good' mothering and thus were also deployed against victim-survivors' mothers as a means of further undermining the credibility of the victim-survivors. In contrast, the 'good men don't rape' narrative provided an easy tool for defence barristers to use to distance defendants from the 'deviant' other of 'rapist' through the use of gendered and classed cultural narratives about respectable masculinities.

References

Ainsworth, J. (2015). Legal discourse and legal narratives: Adversarial versus inquisitorial models. *Language and Law, 2*(1), 1–11.

Allen, K., & Mendick, H. (2013). Keeping it real? Social class, young people and 'authenticity' in reality TV. *Sociology, 47*(3), 460–476.

Anthias, F. (2014). The intersections of class, gender, sexuality and 'race': The political economy of gendered violence. *International Journal of Politics, Culture, and Society, 27*(2), 153–171.

Associated Press. (2016). California passes mandatory sentences for sexual assault after Stanford scandal. *The Guardian*. https://www.theguardian.com/us-news/2016/sep/30/stanford-sexual-assault-case-california-rape-law. Accessed 25 March 2019.

Astor, M. (2018). California voters remove Judge Aaron Persky, who gave a 6-month sentence for sexual assault. *New York Times*. https://search.proquest.com/docview/2050328542. Accessed 25 March 2019.

Atkinson, K., Oerton, S., & Burns, D. (1998). 'Happy families?': Single mothers, the press and the politicians. *Capital & Class, 22*(1), 1–11.

Bailey, L., Griffin, C., & Shankar, A. (2015). "Not a good look": Impossible dilemmas for young women negotiating the culture of intoxication in the United Kingdom. *Substance Use & Misuse, 50*(6), 747–758.

Bar Standards Board. (2020). *The BSB Handbook*. https://www.barstandardsboard.org.uk/the-bsb-handbook.html. Accessed 5 January 2021.

Barker, A. B., Britton, J., Thomson, E., Hunter, A., Breton, M. O., & Murray, R. L. (2019). A content analysis of tobacco and alcohol audio-visual content in a sample of UK reality TV programmes. *Journal of Public Health, 42*(3), 561–569.

Blackman, L., & Walkerdine, V. (2001). *Mass Hysteria*. Macmillan Education UK.

Blume, S. B. (1991). Sexuality and stigma: The alcoholic woman. *Alcohol Health and Research World, 15*(2), 139.

Bourke, J. (2007). *Rape: A history from 1860 to the present day*. Virago Press.

Brooks, P. (2002). Narrativity of the Law. *Law & Literature, 14*(1), 1–10.

Brown, C. (2013). Women's narratives of trauma: (Re)storying uncertainty, minimization and self-blame. *Narrative Works, 3*(1), 1.

Brown, J., Horvath, M., Kelly, L., & Westmarland, N. (2010). *Connections and disconnections: Assessing evidence, knowledge and practice in responses to rape* (Project Report). Government Equalities Office.

Brown, R., & Gregg, M. (2012). The pedagogy of regret: Facebook, binge drinking and young women. *Continuum, 26*(3), 357–369.

Brownmiller, S. (1975). *Against our will*. Secker.

Buchwald, E., Fletcher, P. R., & Roth, M. (1993). *Transforming a rape culture*. Milkweed Editions.

Bullock, H. E., Fraser Wyche, K., & Williams, W. R. (2001). Media images of the poor. *Journal of Social Issues, 57*(2), 229–246.

Button, M., & Tunley, M. (2015). Explaining fraud deviancy attenuation in the United Kingdom. *Crime, Law and Social Change, 63*, 49–64.

Byrne, B. (2006). *White lives: Gender, 'race' and class in contemporary London*. Routledge.

Carabine, J. (2001). Constituting sexuality through social policy: The case of lone motherhood 1834 and today. *Social & Legal Studies, 10*(3), 291–314.

Christie, N. (1986). The ideal victim. In E. A. Fattah (Ed.), *From crime policy to victim policy* (pp. 17–30). Palgrave Macmillan.

Clark, A. (1987). *Women's silence, men's violence: Sexual assault in England, 1770–1845*. Pandora.

Coltrane, S. (1996). *Family man*. Oxford University Press.

Cozzarelli, C., Tagler, M., & Wilkinson, A. (2002). Do middle-class students perceive poor women and poor men differently? *Sex Roles, 47*(11), 519–529.

Day, K., Rickett, B., & Woolhouse, M. (2020). *Class discourse and the media*. Springer.

DeGroot, J. M., & Vik, T. A. (2019). "The weight of our household rests on my shoulders": Inequity in family work. *Journal of Family Issues, 41*(8), 1258–1281.

Department for Communities and Local Government. (2015). *The English Indices of Deprivation 2015. Statistical Release*. Department for Communities and Local Government.

Dermott, E., & Pomati, M. (2016). The parenting and economising practices of lone parents: Policy and evidence. *Critical Social Policy, 36*(1), 62–81.

Derzakarian, A. (2017). The dark side of social media romance: Civil recourse for catfish victims. *Loyola of Los Angeles Law Review, 50*(4), 741–764.

DiBennardo, R. A. (2018). Ideal victims and monstrous offenders: How the news media represent sexual predators. *Socius, 4*.

Dush, C. M. K., Yavorsky, J. E., & Schoppe-Sullivan, S. J. (2018). What are men doing while women perform extra unpaid labor? Leisure and specialization at the transition to parenthood. *Sex Roles, 78*(11–12), 715–730.

Edwards, S. (2016). *California Passes Mandatory Minimum Bill in Response to Brock Turner Controversy*. https://jezebel.com/california-passes-mandatory-minimum-bill-in-response-to-1787289987. Accessed 19 October 2020.

Effron, D. A. (2012). Hero or hypocrite: A psychological perspective on the risks and benefits of positive character evidence. *Jury Expert, 24*(4), 46–51.

Fanghanel, A. (2020). *Disrupting rape culture*. Bristol University Press.

Feagin, J. R. (2020). *The white racial frame* (3rd ed.). Routledge.

Fivush, R. (2010). Speaking silence: The social construction of silence in autobiographical and cultural narratives. *Memory, 18*(2), 88–98.

Franiuk, R., Seefelt, J., & Vandello, J. (2008). Prevalence of rape myths in headlines and their effects on attitudes toward rape. *Sex Roles, 58*(11), 790–801.

Frankenberg, R. (1993). *White women, race matters*. Routledge.

Gathings, M. J., & Parrotta, K. (2013). The use of gendered narratives in the courtroom. *Journal of Contemporary Ethnography, 42*(6), 668–689.

Gavey, N. (2005). *Just sex?* Psychology Press.

Geiger, B. B., Reeves, A., & de Vries, R. (2017). Tax avoidance and benefit manipulation: Views on its morality and prevalence. *British Social Attitudes, 34*.

Gelsthorpe, L. (2010). Women, crime and control. *Criminology & Criminal Justice, 10*(4), 375–386.

Gillies, V. (2007). *Marginalised Mothers*. Routledge.

Glover, T. D. (2003). The story of the Queen Anne Memorial Garden: Resisting a dominant cultural narrative. *Journal of Leisure Research, 35*(2), 190–212.

Griffin, C., Szmigin, I., Bengry-Howell, A., Hackley, C., & Mistral, W. (2013). Inhabiting the contradictions: Hypersexual femininity and the culture of intoxication among young women in the UK. *Feminism & Psychology, 23*(2), 184–206.

Hammack, P. L., & Toolis, E. E. (2016). Putting the social into personal identity: The master narrative as root metaphor for psychological and developmental science. *Human Development, 58*(6), 350–364.

Hancock, L., & Mooney, G. (2011). 'Saints and scroungers': Constructing the poverty and crime myth. *Criminal Justice Matters, 83*(1), 26–27.

Harell, A., Soroka, S., & Ladner, K. (2014). Public opinion, prejudice and the racialization of welfare in Canada. *Ethnic and Racial Studies, 37*(14), 2580–2597.

Harris, A., Carney, S., & Fine, M. (2001). Counter work: Introduction. In M. Fine & A. Harris (Eds.), *Under the covers: Theorising the politics of counter stories* (pp. 6–18). Lawrence & Wishart.

Harvey, D. (2005). *A brief history of neoliberalism*. Oxford University Press.

Haygarth, N. (2018). *UK press discourses surrounding representations of rape in film and the subject of male violence against women* (PhD thesis). http://ethos.bl.uk/OrderDetails.do?uin=uk.bl.ethos.753920

Haylett, C. (2003). Culture, class and urban policy: Reconsidering equality. *Antipode, 35*(1), 55–73.

Herman, D. (1984). The rape culture. In J. Freeman (Ed.), *Women: A feminist perspective* (pp. 45–53). Mayfield.

Hester, M. (2013). *From Report to Court: Rape cases and the criminal justice system in the Northeast*. University of Bristol in association with the Northern Rock Foundation.

Hlavka, H. R., & Mulla, S. (2018). "That's how she talks": Animating text message evidence in the sexual assault trial. *Law & Society Review, 52*(2), 401–435.

Hsu, R. (1996). 'Will the model minority please identify itself?': American ethnic identity and its discontents. *Diaspora, 5*(1), 37–63.

Humphreys, C., Mullender, A., Thiara, R., & Skamballis, A. (2006). Talking to My Mum. *Journal of Social Work, 6*(1), 53–63.

Hunt, J. S., & Budesheim, T. L. (2004). How jurors use and misuse character evidence. *Journal of Applied Psychology, 89*(2), 347–361.

Hutton, F., Griffin, C., Lyons, A., Niland, P., & McCreanor, T. (2016). "Tragic girls" and "crack whores": Alcohol, femininity and Facebook. *Feminism & Psychology, 26*(1), 73–93.

Jensen, T. (2014). Welfare commonsense, poverty porn and doxosophy. *Sociological Research Online, 19*(3), 1–7.

Jozkowski, K. N. (2016). Why does rape seem like a myth? In J. Manning & C. Noland (Eds.), *Contemporary studies of sexuality & communication: Theoretical and applied perspectives* (pp. 239–262). Kendall/Hunt Publishing.

Jun, M. (2019). Stigma and shame attached to claiming social assistance benefits: Understanding the detrimental impact on UK lone mothers' social relationships. *Journal of Family Studies* [online first].

Kendall, D. E. (2005). *Framing class: Media representations of wealth and poverty in America*. Rowman & Littlefield Publishers.

Kitzinger, J. (2009). Rape in the media. In M. Horvath & J. Brown (Eds.), *Rape: Challenging contemporary thinking* (pp. 74–98). Willan.

Kovac, L. D., & Trussell, D. E. (2015). 'Classy and never trashy': Young women's experiences of nightclubs and the construction of gender and sexuality. *Leisure Sciences, 37*(3), 195–209.

Lafrance, M. N., & McKenzie-Mohr, S. (2014). Women counter-storying their lives. In S. McKenzie-Mohr & M. N. Lafrance (Eds.), *Women voicing resistance* (pp. 1–15). Routledge.

Lawler, S. (2005). Disgusted subjects: The making of middle-class identities. *The Sociological Review, 53*(3), 429–446.

Lawler, S. (2012). White like them: Whiteness and anachronistic space in representations of the English white working class. *Ethnicities, 12*(4), 409–426.

Lees, S. (2002). *Carnal knowledge: Rape on trial* (2nd ed.). Women's Press.

Lehtonen, A. (2018, July). *The sexual and intimate life of UK austerity politics* (PhD thesis). http://etheses.lse.ac.uk/3800/

Lennox, J., Emslie, C., Sweeting, H., & Lyons, A. (2018). The role of alcohol in constructing gender & class identities among young women in the age of social media. *International Journal of Drug Policy, 58*, 13–21.

Levin, S. (2016). Stanford sexual assault: Read the full text of the judge's controversial decision. *The Guardian*. https://www.theguardian.com/us-news/2016/jun/14/stanford-sexual-assault-read-sentence-judge-aaron-persky. Accessed 21 August 2020.

Limmer, M. (2016). "I don't shag dirty girls": Marginalized masculinities and the use of partner selection as a sexual health risk reduction strategy in heterosexual young men. *American Journal of Men's Health, 10*(2), 128–140.

Loseke, D. R. (2001). Lived realities and formula stories of 'battered women.' In J. F. Gubrium & J. A. Holstein (Eds.), *Institutional selves: Troubled identities in a postmodern world* (pp. 107–126). Oxford University Press.

Loseke, D. R. (2007). The study of identity as cultural, institutional, organizational, and personal narratives: Theoretical and empirical integrations. *The Sociological Quarterly, 48*(4), 661–688.

Lovett, J., & Horvath, M. A. H. (2009). Alcohol and drugs in rape and sexual assault. In M. Horvath & J. Brown (Eds.), *Rape: Challenging contemporary thinking* (pp. 125–160). Willan.

Lowe, E., Britton, J., & Cranwell, J. (2018). Alcohol content in the 'hyper-reality' MTV Show 'Geordie Shore.' *Alcohol and Alcoholism, 53*(3), 337–343.

Lundström, R. (2013). Framing fraud: Discourse on benefit cheating in Sweden and the UK. *European Journal of Communication, 28*(6), 630–645.

MacDonald, R., Shildrick, T., & Furlong, A. (2020). 'Cycles of disadvantage' revisited: Young people, families and poverty across generations. *Journal of Youth Studies, 23*(1), 12–27.

Mackiewicz, A. (2015). *Alcohol, young women's culture and gender hierarchies.* Policy Press.

Maeder, E. M., & Hunt, J. S. (2011). Talking about a Black Man: The influence of defendant and character witness race on jurors' use of character evidence. *Behavioral Sciences & the Law, 29*(4), 608–620.

Mannay, D. (2015). Achieving respectable motherhood? Exploring the impossibility of feminist and egalitarian ideologies against the everyday realities of lived Welsh working-class femininities. *Women's Studies International Forum, 53,* 159–166.

Martinez, T., Wiersma-Mosley, J. D., Jozkowski, K. N., & Becnel, J. (2018). 'Good guys don't rape': Greek and Non-Greek College student perpetrator rape myths. *Behavioral Sciences, 8*(7), 60.

McKenzie-Mohr, S., & Lafrance, M. N. (2011). Telling stories without the words: 'Tightrope talk' in women's accounts of coming to live well after rape or depression. *Feminism & Psychology, 21*(1), 49.

McLean, K. C., Lilgendahl, J. P., Fordham, C., Alpert, E., Marsden, E., Szymanowski, K., & McAdams, D. P. (2018). Identity development in cultural context: The role of deviating from master narratives. *Journal of Personality, 86*(4), 631–651.

McLean, K. C., & Syed, M. (2016). Personal, master, and alternative narratives: An integrative framework for understanding identity development in context. *Human Development, 58*(6), 318–349.

McRobbie, A. (2013). Feminism, the family and the new 'mediated' maternalism. *New Formations, 80*(80), 119–137.

Meeussen, L., Laar, C. V., & Verbruggen, M. (2019). Looking for a family man? Norms for men are toppling in heterosexual relationships. *Sex Roles, 80*(7), 429–442.

Messner, M. A. (2016). Bad men, good men, bystanders: Who is the rapist? *Gender and Society, 30*(1), 57–66.

Moran, P., Ghate, D., & van der Merwe, A. (2004). *What works in parenting support?: A review of the international evidence.* Department for Education and Skills.

Morris, C., & Munt, S. R. (2019). Classed formations of shame in white, British single mothers. *Feminism & Psychology, 29*(2), 231–249.

Morrison, J. (2019). *Scroungers: Moral panics and media myths.* Zed Books.

Morrison, M. A., Morrison, T. G., Harriman, R. L., & Jewell, L. M. (2008). Old-fashioned and modern prejudice toward aboriginals in Canada. In M. A. Morrison & T. G. Morrison (Eds.), *The psychology of modern prejudice* (pp. 277–305). Nova Science Publishers.

Moulding, N. T., Buchanan, F., & Wendt, S. (2015). Untangling self-blame and mother-blame in women's and children's perspectives on maternal protectiveness in domestic violence: Implications for practice. *Child Abuse Review*, *24*(4), 249–260.

Murray, C. (1990). The British underclass. *Public Interest*, 4–28.

Murray, C. (1994). *Underclass: The crisis deepens*. IEA Health and Welfare Unit.

Murray, C. (2001). The British underclass: Ten years later. *Public Interest*, 25.

Nelson, H. L. (2001). *Damaged identities, narrative repair*. Cornell University Press.

Nilsson, G. (2019). Rape in the news: On rape genres in Swedish news coverage. *Feminist Media Studies*, *19*(8), 1178–1194.

Nunn, H., & Biressi, A. (2010). Shameless?: Picturing the "underclass" after Thatcherism. In L. Hadley & E. Ho (Eds.), *Thatcher & After* (pp. 137–157). Palgrave Macmillan.

Nunn, H., & Biressi, A. (2013). Class, gender, and the docusoap: The only way is Essex. In C. Carter, L. Steiner, & L. McLaughlin (Eds.), *The Routledge Companion to Media and Gender* (pp. 269–279). Routledge.

O'Hara, S. (2012). Monsters, playboys, virgins and whores: Rape myths in the news media's coverage of sexual violence. *Language and Literature: Journal of the Poetics and Linguistics Association*, *21*(3), 247.

Owen, D. (2016). "Hillbillies", "welfare queens", and "teen moms": American media's class distinctions. In S. Lemke & W. Schniedermann (Eds.), *Class divisions in serial television* (pp. 47–63). Palgrave Macmillan.

Pascoe, C. J., & Hollander, J. A. (2016). Good guys don't rape. *Gender & Society*, *30*(1), 67–79.

Patrick, R. (2016). Living with and responding to the 'scrounger' narrative in the UK: Exploring everyday strategies of acceptance, resistance and deflection. *Journal of Poverty and Social Justice*, *24*(3), 245–259.

Payne, G. (2013). Models of contemporary social class: The Great British class survey. *Methodological Innovations*, *8*(1), 3–17.

Payne, H. M. (2016). *'Really damn sexist': A discourse analysis of the language used to portray gender inequality within reality television*. http://e-space.mmu.ac.uk/617867/. Accessed 23 April 2020.

Peat, J. (2020). *Amber Heard was booed and dubbed a 'liar' as crowds threw flowers at Depp's car*. https://www.thelondoneconomic.com/opinion/amber-heard-was-booed-and-dubbed-a-liar-as-crowds-threw-flowers-at-depps-car/02/11/. Accessed 5 February 2021.

Phipps, A. (2009). Rape and respectability: Ideas about sexual violence and social class. *Sociology*, *43*(4), 667–683.

Pierre, J. (2004). Black immigrants in the United States and the 'cultural narratives' of ethnicity. *Identities (yverdon, Switzerland)*, *11*(2), 141–170.

Powell, A. J., Hlavka, H. R., & Mulla, S. (2017). Intersectionality and credibility in child sexual assault trials. *Gender & Society, 31*(4), 457–480.

Rasmussen, B. B., Klinenberg, E., Nexica, I. J., & Wray, M. (2001). *The making and unmaking of whiteness*. Duke University Press.

Richardson, L. (1997). *Fields of play*. Rutgers University Press.

Riemer, A. R., Gervais, S. J., Skorinko, J. L. M., Douglas, S. M., Spencer, H., Nugai, K., et al. (2018). She looks like she'd be an animal in bed: Dehumanization of drinking women in social contexts. *Sex Roles, 80*(9–10), 617–629.

Roberts, K. (2011). *Class in Contemporary Britain* (2nd ed.). Palgrave.

Robinson, P. M. (1984). The historical repression of women's sexuality. In C. S. Vance (Ed.), *Pleasure and danger: Exploring female sexuality* (pp. 251–266). Routledge.

Romano, S. (2017). *Moralising poverty: The 'undeserving' poor in the public gaze*. Routledge.

Ross, J. (2004). 'He looks guilty': Reforming good character evidence to undercut the presumption of guilt. *University of Pittsburgh Law Review, 65*, 227–279.

Salter, E. (2018). A media discourse analysis of lone parents in the UK: Investigating the stereotype. In L. Bernardi & D. Mortelmans (Eds.), *Lone parenthood in the life course* (pp. 55–74). Springer.

Schwark, S. (2017). Visual representations of sexual violence in online news outlets. *Frontiers in Psychology, 8*, 774.

Selseng, L. B. (2017). Formula stories of the "substance-using client": Addicted, unreliable, deteriorating, and stigmatized. *Contemporary Drug Problems, 44*(2), 87–104.

Skeggs, B. (1997). *Formations of class & gender*. Sage.

Skeggs, B. (2004). *Class, self, culture*. Routledge.

Skeggs, B. (2005). The making of class and gender through visualizing moral subject formation. *Sociology, 39*(5), 965–982.

Skeggs, B. (2011). Imagining personhood differently: Person value and autonomist working-class value practices. *The Sociological Review, 59*(3), 496–513.

Skeggs, B., & Wood, H. (2012). *Reacting to reality television*. Routledge.

Smart, C. (1992). The woman of legal discourse. *Social & Legal Studies, 1*(1), 29–44.

Smart, C. (1995). *Law, crime and sexuality*. Sage.

Smith, O. (2018). *Rape trials in England and Wales: Observing justice and rethinking rape myths*. Palgrave Macmillan.

Spencer, B. (2016). The impact of class and sexuality-based stereotyping on rape blame. *Sexualization, Media, & Society, 2*(2), 1–8.

Stanley, C. A. (2007). When counter narratives meet master narratives in the journal editorial-review process. *Educational Researcher, 36*(1), 14–24.

Stepney, M. (2015). The challenge of hyper-sexual femininity and binge drinking: A feminist psychoanalytic response. *Subjectivity, 8*(1), 57–73.

Stewart, J. (2016). *Child guidance in Britain, 1918–1955: The dangerous age of childhood.* Routledge.

Sue, D. W., Capodilupo, C. M., Torino, G. C., Bucceri, J. M., Holder, A. M. B., Nadal, K. L., & Esquilin, M. (2007). Racial microaggressions in everyday life. *The American Psychologist, 62*(4), 271–286.

Swain, S., & Howe, R. (1995). *Single mothers and their children: Disposal, punishment and survival in Australia.* Cambridge University Press.

Tihelková, A. (2015). Framing the 'scroungers': The re-emergence of the stereotype of the undeserving poor and its reflection in the British press. *Brno Studies in English, 41*(2), 121–139.

Vagni, G. (2019). Alone together: Gender inequalities in couple time. *Social Indicators Research, 146*(3), 487–509.

van Doorn, B., & Bos, A. (2017). Are visual depictions of poverty in the US gendered and racialized? In W. van Oorschot, F. Roosma, B. Meuleman, & T. Reeskens (Eds.), *The social legitimacy of targeted welfare* (pp. 113–126). Edward Elgar Publishing.

Vera-Gray, F. (2017). Outlook: Girlhood, agency, and embodied space for action. In B. Formark, H. Mulari, & M. Voipio (Eds.), *Nordic Girlhoods* (pp. 127–135). Palgrave Macmillan.

Walkerdine, V., & Lucey, H. (1989). *Democracy in the kitchen.* Virago.

Watt, P. (2006). Respectability, roughness and 'race': Neighbourhood place images and the making of working-class social distinctions in London. *International Journal of Urban and Regional Research, 30*(4), 776–797.

Welshman, J. (2013). *Underclass: A history of the excluded since 1880* (2nd ed.). Bloomsbury.

Wingfield, A. H. (2010). Are some emotions marked 'whites only'? Racialized feeling rules in professional workplaces. *Social Problems, 57*(2), 251–268.

Wolfinger, E. (2014). Australia's welfare discourse and news: Presenting single mothers. *Global Media Journal: Australian Edition, 8*(2), 1–16.

Wood, H. (2017). The politics of hyperbole on Geordie Shore: Class, gender, youth and excess. *European Journal of Cultural Studies, 20*(1), 39–55.

Wood, H., & Skeggs, B. (2008). Spectacular morality: Reality television, individualisation and the re-making of the working class. In D. Hesmondhalgh & J. Toynbee (Eds.), *The media and social theory* (pp. 177–193). Routledge.

Yamamoto, E. K., Haia, M., & Kalama, D. (1994). Courts and the cultural performance: Native Hawaiians' Uncertain Federal and State Law Rights to Sue. *University of Hawai'i Law Review, 16*, 1–493.

CHAPTER 4

Honesty and Excuses

Abstract This chapter explores how victim-survivors were framed as untrustworthy through intersecting gendered and classed cultural narratives, thus re/producing the misconception that false allegations of rape are common. Through framing victim-survivors as untrustworthy and unreliable, barristers bolstered their narratives that provided excuses for defendants' behaviour or framed them as deserving of sympathy. This established a high bar of credibility for victim-survivors and a comparatively low bar for defendants.

Keywords Rape myths · Court · Rape trials · Cultural narratives · False allegations · Mental health

Credibility is considered central to rape and sexual assault trials across Westernised jurisdictions and there exists a pervasive misconception that false allegations of rape are common despite evidence to the contrary (CPS, 2013; Kelly, 2010; Weiser, 2017). Indeed, as former Canadian Supreme Court Justice asserted:

> The most injurious myth is that women and children are not credible in this area of criminal law. (L'Heureux-Dubé, 2012, cited in Cossins, 2020)

© The Author(s), under exclusive license to Springer Nature
Switzerland AG 2022
E. Daly, *Rape, Gender and Class*,
https://doi.org/10.1007/978-3-030-93925-0_4

This chapter therefore explores the way narratives of belief and disbelief were constructed through gendered narratives that intersect with pejorative narratives about age and mental ill-health. These narratives of honesty further intersect with social class with a clear overlap with the respectability narratives discussed in Chapter 3.

Women as Liars

The misconception that false allegations of rape are common is often articulated through narratives that position women as liars with various malicious motives, including that they are scorned and looking for vengeance or that they had drunken sex which they later regretted. Narratives that positioned women as lying about being raped or assaulted were present in all of the observed trials with adult victim-survivors. In the remaining trial, the victim-survivor, a boy child, was positioned as a lying 'problem child', and this is discussed further later.

The idea that women are inherently untrustworthy and deceitful and therefore lie about rape has been around for centuries (Bourke, 2007; Jordan, 2004). Sir Matthew Hale infamously stated that rape "is an accusation easily to be made and hard to be proved, and harder to be defended by the party accused, tho never so innocent" (Hale, 1726, cited in Rumney, 2006). Assertions such as this persisted through the nineteenth and twentieth centuries (Bourke, 2007), and the following example from an American judge highlights how this notion was clearly articulated in ways that framed women as irrational:

> There are few crimes in which false charges are more easily or confidently made than in rape. Experience has shown that unfounded charges of rape are brought for a variety of motives. The adage, 'Hell hath no fury like a woman scorned', is frequently encountered in rape prosecutions. (Ploscowe, 1951, cited in Jordan, 2004, p. 32)

More contemporarily, an analysis of Twitter posts from 2016 showed that tweets accusing women of lying about rape were almost three times more common than posts validating victim-survivors (Stabile et al., 2019), which helps demonstrate the continued pervasiveness of the misconception that false allegations of rape are common.

In my observations, all victim-survivors were portrayed as liars. The accusations of lying were put directly to the victim-survivors in cross-examination in some trials, whereas in others there were micro-examinations that lay the groundwork for the point to be made during closing speeches. For example, in T2, there were suggestions that the victim-survivor felt scorned or jealous of the defendant's new girlfriend, with the implication being she was lying for revenge. The defence began without making direct comment on motive for lying:

> *Defence*: [You had a work colleague at [place of employment] and at the end of that year you had concerns about how close they were getting, then in the [month] she moved into [house victim-survivor had shared with defendant]. Originally it was a platonic, financial arrangement, but then later it became a relationship and remains so to this day].
> *Victim-survivor*: Yeah.
> *Defence*: You found out [the month before reporting], how did you feel?
> *Victim-survivor*: I didn't really care at that point. (T2)

The defence barrister was setting the background for when she later asked about the timing of the victim-survivor's first disclosure of the alleged rape:

> *Defence*: By this time you knew that [defendant's new girlfriend] had moved in.
> *Victim-survivor*: I suspected but I didn't know for sure. (T2)

This built on the questioning in the preceding excerpt to imply the victim-survivor was lying out of jealousy. Later in the trial, the defendant's police interview was read into court. In it, he said: "[It] sounds like she is trying to get back at me for all of this" (T2). The prosecution cross-examined the defendant to address the suggestion the victim-survivor was jealous of his new relationship:

> *Prosecution*: So she had no reason to think that she couldn't have you back if she wanted?
> *Defendant*: No.
> *Prosecution*: She had no reason to be jealous of [girlfriend] [...] It is your argument that she made the accusation up because she was jealous of [girlfriend].
> *Defence*: [Not relevant, that is not our argument, our argument is that there was no non-consensual sex].
> *Prosecution*: There is a huge passage in his interview that talks about jealousy.

Judge: What's been put to him in interview is not put as motive.
Prosecution: Can we have the jury out please? (T2)

With the jury out, there was a back and forth about the defence case and what wording the prosecutor was permitted to use in her questioning:

Prosecution: [He's put forward that she was jealous, it is repeatedly referred to as about [the girlfriend], the only inference that can be made from that is that he is saying she is making it up].
Judge: Where is jealousy referred to in this interview?
Prosecution: The word 'jealous' is not necessary in interview for me to raise it here.

[Long discussion about whether he had accused her of lying or being jealous of the new girlfriend]

Defence: [My concern is that [defendant] has not put forward a motive to get back at him, [defendant] is replying to questions, he is not asserting anything. It's not right to say that is his argument, all his case is, is that he did not rape her].
Prosecution: [Because he says she is making it up, I can't be confined to only asking questions using words from his interview.] Otherwise no-one would be able to ask anything!
Judge: [I agree, but that was not my point. You said jealous, I asked where in the interview that was said, you did not point it out] [...]
Prosecution: [It has been edited out, my mistake. But am I entitled to ask without the word jealous?]
Judge: Yes. [...]. (T2)

Although the defence had been allowed to imply this reasoning in her cross-examination of the victim-survivor, the prosecution was limited in the way she was permitted to address that implication. The defence barrister chose to interpret what counts as a 'legal argument' narrowly in an attempt to limit the prosecution's ability to challenge previous assertions made by the defendant. It seemed, however, that the judge had not noticed or remembered that the defendant had said "she is trying to get back at me" in the police transcript that was read into court. It was a clear suggestion of motive for lying. It seemed unnecessarily harsh to limit the prosecution's line of questioning in this way, and further interrogation of the defence's position by the judge may have made that clearer by, for example, taking time to properly review the transcript. Nevertheless,

the prosecution barrister did however go on to effectively counter the
assertion within her limited scope:

> *Prosecution*: So you said in interview that [victim-survivor] would know
> from your contact that she was welcome back as your girlfriend.
> *Defendant*: Yes.
> *Prosecution*: She was welcome to move back to the flat.
> *Defendant*: Yes.
> *Prosecution*: And to engage in sexual relations.
> *Defendant*: Yes.
> *Prosecution*: You loved her and wanted to marry her.
> *Defendant*: Yes.
> *Prosecution*: So you couldn't have made it clearer.
> *Defendant*: No.
> *Prosecution*: So she had nothing to worry about.
> *Defendant*: No.
> *Prosecution*: She had no reason to do anything nasty to you because of
> [girlfriend].
> *Defendant*: No.
> *Prosecution*: So in terms of [girlfriend] getting between you, we can forget
> about that?
> *Defendant*: Yes. (T2)

The prosecution skilfully challenged the defence's insinuation here by
clearly and simply getting confirmation from the defendant that the
suggested motive was immaterial. Whilst the defence had argued that their
case was not that the victim-survivor was lying out of jealousy, and had
limited the prosecution's cross-examination accordingly, in her closing
argument the defence directly stated it:

> [As for motive, it is not for him to prove, but you may be interested
> in the timing of the reports to the friend and the police. At that time
> we know that [girlfriend] had moved in and [victim-survivor] has said
> that she thought that had happened and said that she wasn't bothered by
> that time.] But what do you make of the timing? ... [Every jury brings
> common sense. Yes you might agree that there is no such thing as a stan-
> dard response to rape, but I ask you to look at the timing of that report.]
> (Defence, T2)

It is significant that the defence had explicitly said that she was not
arguing that the victim-survivor was lying out of jealousy but then went

on to make exactly that point in her closing statement. This highlights precisely why it was important for the prosecution to be able to cross-examine the defendant on the issue, rather than being limited by the defence and the judge. At the time of this trial, there was a considerable amount of media attention given to cases with disclosure failings that lead to the CPS dropping cases (e.g. Bowcott, 2018; Evans, 2018). This had resulted in a heightened rhetoric around false allegations throughout 2018 and 2019 (e.g. Davies, 2019; Fouzder, 2019; McKinney, 2019; Osborne, 2018). It seems fair to assert, then, that jurors may likely have been aware of this high-profile media attention, which could have made the defence argument more compelling to them. Particularly because the defence barrister stated in her closing speech:

> [Rape is a word that stirs up strong feelings. There is a lot in the news,] there's #metoo, it is a hot topic. (Defence, T2)

Saying "there is a lot in the news" arguably directed the jurors to think about the false allegations rhetoric, as that is what was dominating the British press regarding rape at the time. Pointing to this rhetoric, therefore, arguably made the value of drawing on the 'jealous women lie' narrative much stronger.

Another 'motive for lying' was put forward in T1. In this case, the victim-survivor and defendant were friends who had been out drinking together and the defendant had unrequited romantic feelings for the victim-survivor. The victim-survivor was accused of regretting consensual sex seven times during cross-examination. One such example:

> *Victim-survivor*: I cried for half an hour first, because I knew something had happened.
> *Defence*: I suggest you do remember and you know what happened. You felt disgusted and guilty out of regret for it happening again, and that's why you got hysterical. (T1)

The use of the descriptor "hysterical" was significant because historically 'hysterical' women were viewed as prone to making false allegations (Bourke, 2007; Jordan, 2004). It also has connotations with mental ill-health and served to further undermine the victim-survivor's credibility by portraying her as unstable (discussed further later). 'Regret' as a motive for lying was a strong theme in the defence's closing:

She did remember. She did consent, she knows she did. She was embarrassed. She knew, that she said 'I really hope we didn't have sex' is a clear indication that she remembered but regretted it... She said she felt disgusted, but was she not disgusted at herself for what she was doing to the defendant's feelings? ... My learned friend says she has no motive for lying, I suggest that her motive is regret and disgust and embarrassment. The defendant is telling the truth. She is lying. (Defence, T1)

These were the final words of the defence. Previous court observation studies have also found the notion of 'regretted drunken consent' to be used by defence counsel (Lees, 2002; Temkin et al., 2018). The idea that women make false allegations after regretful sex is deeply embedded in society, which makes this a valuable argument for defence barristers to put forth and probably a powerful note to end on. For example, Gunby et al. (2012) asked four focus groups to discuss a rape vignette and found that the idea of 'regretting it after' was discussed in three out of their four groups. Their findings also indicated that it was held against the victim-survivor that she did not immediately recognise the experience as rape, which was also the case for the victim-survivor in T1. The participants in Gunby et al. (2012) also framed alcohol as a factor in 'causing' women to make false allegations after regretful sex. Again, alcohol was a significant factor in T1.

These assumptions and narratives are rooted in patriarchal values where women were historically denied sexual desire and agency. For example, Degler (1974) documented some narratives in which women in nineteenth-century Britain and America were viewed as having no sexual desire except in exceptional circumstances and those exceptions were viewed as abnormal and associated with the working-classes. Though Degler (1974) went on to argue that the ideologies prescribed through those narratives were not necessarily bought into by the majority of the public, the continued pervasiveness of such narratives cannot easily be denied. Indeed, Webb (2015) traced the existence of 'slut-shaming' as a means of suppressing women's sexuality back to ancient Rome, where, for example, type of clothing was used to distinguish between married women and prostitutes and female adultery was punishable by exile or death.

Robinson (1984) noted how women's sexuality had historically been denied and obscured, which therefore shrouded acknowledgement or performance of female sexuality in contemporary times with shame. The chastity of women was historically a primary marker of respectability and honour (Gowing, 1996), and this was clearly reflected in early rape law which conceived of women as property of their fathers or husbands (Edwards et al., 2011). The value given to 'chastity' led to 'unchaste' women being viewed as dishonourable (Gowing, 1996). It was therefore thought of as a reason for women to lie to avoid scorn and shame when they were caught having sex and as a reason that men needed to be protected from these 'false' allegations (Sanday, 1997). This highly gendered narrative intersects with the 'respectable' ideals that framed the expectations for women's sexuality. For example, women in the nineteenth century were characterised in a false dichotomy that positioned women as either chaste and virtuous and therefore respectable or unchaste and unvirtuous and often labelled as prostitutes, thereby being *un*respectable (Sanday, 1997).

Women were also historically thought of as conniving and cunning in their 'false allegations' (Bourke, 2007) and this, too, was reflected in my observations of T3 and T6. Similar accusations of women conniving were made in T1 and T5, where the victim-survivors' mothers were also implicated in the accusations of lying, and this is discussed separately in the next section. Defence counsel in T3 appeared to suggest that a gap in digital messaging between the victim-survivor and the defendant, which was taking place in the hours after the assault, provided an opportunity for her to be influenced by a friend:

> *Defence*: [There is an 11-min gap].
> *Victim-survivor*: Yes.
> *Defence*: Then that's where you claim he had massaged inside your vagina?
> *Victim-survivor*: Yes.
> *Defence*: Did you speak to anyone in those 10 minutes?
> *Victim-survivor*: Maybe.
> *Defence*: Did you speak to [friend A]?
> *Victim-survivor*: No, that was later.
> *Defence*: <long pause> but maybe [friend B]?
> *Victim-survivor*: Yes. (T3).

This is where the cross-examination ended. By first identifying a gap in the communications and determining that it was after that gap that the victim-survivor 'claimed' (in the messages) the defendant had sexually assaulted her, the defence was able to cast suspicion on the gap. Although it was not explicitly mentioned, it seemed that the defence barrister was listing friends until the victim-survivor said 'yes'. The long pause before "but maybe [friend H]?" could be indicative of this. There is no confirmation of communication nor any evidence of it, merely a suggestion from defence that there *could* have been and an acknowledgement from the victim-survivor that there *could* have been. Yet to an observer, such as jurors, this could easily have added weight to the accusation that the victim-survivor was lying, by leaning on cultural narratives that position women as untrustworthy and conniving. This was also bolstered through portraying the victim-survivor as sexually provocative. Indeed, in the closing speech, the defence said:

> [there has been a lot of sexual banter, sexually charged, sexual discussion. We have messages directly after, where [victim-survivor] says <reads messages>, then there's a gap of 11 minutes then she says] 'but why did he massage inside my vagina?'. Her evidence is that she may have spoken to one of her friends between. (Defence, T3)

As noted in Chapter 3, gendered narratives of women's sexualities intersect with classed notions of what counts as 'respectable'. In the above example, the defence barrister pointed the jury to his earlier characterisation of the victim-survivor as 'promiscuous' and linked that to his implicit suggestion that she was influenced in making her allegation after speaking to a friend. The prosecution addressed the accusation that the victim-survivor was lying in his closing speech:

> Unless mentally unhinged, [you don't go around making these things up. What reason could there be? You may be really struggling to come up with a logical reason for why [victim-survivor] might]. I can, and this is really stretching for an example, maybe [victim-survivor] is scorned, she could logically make something up. But that is not what has happened here. [According to [defendant] nothing happened, just a massage, then she immediately decides to make this up?] Why? There is no reason, what logical process might explain why she made it up? ... You must find him guilty. (Prosecution, T3)

The prosecutor attempted to resist the false allegations myth by acknowledging the gendered narratives of 'scorned women' and arguing that that reasoning was illogical in this case. Whilst it is good that it was addressed, the way in which the argument was framed continued to reference the myth that in certain circumstances women do lie about rape and that it is women with mental ill-health who lie, not this 'ideal victim' in front of the jury. This framing drew on the notion that 'hysterical' women lie about rape (discussed further later). The victim-survivor in this trial did in many ways match up to the 'ideal victim' image (Christie, 1986), and even in the ways she deviated from that image they were what could be considered exceptional. For example, although 'sexting' deviates from the idea of 'chastity' associated with an ideal victim, this victim-survivor was demonstrably hesitant and reserved in the images she sent to the defendant; therefore, she only minimally, and 'reasonably', deviated from the ideals of respectability that formulate the 'ideal victim' stereotype. Another factor that could lend favour to the victim-survivor in this regard was that she thrice interrupted the defence barrister in order to rebut or preempt victim-blaming assertions. This is significant because Larcombe (2005) argued that

> the 'successful rape complainant' is not necessarily one with an unblemished sexual history. Rather, she has a strong sense of herself and takes overt offence at…alternative or derogatory constructions of her character and credibility. (p. 73)

The following excerpt from the defence's closing remarks demonstrates how easy it is to form a 'women lie' narrative with regard to even those who bear close resemblance to the 'ideal victim':

> [It is simply one word against another. Does [victim-survivor's] word have enough weight… or was it a young woman] a bit prone to exaggeration, perhaps very embarrassed as to the position she found herself in… 'I've been duped, [he's not who he says he is]'. Imagine how she'd feel having to tell people about it. [Remember her messages, she suspected. Did she, as a result of embarrassment, knowing she'd be told off by her friend, think] the way out of this is to…play the victim. ['I'm going to say I was sexually assaulted…create a wave of sympathy rather than intense embarrassment…and people thinking I'm stupid']… 'you've been playing with my feelings, I'm gonna make your life really difficult now'…and be really vindictive. (Defence, T3)

The defence barrister chose words and phrases with clear negative connotations: "exaggeration", "embarrassed", "play the victim", and "vindictive". This relied on the gendered and classed narratives already discussed that posit that women lie about rape in order to avoid shame (Bourke

2007; Clark, 1987; Sanday, 1997; Stevenson, 2000). For example, Bourke noted a belief that "even 'respectable women' [could] 'imagine themselves the victims of a man's sexual passion'" (2007, p. 33). The connotation of 'exaggeration' in the defence counsel's closing speech reflected the idea that women 'imagine themselves the victims'. Again, as with T2, the defence arguably took advantage of the strength of the 'women lie about rape' narratives in news and social media at the time of the trial observations.

As with T3, there were insinuations of conniving in T6. The case involved two sisters as victim-survivors who had made allegations against a previous partner of their mother. Defence counsel in this trial used the sisters' relationship to undermine their claims by alluding to collusion. For example:

> *Defence*: Is it because it didn't happen?
> *Victim-survivor1*: No. It did. I won't be called a liar.
> *Defence*: … isn't it the case that you made up the bus allegations to support your sister's allegations?
> *Victim-survivor1*: No. (T6)

This assertion was then repeated in the context of inconsistencies with dates in the victim-survivor's accounts:

> *Defence*: I'm going to suggest you brought it forward three months.
> *Victim-survivor1*: No.
> *Defence*: Brought it forward to support [victim-survivor2's] allegations.
> *Victim-survivor1*: No! (T6)

The defence framed both sisters as vindictive liars in her closing remarks:

> … is she trying to make it worse for this defendant? It's not enough to accuse him of sex when she was 15, let's make it worse for him … [having made up allegations about kissing when she was a child which none of us had heard before] (Defence, T6)

Here the defence clearly articulated a motive of vindictiveness and malice and used victim-survivor1's inconsistencies to bolster that assertion. Victim-survivor2 was also framed as a vindictive liar:

> Members of the jury you may think it quite telling that she says at the
> end of the ABE about being angry with [victim-survivor1] 'stealing her
> boyfriend', but no one says anything about that...[recaps burden of proof]
> ... [Defendant] says she's odd ... does this rivalry give an insight as to how
> [victim-survivor2's] mind works? (Defence, T6)

The defence barrister portrayed victim-survivor2 as jealous, a narrative
put forward by the defendant on multiple occasions, and vindictive and
implied that a rivalry between the sisters could be seen as an indication
of that vindictiveness. This characterisation of rivalry contrasts with the
earlier assertion that one sister had made up allegations in support of
the other. Both characterisations, however, portray the victim-survivors
as untrustworthy and provide motive for lying. These narratives drew
on the gendered and classed narratives previously discussed that position
working-class women as untrustworthy.

In contrast to the other trials discussed in this section, the victim-
survivor in T4 had not used the word rape in her allegation, which closed
off the opportunity for the defence to put a 'motive' for false allegations in the ways outlined above. Therefore, the defence barrister instead
constructed the victim-survivor as a liar through focusing on her actions
at the time of the rapes, rather than focusing on providing the jury with
a motive for lying.

> Even the most socially adept people can be deceived by the actions of
> someone so intent on misleading. [That's what this case is about. [Victim-
> survivor] told you she was scared, in her mind felt scared of [defendant].
> So whilst [victim-survivor] told you that she had fear in her mind, she
> sought to deceive [defendant] because she wanted him to believe they
> were back together...]. (Defence closing, T4)

This remark ignored the context of the history of domestic abuse perpetrated by the defendant against the victim-survivor. He referred to the
victim-survivor as deceitful for not communicating her fear to the defendant and framed it as intentional manipulation. A later remark in his
closing argument reasserted this:

> if this was a woman who was genuinely fearful and desperate to escape,
> she was masterful at hiding it. (Defence closing, T4)

The assertions in both these extracts ignored and obscured what is known about the power dynamics in intimate partner violence and draws on the myth that women should and always do actively resist rape (see Chapter 2). Men who are violent towards their partners often do not need to resort to violence or threat in order to have their wishes met because the underlying pattern of abuse works as an effective tool of coercion (Hamby & Koss, 2003; Kelly, 1987). Cultural narratives, however, tend to obscure this by trivialising intimate partner rape, and this has been shown to influence charging decisions in a US context (O'Neal et al., 2015) and in mock jury research (Lynch et al., 2019).

Mothers as Liars

So far, this chapter has demonstrated that all the adult victim-survivors were accused of lying by the defence barristers through the use of gendered and classed narratives that reflect hundreds of years of disbelief of women and shaming of their sexualities. The gendered nature of these narratives was further demonstrated in the ways in which victim-survivors' mothers were also framed as untrustworthy liars by defence counsel. Whilst there was one male victim-survivor, he was a child and so narratives about his age were used to illustrate his untrustworthiness (discussed in following section); however, this was bolstered by gendered and classed narratives about his mother.

In Chapter 3, I set out the ways in which the child victim-survivor's mother in T5 was cast as a 'bad' mother through gendered and classed narratives. During cross-examination, she was asked about the timing of the report to the police in relation to her being annoyed with the defendant for cancelling planned contact with the children:

> *Defence*: Were there some messages after the breakup where [defendant] had to rearrange seeing the boys because of work?
> *Mother*: No, it was because of his back.
> *Defence*: I suggest there was a time he had to rearrange because he had a few days of work come up.
> *Mother*: Maybe, I don't remember.
> *Defence*: And shortly after it is when you call the police?
> *Mother*: I don't remember, I mean I remember what you're saying but I don't remember when it was. (T5)

Casting suspicion on the timing of the allegations in this way drew on pervasive cultural narratives that wrongly suggest mothers often make false child sexual abuse allegations against their former partners (Penfold, 1995; Trocmé & Bala, 2005). These assumptions draw on gendered and classed narratives that position women as vindictive liars. For example, Bourke (2007) noted that during the nineteenth century working-class children were thought to often make malicious allegations and were spurred on to do so by their mothers. Given the classed narratives constructed around the mother in T5 by the defence, the casting of suspicion over the timing of the allegations seems to reflect this historic narrative. This narrative was also reflected in T6, where the victim-survivors had been accused of fabricating their allegations and conniving together. Their mother was brought into this narrative in the defence's closing speech:

> [Did you think all three of them were challenged and backtracked to say 'I can't remember'. Are they helping you? Especially [mother]? That] throwaway remark 'I got dementia', really?! Really, members of the jury? (Defence, T6)

The defence barrister suggested that all three had given untruthful accounts and "backtracked" when they were challenged over details. She pointed particularly to the mother. This mother, like the mother in T5, had been painted as a 'bad' mother by the defence through the use of classed and gendered narratives. This intersected with unrealistic expectations that wholly accurate and consistent accounts of sexual violence are given.

As earlier examples have shown, the victim-survivor in T1 was accused of lying about being raped because she regretted having sex with the defendant. This narrative was bolstered through implying that the victim-survivor had conceded to a suggestion from her mother that it was rape, which was put forward as the source of the lie:

> *Defence*: You accused him of 'taking advantage'. Not rape.
> *Victim-survivor*: I don't know what went on.
> *Defence*: Exactly. You didn't accuse him of rape. You didn't tell your mum it was rape.
> *Victim-survivor*: I didn't want to believe it.
> *Defence*: It was your mum who first said it was rape. She put the idea in your head.

Victim-survivor: I don't agree.
Defence: You were not truthful to your mum about what happened. Then she suggested it was rape. (T1)

Here the defence used the term "put the idea in your head", which has clear negative connotations, to suggest that the victim-survivor had not believed it was rape. By then suggesting that the victim-survivor had not been truthful with her mother, he implied that she had misled her and did not correct her suggestion that it was rape. The implication was that she *should* have corrected her mother. This suggested that because the victim-survivor had not herself immediately labelled her experience as rape, her mother's assertion was invalid. This assumes that all 'true' victim-survivors are able to immediately accept or understand what has happened to them as rape, which ignores the difficulty women have in naming their experiences (McKenzie-Mohr & Lafrance, 2011). Indeed, Brooks-Hay (2019) found that it is common for victim-survivors to discuss their experiences with third-parties before reporting to the police and that these discussions are helpful in enabling them to 'name' their experiences. Nevertheless, the defence in T1 furthered his narrative in his cross-examination of the mother:

Defence: [Am I right that...all she said was '[defendant] did things to me'. You thought she was embarrassed because you're her mum, and she said 'I was aware that he was doing stuff but I couldn't move'], she never said what 'stuff' is.
Mother: But I knew what she was saying, I know her, I'm her mum. I know what she meant when she said 'stuff'.
Defence: You assumed.
Mother: I don't think that's an assumption.
Defence: You assumed.
Mother: I know what she meant by how she said 'you know mum, '*stuff*''. [She was so upset, but she was fine a few hours earlier.]
   ...
Defence: So, you made an assumption about what 'stuff' means.
Mother: No! (T1)

The defence barrister repeatedly used the word 'assumption' to cast doubt on the mother's account. He then continued by asking closed questions about the use (or not) of specific words:

Defence: Did she use the word rape?
Mother: No.
Defence: Did she use the word penis?
Mother: No.
Defence: Did she use the word vagina?
Mother: No.
Judge: Do you use different words for body parts? You know some people have different words for things within families.
Mother: No. (T1)

The implication of the above exchange was that a victim-survivor's account must be clear and specific; however, as noted above regarding T6, this is an unrealistic expectation. The cross-examination continued with the defence barrister returning to calling the mother's interpretation of her daughter's words an assumption:

Judge: So you just thought that's what she meant from what she was saying?
Mother: Yes.
Defence: That's an assumption. She said the defendant had done 'stuff' to her, you made an assumption about what that meant. So the word rape came from you?
Mother: Yeah, and so what?!
Judge: You were first to use the word rape, that's what he's asking.
Mother: Yes.
Defence: Nothing further. (T1)

This whole line of questioning focuses in of the meaning of words. A pattern that has been clear in this and two other trials (T2 and T3; see Daly, 2021) is that commonly used words and phrases that are well established colloquially as referring to sexual activity were drilled down on and given alternative meanings. In this case, that word is 'stuff'. It seems, therefore, that the language used to describe rape has to be precise; otherwise, it is questioned and positioned as incredible or insignificant. This is a worrying finding, given the frequency of colloquialisms in the English language. Guidance for ABE interviewers recognises that descriptions contain imprecise language (MoJ, 2011), and indeed, the use of imprecise language to give an account of rape is not a new phenomenon (see Bourke, 2007, p. 21, for an example account from

1880). Women's accounts of sexual violence are shaped by cultural narratives that blame and shame them (Brown, 2013) and medicalise their experiences (McKenzie-Mohr & Lafrance, 2011). Their narratives of trauma are thus often filled with uncertainty and minimisation (Brown, 2013). It is, therefore, unrealistic to expect precise medicalised language in victim-survivors' accounts, most especially in their first accounts.

In the above extract, the act of a mother comforting her child and helping her identify what had happened to her was used to undermine the victim-survivor's credibility and position her as a liar. The defendant also made use of this narrative during his cross-examination:

> *Prosecution*: Why would she say she didn't consent?
> *Defendant*: Well, to be honest I think it was down to her mum.
> *Judge*: That is speculation. (T1)

Whilst the judge rightly asserted that the defendant was speculating, she did not go further to explain to the jury that they should not give any consideration to speculation. As is standard, the judge did direct the jury in her summing-up that there is no place for speculation in a criminal trial; however, she did not refer back to this intervention. It seems unlikely that the jury would independently remember this intervention by the end of trial when the judge gave her directions. Instead, they were left with the defence's narrative of calculating women, involving the mother as well as the victim-survivor, implied through the defence's closing remarks:

> She never told her mum using words rape, penis or touching. Rape was her mother's idea. The timing of it all is interesting. Her mother said it was rape and off they went to the police station that very morning. In the time between her report and ABE she messaged people to tell them something really bad had happened that was so difficult for her to talk about, yet she keeps telling people. This, we submit, is a way for her to garner support and sympathy to keep up her charade. (Defence, T1)

The word "idea" carries connotations of scheming and brings the mother clearly into the narrative. Stating that "the timing of it all is interesting" again casts suspicion over the mother and daughter's intentions, seemingly implying an element of scheming. The victim-survivor confiding in her friends is treated as suspicious and a function of her "charade". This was made possible through digital evidence because what might previously have been offline conversations had taken place online and were thus recorded and made readily accessible for the defence to mould to their narrative. As noted in Chapter 2, this produces a 'damned if they do, damned if they don't' predicament for victim-survivors, where they are criticised for not telling but are also criticised when they do.

Children as Liars

Best practice for the cross-examination of child witnesses is guided through the Equal Treatment Bench Book (ETBB; Judicial College, 2020b), which outlines considerations and adjustments that can be made at the judge's discretion. For example, it specifies the manner in which questions should be phrased, that the defence case should not be directly put to the child, and that inconsistencies should be pointed out to the jury after rather than during the child's evidence. T5, the only observed trial with a child victim-survivor, provided an example of excellent practice in this regard. The questions were agreed in advance with the judge and intermediary, were phrased according to the guidelines in the ETBB, and were stuck to during cross-examination. The defence barrister used a manner appropriate for a child witness; that is, it was not aggressive or cold; rather, it was friendly in tone. The mother of the child, however, was cross-examined in a manner akin to the cross-examination of adult victim-survivors, during which questions pertaining to child's motive for lying were put to her.

> *Defence*: What was [victim-survivor's] reaction to [sibling] being born?
> *Mother*: He loved him.
> *Defence*: Wasn't he insanely jealous?
> *Mother*: No.
> *Defence*: Didn't he say he wanted him to die?
> *Mother*: No. (T5)

The above extract shows how the victim-survivor was portrayed as harbouring extreme jealousy towards his then-newborn half-brother. This reflects the gendered jealousy narrative discussed earlier, and whilst that narrative was formed around women, as recently as the 1970s the belief that boys lie has been clearly articulated by the judiciary:

> It is well known that women in particular, and small boys, are liable to be untruthful and invent stories. (Judge Sutcliffe, 1976, cited in Jordan, 2004)

Bourke (2007) traced historical narratives about children being disbe-
lieved when making claims of sexual abuse, particularly children from
working-class families. The classed nature of this misconception is significant because in T5 the mother's parenting skills were routinely called into
question by the defence, arguably in an attempt to bolster the image of
her child as a lying 'problem child':

> *Defence*: Do you recall [victim-survivor] saying he was going to go to
> school and say you stabbed him?
> *Mother*: Yep.
> *Defence*: Did you stab him?
> *Mother*: No. (T5)

Four other instances of historical lying were laid out in the same manner
one after the other, building a concentrated image of this child's past
behaviour. This painted the victim-survivor as a child who tells lies in
order to get people into trouble. 'Fanciful lying' is a trait associated with
narratives of the 'problem child' (Horn, 1993). Horn (1993) demonstrated how the 'problem child' was constructed based on middle-class
ideals in the twentieth century, where the 'proper' raising of children was
seen to ameliorate social problems. Given that behavioural problems are
associated with acquittals in child sex offences trials (Lewis et al., 2014),
drawing on the 'problem child' narrative could have been compelling for
the jury. Indeed, a similar narrative has been observed in a US context,
where Powell et al. (2017) identified narratives about 'rebellious adolescents' and 'dysfunctional families' as undermining the credibility of child
victim-survivors.

> *Defence*: Has he ever told you anything bad about [current partner]?
> *Mother*: No.
> *Defence*: As far as you're concerned he loves him?
> *Mother*: He sees him as a friend, likes him not love.
> *Defence*: Has he ever told you he hates him?
> *Mother*: Sometimes.
> *Defence*: No more questions. (T5)

These lines of questioning ignored the fact that it is not unusual for young
children to lie (Talwar & Crossman, 2012) or say they hate someone as
a reaction to a perceived slight or to being told off (Einon & Potegal,
1994). Furthermore, lying about one thing does not mean they are lying
about the alleged offences. This issue with credibility and past lies is a

narrative that is applied to children in court as well as adults, and school records are commonly used to evidence histories of lying (e.g. Baird & Newlove, 2018; Busby, 1997; Temkin & Krahe, 2008). The prosecution in T5 addressed the narratives of both mother and child as liars directly with the defendant:

> *Prosecution*: [The mother] never showed any antagonism to you?
> *Defendant*: No.
> *Prosecution*: So if you're right, and he has made this up.
> *Defendant*: Yeah.
> *Prosecution*: There's nothing in your experience of him that gives any indication that he would?
> *Defendant*: Well, when [sibling] was born I felt [victim-survivor] was jealous.
>
> …
>
> *Prosecution*: So you're saying there were enough things she would be aware of to show that [victim-survivor] was hostile towards [sibling]?
> *Defendant*: Yes.
> *Prosecution*: So that's a pretty big lie from [mother]?
> *Defendant*: Yes, it is.
> *Prosecution*: … Are you sure you're not making this up?
> *Defendant*: Yes.
>
> …
>
> *Prosecution*: Or is it just a motive you have made up for [victim-survivor]?
> *Defendant*: No. (T5)

The prosecution also addressed this, along with other rape myths, well in her closing speech:

> [You have to assess whether [victim-survivor] is fundamentally telling the truth]. You may think that all boys and girls lie, sometimes about important things, sometimes about trivial things. [… what we do know] is that as soon as he's challenged he has retracted [his lies]… that is not something that happened here, [lying is not something that runs through the time of [defendant] and [mother's] relationship, it comes after]. (Prosecution, T5)

The defence's closing focused on positioning the victim-survivor as a liar and countering the prosecutions reasoning for viewing him as credible. She talked about children being known to lie and she couched her argument by saying perhaps he did not mean to tell such a lie:

> He may not have set out deliberately doing this, it takes courage to say you were lying, imagine how hard it is for a child to admit to mum, school, grandmother, aunts, that it wasn't true. (Defence, T5)

She then, however, continued to draw on her earlier 'problem child' narrative:

> Very often in the experience of the court, perpetrators of child abuse will tell children to keep it a secret, very often that's the reason genuine abuse victims take so long to come forward. Here it was never suggested it was a secret, given what we know about him, do you really think he wouldn't have told anyone? For all these years? (Defence, T5)

It could be argued that presenting a monologue attacking a 9-year-old child would not be a good look to a jury; therefore, carefully couching it as outlined above lessens the severity thereby protecting the argument from potentially repelling the jury. In this last extract, the defence was othering the child, seemingly simultaneously invoking an 'ideal victim' and a 'real child abuse' stereotype. Whilst 'secret keeping' is a common tactic used by perpetrators (e.g. Somer & Szwarcberg, 2001), the absence of such a tactic is being used here to cast doubt on the legitimacy of the child's claims. Interestingly, in a review of transcripts from 133 child sexual abuse trials in Victoria (Australia), Lewis et al. (2014) found that evidence of a child 'acting out' after alleged sexual abuse was most strongly associated with guilty verdicts. As noted above, the prosecution in T5 pointed out that the victim-survivor's 'acting out' behaviour began after the alleged assaults; therefore, the defence's reframing of the child's behaviour as an issue related to 'bad' mothering served to work against the prosecution's narrative and subvert any causal association jurors may have made between the victim-survivor's behaviour and the allegations.

MENTAL ILL-HEALTH AS AN INDICATOR
OF UNTRUSTWORTHINESS AND UNRELIABILITY

Kelly et al. (2006) found that third-party evidence relating to victim-survivors' health and social care history is often sought, usually via records from social services, medical records, and/or counselling records (see also, Smith & Daly, 2020). Concerns have been raised regarding defence barristers' use of mental health records as a tool for undermining victim-survivor credibility (Ellison, 2009; Temkin, 2002). It is argued that such records are used to portray victim-survivors as 'crazy', damaged, disturbed, and untrustworthy, and thus someone who cannot be trusted to provide reliable evidence (Ellison, 2009; Temkin, 2002). Indeed, precisely these attitudes were highlighted in research related to earlier CJS stages (Hester, 2013; Stanko & Williams, 2009). These portrayals play into rape myths regarding false accusations and stereotypes about 'hysterical' women. They also play into prejudices and misconceptions about mental health more generally which are common in the English population (Evans-Lacko et al., 2013; Mehta et al., 2009).

Ellison (2009) outlined a case where a depression diagnosis was seemingly used to imply that the victim-survivor was 'emotionally unstable' and was therefore likely to have lied. In another example discussed by Ellison (2009), a victim-survivor's childhood self-harming was used to imply that she deliberately sought out harm and thus consented to the incident in question. In both these cases, the mental health issues discussed were historic rather than current (Ellison, 2009), arguably further adding to their irrelevance to the cases on trial. Repeat victimisation, despite being common, is also used to undermine the credibility of victim-survivors. International research has indicated that diagnoses of post-traumatic stress disorder/syndrome have been used to suggest that victim-survivors were experiencing flashback at the time of the assault and were therefore confused about the nature of the encounter (Wilkinson-Ryan, 2005).

The Court of Appeal ruling in *R v Tine* (in relation to burglary) upheld that psychiatric history was irrelevant to the credibility of the witness and was therefore disallowed; however, the ruling offered no guidance as to determining relevance nor to the potential prejudicial impact of such questioning (Ellison, 2009). This means it remains up to individual judges to determine whether mental health history can be relevant for cross-examination. Ellison (2009) argued that even where evidence regarding mental health history is disallowed during trial by the judge, the prejudicial damage with regard to juror perceptions of credibility may already have been done. Notably, looking to Scots Law, the appeal court in *Branney v HM Advocate* [2014] HCJAC 78 asserted that:

> It is by no means clear that...a bare statement that a complainer had suffered from severe depression as a result of the appellant's conduct would have provided legitimate ground for exploring her mental health in evidence. We are unaware of any automatic association between depression and lack of credibility.

This reflects Ellison's (2009) argument that "cross-examination intended to impugn credibility should be allowed only if it is shown that a witness's capacity or disposition to provide reliable evidence is negatively affected by a mental illness or disorder" (p. 43). This has, however, not been successfully taken up as a matter for reform in England and Wales so victim-survivors continue to have limited protections with regard to mental health history being used to undermine their credibility during cross-examination (Ellison & Munro, 2016).

In addition to the potential impact on perceived credibility and juror decision-making, the use of third-party records relating to mental health can negatively impact a victim-survivor's recovery. This is because it is widely acknowledged within the CJS that these records are regularly used at trial by defence barristers, so victim-survivors were often advised by police and CPS not to seek therapy or counselling prior to trial because the defence could use it to challenge the validity of their evidence (Rossetti et al., 2017; Temkin, 2002). This limits victim-survivors' access to support following victimisation and is counter to the Government's *Victims Strategy* (HM Government, 2018) which includes a promise to "make it easier for people who have suffered a crime to cope, recover, and move on with rebuilding their lives" (p. 6). It is reassuring that the CPS recognises and seeks to address this issue through revised guidance for prosecutors (CPS, 2020); however, it is too soon to tell what the impacts of this change will be going forward.

Narratives about mental ill-health were another way in which defence barristers relied on broader cultural narratives to undermine victim-survivors. As noted earlier, the defence barrister in T1 described the victim-survivor's reaction as "hysterical". Two witnesses in the trial also described her reaction as such. Studies have repeatedly found that the word 'hysterical' is associated both with femininity and with mental illness

(Epting & Burchett, 2019). Indeed, Ussher (2013) noted that narratives about 'hysteria' can be traced as far back as the ancient Greeks, with the narratives later becoming commonplace in the seventeenth century. Though 'hysteria' was later broadened in diagnostic terms so that men too could receive such a 'diagnosis', the cultural narratives surrounding it remained clearly gendered, with women's hysteria considered innate and men's hysteria considered an illness (Ussher, 2013). In T1, the hysteria narrative fed into a wider narrative about the victim-survivor's mental health that was used to discredit her. The victim-survivor's depression was first adduced during her cross-examination through digital evidence:

> *Defence*: <Reads messages> [You said that you had come back off holiday feeling much more confident, that you were feeling much better especially since] you had been taking happy pills. I guess by that you don't mean anything illegal?
> *Victim-survivor*: Anti-depressants. (T1)

Her anti-depressant use was also included in the toxicology report. According to the CPS, "where it is alleged that the victim was incapable, through alcohol consumption or drug inducement, toxicological evidence may provide strong support for a lack of capacity to consent" (CPS, undated, unpaginated). Since the substance at issue in this trial was alcohol, it is unclear why the result pertaining to anti-depressants could not have been redacted from the report provided to the jury. The victim-survivor's anti-depressant use was also mentioned by the defendant in his police interview when discussing what others characterised as the victim-survivor's "hysterical" reaction:

> she's on anti-depressants, you dunno what that can do to someone if like they, like, haven't taken their tablets or something. (Defendant, police interview, T1)

The defendant brought up the victim-survivor's anti-depressants a further two times during his interview in much the same manner. The assertion the defendant made here was that the victim-survivor's behaviour was unprovoked and must have occurred because of her depression, insinuating that she behaved irrationally and that it was because she was on anti-depressants (not because he had raped her). During cross-examination of the defendant, the prosecution provided an avenue for this assertion to be made once again:

Prosecution: You were shouting at her.
Defendant: I was trying to calm her down.
Prosecution: ...it's not like she had mental problems.
Defendant: Yes, she was on anti-depressants. (T1)

It is disappointing that the prosecutor opened such an avenue for the defendant to reinforce his narrative. According to the testimony of multiple witnesses and the defendant's police interview, the defendant had in the immediate aftermath of the second alleged rape called the victim-survivor "crazy", "paranoid", a "psycho", and said she was "having a breakdown". These words demonstrate the reliance on this narrative as a tool for undermining the victim-survivor's credibility. Indeed, in the context of parental custody hearings, Zaccour (2018) found that mental health labels are used in court to undermine women's credibility. It has long been recognised that defence barristers adduce mental health evidence in rape trials as a way of undermining victim-survivors' credibility (Ellison, 2009; Temkin, 2000). When this type of evidence is adduced with no relevance, it infringes on victim-survivors' right to privacy and protection of medical details. As noted earlier, a Court of Appeal ruling in *R v Tine* [2006] EWCA Crim 1788 upheld that psychiatric history was irrelevant to the credibility of the witness, although this was in relation to burglary (Ellison, 2009), and a similar assertion was made in *Branney v HM Advocate* [2014] HCJAC 78.

The usefulness of defence counsel adducing mental health evidence stems from the long history of women's distress being framed as madness (Busfield, 1996; Ussher, 2011). The continued pervasiveness of such narratives can arguably be demonstrated by the worldwide popularity of a song entitled '*Sweet but psycho*' which spent four weeks at number 1 and 12 weeks in the top 10 of the UK music singles chart over the time period of this trial (Official Charts, undated). The lyrics of this song and accompanying video were widely criticised as sexist and stigmatising of mental illness (e.g. *Daily Mail*, 2019; Meaney, 2018). The characterisation of the victim-survivor in T1 as 'crazy' was further galvanised by the defendant's following assertion during his cross-examination:

Prosecution: Did you feel scared about telling her about what had happened?
Defendant: Yeah, course.
Prosecution: ...you were scared about how she would react?
Defendant: Yeah cos she's always had a temper. (T1)

This 'crazy woman' narrative draws on pervasive gendered stereotypes of women as overly emotional (Shields, 2013) and irrational (McCormick et al., 2016). Women are perceived to be more emotional than men, with women often being viewed as *being* emotional as opposed to men *having* emotions (McCormick et al., 2016). Similar trial narratives were found by Smith (2018) which characterised women as, for example, delusional and erratic and therefore untrustworthy. It is well established that gendered stereotypes based on emotion impact people's assessment of other's emotion (Shields, 2013); therefore, these narratives are likely to play a role in jurors' assessments at trial.

As Gilmore (2017) argues, "women's testimony is frequently associated with unreliability *because* it is women's testimony" (p. 19, emphasis added). Gilmore's (2017) analysis explores the intersections of race and class with gender, demonstrating that Black women's emotions and associated credibility are judged against different criteria than white women. All the victim-survivors in the observed trials were white women, so the classed narratives present in the trials demonstrate how they are both privileged and oppressed at the same time. Indeed, Wingfield (2010) found that rules regarding what is considered appropriate ways of displaying emotions are differently constructed for different racialised and classed groups. Wingfield (2010) posits that white, middle-class ideals shape what is considered appropriate emotional behaviour, characterised by calmness and congeniality. That the victim-survivor was framed using cultural narratives about young white working-class women therefore bolstered this narrative of her as being highly emotional because of mental ill-health rather than because of trauma.

The gendered narratives about emotionality and mental ill-health were also present in T2, T4, and T6 to varying extents. For example, similarly to T1, the victim-survivor in T2 was referred to as "paranoid" by the defendant and portrayed as behaving irrationally within their relationship:

> We were arguing all the time, she was paranoid about [defendant's new girlfriend], we had pathetic arguments...she had been having a go at me for having a password on my phone even though she had loads and a thing where it took a photo of whoever tries to unlock your phone... but she knows how to wind me up, she would just dig, dig, dig, pushing me to the point when I feel like a cunt, then I shout. (Defendant, police interview, T2)

In this trial, there was contestation over whether the breakdown of the relationship was due to the alleged rape, as was the prosecutions position, or not. By portraying the victim-survivor as irrational, the defendant was able to refute that assertion and distance himself from his poor behaviour within the relationship.

> [I would always give her a kiss and a cuddle before I left for work no matter how early it was because she would get upset when I didn't]. (Defendant, police interview, T2)

In the following example, the prosecution cross-examined the defendant about the reasons for the breakdown of the relationship:

> *Defendant*: Arguments, just too many arguments.
> *Prosecution*: Like what?
> *Defendant*: [The woman who later became defendant's new girlfriend], I wasn't doing the cleaning, wasn't helping out around the house, bills, silly little things like passwords on phones.
> *Prosecution*: Okay, so let's take each of those things, not cleaning or helping around the house, presumably that was throughout the relationship?
> *Defendant*: [No cos I got the new job and was working silly hours and she wanted me to clean when I'd get home, at like 3 or 4 in the morning she would want me to hoover].
> *Prosecution*: *Right*. (T2)

The intonation in the prosecution's final word here seemed to be expressing disbelief at the defendant's explanation about the hoovering. In this same trial, the prosecution made plain that she did not accept some of his other explanations, including regarding what the prosecution alleged was an admission to rape (Daly, 2021). In her closing speech, she therefore twice told the jury that the defendant "insults your intelligence" (T2); however, the not guilty verdict in this case suggests that the jury did not find his explanations as ludicrous as the prosecutor did. Given the pervasiveness of gendered stereotypes about emotion and mental health, the 'crazy woman' narrative employed by the defendant could well have had an impact on the jurors' assessments of credibility.

In contrast, the prosecution in T3 drew on this same stereotype as a means of bolstering the credibility of the victim-survivor by contrasting her against that stereotype:

> Unless mentally unhinged, you don't go around making these things up. What reason could there be? (Prosecution closing, T3)

The implication in this extract is that 'unhinged' women do lie about rape and this is presented as the only reason a woman would lie about rape. Furthermore, it produces a simplistic dichotomy that says parties are either being wholly truthful or wholly dishonest (Smith & Skinner, 2017), which does not allow for people holding differing interpretations of the same facts and thus hold differing truths of the same situation (Smart, 1989). Whilst perhaps not a damaging remark with regard to this victim-survivor's credibility in this trial, it is a remark that nevertheless demonstrates the pervasiveness of damaging narratives at trial and serves to generally reinforce these damaging social stereotypes.

MAKING EXCUSES AND CONSTRUCTING SYMPATHY FOR THE DEFENDANT

In all trials, defence counsel attempted to construct narratives that elicited sympathy and made excuses for the defendants. In two cases (T3 and T5), this built on the defence counsel's narratives that sought to portray the defendants as objectively 'good' men.

In T5, the defence began her closing argument by encouraging the jury to identify with the defendant:

> Any single one of you who has contact with a child could be sitting where he is sitting. (Defence, T5)

This urged the jury to empathise with the defendant; it asked them to 'put themselves in his shoes'. Asking the jurors to imagine themselves in that position makes it harder for them to deliver a guilty verdict because they see themselves in the dock. This type of reasoning is known as Golden Rule reasoning and stems from the Christian edict "do unto others as you would have them do unto you" (The Bible, Matthew 7:12). Urging jurors to engage in such reasoning is a practice that has long (see *Duchaine v Ray* [1939] 110 Vt. 313) been deemed improper in US courts because it encourages a departure from impartiality (Conner, 2001; Mangrum, 2015):

A golden rule argument—which asks 'jurors to place themselves in the position of a party'—is 'universally condemned' because it encourages the jury to depart from neutrality and to decide the case on the basis of personal interest and bias rather than on evidence. (*Caudle v District of Columbia* [2013] 707 F.3d 354)

In T5, the defence's 'Golden Rule' argument also drew on the misconception that false allegations are common, especially the 'easy to make, hard to disprove' trope. Encouraging the jury to put themselves in the defendant's shoes was also a tactic used in T6:

Put yourself in his shoes, you may think you would struggle to give an account of what you were doing 10-15 years before, then imagine that in the pressure of a police interview. Then four months later there are more allegations, a further interview. (Defence, T6)

These appeals for empathy are in stark contrast to this defence barrister's later claims that "emotion plays no role" and "moral judgement plays no part" in reference to the prosecution's case. The jury were encouraged to consider emotions so that they can empathise with the defendant, but then told that they should not consider emotion when assessing the victim-survivors' evidence or the prosecution's case.

In other trials, the narratives constructing sympathy were woven throughout using micro-examinations. For example, in T1, the defence elicited reference to low self-esteem from the defendant on three occasions. To give one such example:

Defence: Did you say anything to her about it?
Defendant: No.
Defence: Did you want to?
Defendant: Yeah.
Defence: Why didn't you?
Defendant: Cos I've got low confidence. (T1)

This narrative sought to elicit sympathy for the defendant. It was later expanded upon by positioning the defendant as the victim of unrequited love who was having his feelings knowingly hurt by the victim-survivor's sociable behaviour, which had been implied as flirtatious by the defence:

Defence: Where was [victim-survivor] throughout the night?
Defendant: She kept disappearing, coming back with a boy or group of boys.
Defence: You weren't with them?

Defendant: No.
Defence: You saw [victim-survivor] later?
Defendant: Yeah she kept coming back to me and [friend].
Defence: How did you feel seeing her with other boys?
Defendant: I wasn't happy about it, I didn't wanna see that.
Defence: And [friend]?
Defendant: Not happy at all either. (T1)

The final question in this exchange asked what the defendant's female friend's feelings were about the victim-survivor "disappearing". This sought to bolster the defendant's characterisation of the behaviour as negative or morally improper. That the defence asked how the defendant (and his friend) felt seeing the victim-survivor with other men is significant because earlier in the trial the judge had intervened when the prosecution asked the victim-survivor a 'how did that make you feel question', saying: "How someone feels is not relevant" (Judge, T1). The judge did not intervene in the above example in relation to the defendant (and his friend), which demonstrates an imbalance in the application of practice rules. The defence were allowed to seek sympathy for the defendant in ways that were not allowed for the prosecution and victim-survivor. This is reflective of Manne's (2020) concept of 'himpathy': "the way…boys and men who commit acts of sexual violence or engage in other misogynistic behaviour often receive sympathy and concern over their female victims" (p. 5).

Similarly, in T2, 'himpathy' was used to reframe the defendant as the victim of a capricious woman:

I don't know why she's done this to me, the girl I wanted to marry, she hasn't even said if we have broken up or not. (Defendant, police interview, T2)

Here the defendant employed a narrative that portrayed himself as being strung along and hurt by the victim-survivor and this was built upon during his live evidence at trial:

Defence: You refer to your head being a bit of a mess at the moment.
Defendant: Yes.
Defence: Were you clear in your mind whether she did or did not want to be with you?
Defendant: No.

Defence: [So before, had there been times when she said she didn't want contact but then had been happy to have sex with you?]
Defendant: Yes. (T2)

Here the defendant, who cried often throughout his testimony, exhibited remorse for his admitted anger and aggression towards the victim-survivor, for example "then I shout and she leaves and I sit and cry cos it's not how I meant to be" (T2), and when asked how he would feel afterwards: "Dreadful, I was ashamed of myself as well" (T2). Research has long shown that when defendants display emotions such as sadness, distress, and remorse, they elicit more sympathy from the 'guilt assessor' (e.g. a jury) and improve their perceived credibility (MacLin et al. 2009; Robinson et al., 1994; Rumsey, 1976; Savitsky & Sim, 1974). In T2, then, admitting aggression towards the victim-survivor whilst showing remorse may have worked in the defendant's favour. Indeed, this construction of sympathy was built into the defence's closing arguments:

His head was a mess. Of course it was. [If someone says they don't want anything to do with you but then 2 days later has sex with you, maybe your head would be a mess, so to say 'won't take no for an answer',] well that is one interpretation, but bear in mind this is a young man, maybe not as bright as [victim-survivor], [and this is an interpretation too]. He is not a young man who is a sex pest, but a young man whose head is a mess. (Defence, T2)

Here the defence barrister discredited the idea that the defendant was a 'sex pest', thus distancing him from 'deviant rapist', whilst simultaneously constructing sympathy through the use of a classed and gendered portrayal of the victim-survivor as 'promiscuous' and capricious. The defence twice used the term "head is a mess", which points to the notion of not thinking straight and making mistakes, which is not part of the law on consent. The term also has connotations of sadness and distress. As noted above, sadness and distress have been shown to influence juror's perception of defendants, which is important because this defendant frequently displayed these emotions during his evidence and whilst sitting in the dock, including crying and heavy breathing. Wessel et al. (2012) explored the effect of the displays of emotion from men accused of rape and found that expressions of despair strongly increased their perceived credibility. This seemed to benefit the defendant in T2 because he was acquitted. The classed narratives within this trial may also have benefitted the defendant in relation to this because Thompson et al. (2011) found that as well as displaying upset emotions, being of low socioeconomic status made male defendants more likeable and more trustworthy compared to those from a higher socioeconomic status.

The sympathy narrative was most prominent in T3, which the defence constructed using multiple aspects of the defendant's personal life. These included asking about the defendant's disabled child, his troubles at work, and the difficulties in his marriage. For example:

> *Defence*: [How did that affect you?].
> *Defendant*: [It was very hard, our relationship was affected, it affected all aspects of my life including financial, we were living together but it was like we were living separately, I was trying to help her, but she was pushing me away and I felt rejected]. (T3)

The defendant's unsuccessful online dating experiences were added to this to expand on his feelings of rejection:

> *Defendant*: [A lot of rejection, negative comments] some more detrimental than others, [no interest at all], a lot of 'you're not what I'm looking for'.
> *Defence*: Your response to that?
> *Defendant*: [It hurt, it was even more rejection, I felt worthless], ugly...fat...completely worthless in myself. (T3)

The rejection added to an overall construction of a sympathy narrative and was then used to excuse his online deception ('catfishing') of the victim-survivor, first through his evidence-in-chief:

> *Defence*: Why did you use those photos?
> *Defendant*: [Because of the first experience I had, complete rejection, so I chose to use photos that might get more conversation with people]. (T3)

Then in the defence barrister's closing arguments:

> [Remember the space he was in in his life that year: demoted, wife redundant, [disabled] child, and remember he was portrayed as a dreamer.

Affirmation perhaps.] He tried being himself and had been completely rejected [on the first dating site]. (Defence, T3)

The defendant's wife gave a character statement in this trial in which she stated that she wanted to work on the marriage and took responsibility for causing the defendant's actions regarding the online dating:

> [I was not giving him enough attention when I was going through redundancy, [defendant] had work stress. [Defendant] is a wonderful, loving father and [volunteers in the community]. I realise we have taken each other for granted. I do not want to give up on our marriage. I want to have couples counselling]. (Character statement, defendant's wife, T3)

Her statement bolstered the sympathy narrative aimed at absolving or minimising the defendant's deceptive actions and thus attempted to make it seem less likely that he would have sexually assaulted the victim-survivor. The narrative ties into the myth that men have uncontrollable sex drives, which has been wrongly used to justify and explain men's sexual violence and aggression (Bourke, 2007; Carabine, 1992) and is a narrative that has been prevalent in mock jury deliberations (Leverick, 2020). Whilst sexual aggression is not an intrinsic element of maleness, narratives that position it as such form part of what Gavey (2005) calls the 'cultural scaffolding' of rape. These are narratives rooted in patriarchal values that prioritised men's sexual desire and often denied 'respectable' women any sexual desire at all (Seidman, 1991; Shorter, 1991).

Women were, and often continue to be, positioned as sexually passive objects that are awaiting to fulfil men's sexual urges rather than actively seeking to satisfy their own (Gavey, 2005). This situates women as gatekeepers to sex and excuses and minimises men's sexual aggression (Carabine, 1992). Positioning women as gatekeepers to sexual interactions is reflective of the embedded gendered and classed narratives that value women's chastity (Clark, 1987; Robinson, 1984). This positioning of women as passive gatekeepers therefore also implies that women who do not behave with sexual passivity and chastity are to blame for their sexual victimisation through 'inviting' men's sexual aggression. As demonstrated earlier in this book, this consequently provides a space for gendered and classed cultural narratives to intersect and cast women against the idea of an 'ideal victim' (Christie, 1986). Narratives that draw on the notion of 'uncontrollable male urges' therefore also seek to excuse defendants' behaviour.

Over the course of the trials, most defendants admitted some level of harm to the victim-survivors. In some instances, those admissions related to behaviour peripheral to the allegations (T1, T2 and T4), such as aggression within an intimate relationship.[1] This is particularly true in T4 where the defendant pleaded guilty to a charge relating to domestic abuse at the outset of the trial and coercion was central to the arguments about consent. In other instances, the admissions of harm related directly to the allegations of sexual violence being put to the defendants (T2 and T3). In these two trials, the victim-survivors had both confronted the defendants in digital messaging; therefore, there was digital evidence directly relating to the allegations. I discuss these digital admissions of harm and the excuses used by defendants in depth elsewhere (Daly, 2021), but will briefly illustrate using T2 as an example. In this trial, the defence used a narrative that drew on notions of intelligence and a lack of educational attainment to excuse the defendant. As was set out in Chapter 2, the victim-survivor in T2 had confronted the defendant using the words "you climbed on top of me when I said no" to describe the alleged rape. The defendant claimed that he had thought the victim-survivor was talking about an argument where he had slapped her phone from her hands, which the prosecution characterised as an explanation that 'insulted the intelligence' of the jury. The defence provided an avenue for the jury to accept the defendant's 'nonsensical' explanation by drawing on the defendant's proclamations that he was "not good with words" and "didn't do well at school".

Notions of youth and immaturity were also used as an excuse for harmful behaviour. For example, in T1, the defendant used his youth as an excuse for his admitted bad behaviour towards the victim-survivor, in this case photographing her without her consent whilst she slept in her bra:

Prosecution: [In [month of second incident] you took photos. Do you agree that [victim-survivor] didn't like you seeing her just wearing a bra?]
Defendant: No.

[1] Though of course aggression within a relationship cannot necessarily be separated from rape within a relationship.

Judge: [Wait, that's unclear there are two ways that answer can be interpreted. Did [victim-survivor] let you see her in a bra?]
Defendant: No.
Judge: Why?
Defendant: She's never changed in front of me.
Prosecution: You knew she wouldn't like you taking those photos?
Defendant: Yeah.
Prosecution: You knew you shouldn't take them.
Defendant: Not at the time, I was young then, I didn't understand life.
   (T1)

The prosecution later argued that this behaviour demonstrated a history of the defendant violating the victim-survivor's bodily autonomy whilst she slept:

> It is clear that she didn't want him to see her in her bra. He does take photos of her when she's asleep knowing that she wouldn't like it. There is a clear pattern of him doing things to her that she wouldn't like when she is asleep. (Prosecution, T1)

The defence did not mention this at all during his closing arguments, which reflects a tactic Rosulek (2015) refers to as 'silencing'. That is, omitting a topic in hopes the jury will forget about it in their deliberations. This can be particularly effective because the defence speech comes after the prosecution speech in England and Wales.

In T2, the prosecution asserted that immaturity "is not an excuse for being a rapist". The defence sought to deflect that assertion through excusing and minimising the defendant's admitted bad behaviour towards the victim-survivor. For example, in her closing speech, defence counsel posited that the relationship deteriorated not because of the alleged rape, but because the victim-survivor "outgrew" the defendant. That remark trivialised the defendant's admitted aggression towards and harassment of the victim-survivor, thereby also attempting to excuse the alleged rape. The behaviour he had admitted to throughout the course of the trial was that he was routinely aggressive and domineering in arguments, that he was often angry towards the victim-survivor, that he would ask the victim-survivor to bring home another woman's underwear, and that he had sent messages post-break-up to the victim-survivor requesting sex 10–12 times a day. The defence barrister's insinuation became clear in the final lines of her closing speech:

but bear in mind this is a young man, maybe not as bright as [victim-survivor], [and this is an interpretation too.] He is not a young man who is a sex pest, but a young man whose head is a mess. [Is that an interpretation you could make of his mindset and if it is, is that not something that can cast doubt?] He is probably guilty of not behaving in the best way, what he is *not* guilty of is having sex with her when she said no. He might be stupid and immature, but he is not [victim-survivor's] rapist. (Defence, T2)

Firstly, the suggestion here that lack of consent requires a 'no' was misleading. Aside from this, defence counsel repeatedly referenced the defendant's youth and immaturity in such a way as to minimise and excuse the defendant's admitted and alleged actions. Focusing on these peripheral aspects of the defendant's behaviour enabled the defence to distance the defendant from the cultural image of 'rapist' shaped by the 'real rape' myth that positions rapists as 'deviant other'. Furthermore, narratives that focus on a defendant's youth are useful to defence barristers because evidence suggests that juries are reluctant to convict young men of rape, particularly those under the age of 25 (Topping & Barr, 2018). In T2, the defendant was several years older than the victim-survivor and in his late twenties at the time of the alleged rape. Therefore, highlighting the defendant as young, and contrasting his 'immaturity' against the victim-survivor, invited the jury to consider him a young man and aligned him with the 18–24 age range.

SUMMARY

This chapter has outlined how sexism and classism, and to a lesser extent ableism, intersected in cultural narratives that constructed victim-survivors, and their mothers, as untrustworthy and unreliable. These narratives drew on the common misconception that women routinely lie about being raped. This was also evident for the boy child victim-survivor who was portrayed as a lying 'problem child'. Varying motives for lying were posed, including vengeance and regret, and even where it was not possible for defence barristers to put forward such a motive, the victim-survivor was characterised as unreliable as an alternative means of undermining her. Further, drawing on gendered cultural narratives related to emotionality and mental health enabled defence barristers to characterise victim-survivors as unstable and manipulative. These narratives of victim-survivors as dishonest also intersected with the narratives of respectability set out in Chapter 3, for example in bolstering characterisations of victim-survivors and their mothers as untrustworthy through reference to their sexual behaviour.

In stark contrast to narratives about victim-survivors, narratives about defendants sought to further rely on the 'good men don't rape' fallacy even in cases where defendants had admitted harmful behaviour towards the victim-survivors. Defendants were also distanced from 'rapist' through narratives that sought sympathy and provided excuses for harmful behaviour. Such tactics are indicative of the low bar that is set for defendants' credibility in comparison with the incredibly high bar for victim-survivors.

REFERENCES

Baird, V., & Newlove, H. (2018). *Article by Dame Vera Baird and Baroness Newlove on why disclosure must put victims first!* http://www.northumbria-pcc.gov.uk/article-dame-vera-baird-baroness-newlove-disclosure-must-put-victims-first/. Accessed 15 October 2020.

Bourke, J. (2007). *Rape: A history from 1860 to the present day*. Virago Press.

Bowcott, O. (2018). CPS and police 'routinely failing' to disclose evidence. *The Guardian*. https://www.theguardian.com/law/2018/nov/15/cps-and-police-routinely-failing-to-disclose-evidence. Accessed 15 November 2019.

Brooks-Hay, O. (2019). Doing the "right thing"? Understanding why rape victim-survivors report to the police. *Feminist Criminology, 15*(2), 174–195.

Brown, C. (2013). Women's narratives of trauma: (Re)storying uncertainty, minimization and self-blame. *Narrative Works, 3*(1), 1.

Busby, K. (1997). Discriminatory uses of personal records in sexual violence cases. *Canadian Journal of Women and the Law, 9*(1), 148.

Busfield, J. (1996). *Men, women and madness*. Palgrave Macmillan.

Carabine, J. (1992). 'Constructing women': Women's sexuality and social policy. *Critical Social Policy, 12*(34), 23–37.

Christie, N. (1986). The ideal victim. In E. A. Fattah (Ed.), *From crime policy to victim policy* (pp. 17–30). Palgrave Macmillan.

Clark, A. (1987). *Women's silence, men's violence: Sexual assault in England, 1770–1845*. Pandora.

Conner, T. J. (2001). What you may not say to the jury. *Litigation, 27*(3), 36–67.

Cossins, A. (2020). *Closing the justice gap for adult and child sexual assault*. Palgrave Macmillan.

Crown Prosecution Service. (2013). *Charging perverting the course of justice and wasting police time in cases involving allegedly false rape and domestic violence allegations.* CPS.

Crown Prosecution Service. (2020). *Crown Prosecution Service invites the public to comment on revised pre-trial therapy guidance.* https://www.cps.gov.uk/cps/news/crown-prosecution-service-invites-public-comment-revised-pre-trial-therapy-guidance. Accessed 16 May 2021.

Daily Mail. (2019). *Ava Max's Sweet But Psycho music video draws backlash from mental health advocates.* https://www.dailymail.co.uk/tvshowbiz/article-6618161/Ava-Maxs-Sweet-Psycho-music-video-draws-backlash-mental-health-advocates.html. Accessed 21 June 2020.

Daly, E. (2021). Making new meanings: The entextualisation of digital communications evidence in English sexual offences trials. *Crime, Media, Culture* [online first]. https://doi.org/10.1177/17416590211048251

Davies, G. (2019). Men falsely accused of rape are victims too, says wrongly-charged student as he backs disclosure move. *Telegraph.* https://www.telegraph.co.uk/news/2019/04/29/men-falsely-accused-rape-victims-says-wrongly-charged-student/. Accessed 14 August 2020.

Degler, C. N. (1974). What ought to be and what was: Women's sexuality in the nineteenth century. *The American Historical Review, 79*(5), 1467.

Edwards, K., Turchik, J., Dardis, C., Reynolds, N., & Gidycz, C. (2011). Rape myths: History, individual and institutional-level presence, and implications for change. *Sex Roles, 65*(11), 761–773.

Einon, D., & Potegal, M. (1994). Temper Tantrums in young children. In M. Potegal & J. F. Knutson (Eds.), *The dynamics of aggression* (pp. 175–212). Psychology Press.

Ellison, L. (2009). The use and abuse of psychiatric evidence in rape trials. *The International Journal of Evidence & Proof, 13*(1), 28–49.

Ellison, L., & Munro, V. (2016). Taking trauma seriously: Critical reflections on the criminal justice process. *International Journal of Evidence and Proof, 21*(3), 183–208.

Epting, L. K., & Burchett, J. (2019). Buzzwords: Identifying the language of gender and mental health status. *North American Journal of Psychology, 21*(3), 661–674.

Evans, M. (2018). Rape evidence flaws may have put hundreds of innocents in jail. *Telegraph.* https://www.telegraph.co.uk/news/2018/06/05/hundreds-miscarriages-justice-feared-cps-apologises-disclosure/. Accessed 19 October 2020.

Evans-Lacko, S., Henderson, C., & Thornicroft, G. (2013). Public knowledge, attitudes and behaviour regarding people with mental illness in England 2009–2012. *The British Journal of Psychiatry, 55*(Supplement 55), s51–s57.

Fouzder, M. (2019). *We will not be silenced: Liam Allan joined by protesters outside RCJ*. https://www.lawgazette.co.uk/news/we-will-not-be-silenced-liam-allan-joined-by-protesters-outside-rcj/5070731.article. Accessed 19 October 2020.

Gavey, N. (2005). *Just sex?* Psychology Press.

Gilmore, L. (2017). *Tainted witness: Why we doubt what women say about their lives*. Columbia University Press.

Gowing, L. (1996). Women, status and the popular culture of dishonour. *Transactions of the Royal Historical Society, 6*, 225–234.

Gunby, C., Carline, A., & Beynon, C. (2012). Regretting it after? Focus group perspectives on alcohol consumption, nonconsensual sex and false allegations of rape. *Social & Legal Studies, 22*(1), 87–106.

Hamby, S. L., & Koss, M. P. (2003). Shades of gray: A qualitative study of terms used in the measurement of sexual victimization. *Psychology of Women Quarterly, 27*(3), 243–255.

Hester, M. (2013). *From Report to Court: Rape cases and the criminal justice system in the Northeast*. University of Bristol in association with the Northern Rock Foundation.

HM Government. (2018). *Victims strategy*. Stationery Office.

Horn, M. (1993). Inventing the problem child: "At risk" children in the child guidance. In R. Wollons (Ed.), *Children at risk in America: History, concepts, and public policy* (pp. 141–153). State University of New York Press.

Jordan, J. (2004). *The word of a woman?* Palgrave.

Judicial College. (2020b). *Equal Treatment Bench Book*. https://www.judiciary.uk/wp-content/uploads/2020/05/ETBB-February-2018-amended-March-2020-17.09.20-1.pdf. Accessed 15 September 2021.

Kelly, L. (1987). The continuum of sexual violence. In J. Hanmer & M. Maynard (Eds.), *Women, violence and social control* (pp. 46–60). Macmillan.

Kelly, L. (2010). The (in)credible words of women: False allegations in European rape research. *Violence against Women, 16*(12), 1345–1355.

Kelly, L., Temkin, J., & Griffiths, S. (2006). *Section 41: An evaluation of new legislation limiting sexual history evidence in rape trials*. Home Office.

Larcombe, W. (2005). *Compelling engagements*. Federation Press.

Lees, S. (2002). *Carnal knowledge: Rape on trial* (2nd ed.). Women's Press.

Leverick, F. (2020). What do we know about rape myths and juror decision making? *International Journal of Evidence & Proof, 24*(3), 255–279.

Lewis, T. E., Klettke, B., & Day, A. (2014). The influence of medical and behavioral evidence on conviction rates in cases of child sexual abuse. *Journal of Child Sexual Abuse, 23*(4), 431–441.

Lynch, K., Golding, J., Jewell, J., Lippert, A., & Wasarhaley, N. (2019). "She is his girlfriend—I believe this is a different situation": Gender differences in perceptions of the legality of intimate partner rape. *Journal of Family Violence,* *34*(3), 213–230.

MacLin, M. K., Downs, C., MacLin, O. H., & Caspers, H. M. (2009). The effect of defendant facial expression on mock juror decision-making: The power of remorse. *North American Journal of Psychology, 11*(2), 323.

Mangrum, R. C. (2015). I believe, the Golden Rule, send a message, and other improper closing arguments. *Creighton Law Review, 48*(3), 521.

Manne, K. (2020). *Entitled how male privilege hurts women.* Allen Lane.

McCormick, K. T., MacArthur, H. J., Shields, S. A., & Dicicco, E. C. (2016). New perspectives on gender and emotion. In T. A. Roberts, N. Curtin, L. E. Duncan, & L. M. Cortina (Eds.), *Feminist perspectives on building a better psychological science of gender* (pp. 213–230). Springer.

McKenzie-Mohr, S., & Lafrance, M. N. (2011). Telling stories without the words: 'Tightrope talk' in women's accounts of coming to live well after rape or depression. *Feminism & Psychology, 21*(1), 49.

McKinney, C. J. (2019). *Durham Uni law academic sparks furious Twitter debate after claiming high-profile rape allegation wasn't necessarily 'false'.* https://www.legalcheek.com/2019/04/durham-uni-law-academic-sparks-furious-twitter-debate-after-claiming-high-profile-rape-allegation-wasnt-necessarily-false/. Accessed 19 October 2020.

Meaney, C. (2018). *Sweet but Problematic | Is Ava Max stigmatising mental illness?* https://www.headstuff.org/topical/opinion/ava-max-sweet-psycho/. Accessed 21 June 2020.

Mehta, N., Kassam, A., Leese, M., Butler, G., & Thornicroft, G. (2009). Public attitudes towards people with mental illness in England and Scotland, 1994–2003. *The British Journal of Psychiatry, 194*(3), 278–284.

Ministry of Justice. (2011). *Achieving Best Evidence in Criminal Proceedings.* https://www.cps.gov.uk/sites/default/files/documents/legal_guidance/best_evidence_in_criminal_proceedings.pdf. Accessed 16 July 2020.

O'Neal, E. N., Tellis, K., & Spohn, C. (2015). Prosecuting intimate partner sexual assault: Legal and extra-legal factors that influence charging decisions. *Violence Against Women, 21*(10), 1237–1258.

Osborne, S. (2018, January 30). Liam Allan: Met Police apologise to 22-year-old man falsely accused of rape after failing to disclose crucial text messages. *The Independent.* https://www.independent.co.uk/news/uk/crime/liam-allan-met-police-rape-accusation-false-evidence-disclosure-arrest-mistake-detectives-a8184916.html. Accessed 19 October 2020.

Penfold, P. S. (1995). Mendacious moms or devious dads? Some perplexing issues in child custody/sexual abuse allegation disputes. *The Canadian Journal of Psychiatry, 40*(6), 337–341.

Powell, A. J., Hlavka, H. R., & Mulla, S. (2017). Intersectionality and credibility in child sexual assault trials. *Gender & Society, 31*(4), 457–480.

Robinson, D. T., Smith-Lovin, L., & Tsoudis, O. (1994). Heinous crime or unfortunate accident? The effects of remorse on responses to mock criminal confessions. *Social Forces, 73*(1), 175–190.

Robinson, P. M. (1984). The historical repression of women's sexuality. In C. S. Vance (Ed.), *Pleasure and danger: Exploring female sexuality* (pp. 251–266). Routledge.

Rossetti, P., Mayes, A., & Moroz, A. (2017). *Victim of the system: The experiences, interests and rights of victims of crime in the criminal justice process.* Victim Support.

Rosulek, L. F. (2015). *Dueling discourses: The construction of reality in closing arguments.* Oxford University Press.

Rumney, P. (2006). False allegations of rape. *Cambridge Law Journal, 65*(1), 128–158.

Rumsey, M. C. (1976). Effects of defendant background and remorse on sentencing judgments. *Journal of Applied Social Psychology, 6*(1), 64–68.

Sanday, P. R. (1997). The socio-cultural context of rape: A cross-cultural study. In L. L. O'Toole & J. R. Schiffman (Eds.), *Gender violence: Interdisciplinary perspectives* (pp. 52–66). New York University Press.

Savitsky, J. C., & Sim, M. E. (1974). Trading emotions equity theory of reward and punishment. *Journal of Communication, 24*(3), 140–147.

Seidman, S. (1991). *Romantic longings: Love in America, 1830–1980.* Routledge.

Shields, S. A. (2013). Gender and emotion: What we think we know, what we need to know, and why it matters. *Psychology of Women Quarterly, 37*(4), 423–435.

Shorter, E. (1991). *Women's bodies.* Transaction Publishing.

Smart, C. (1989). *Feminism and the power of law.* Routledge.

Smith, O. (2018). *Rape trials in England and Wales: Observing justice and rethinking rape myths.* Palgrave Macmillan.

Smith, O., & Daly, E. (2020). *Evaluation of the sexual violence complainants' advocate scheme.* Loughborough University.

Smith, O., & Skinner, T. (2017). How rape myths are used and challenged in rape and sexual assault trials. *Social & Legal Studies, 26*(4), 441–466.

Somer, E., & Szwarcberg, S. (2001). Variables in delayed disclosure of childhood sexual abuse. *American Journal of Orthopsychiatry, 71*(3), 332–341.

Stabile, B., Grant, A., Purohit, H., & Rama, M. (2019). "She Lied": Social construction, rape myth prevalence in social media, and sexual assault policy. *Sexuality, Gender & Policy, 2*(2), 80–96.

Stanko, B., & Williams, E. (2009). Reviewing rape and rape allegations in London: What are the vulnerabilities of the victims who report to the police? In M. Horvath & J. Brown (Eds.), *Rape: Challenging contemporary thinking* (pp. 207–225). Willan.

Stevenson, K. (2000). Unequivocal victims: The historical roots of the mystification of the female complainant in rape cases. *Feminist Legal Studies, 8*(3), 343–366.

Talwar, V., & Crossman, A. M. (2012). Children's lies and their detection: Implications for child witness testimony. *Developmental Review, 32*(4), 337–359.

Temkin, J. (2000). Prosecuting and defending rape: Perspectives from the bar. *Journal of Law and Society, 27*(2), 219–248.

Temkin, J. (2002). Digging the dirt: Disclosure of records in sexual assault cases. *Cambridge Law Journal, 61*(1), 126.

Temkin, J., Gray, J. M., & Barrett, J. (2018). Different functions of rape myth use in court: Findings from a trial observation study. *Feminist Criminology, 13*(2), 205–226.

Temkin, J., & Krahé, B. (2008). *Sexual assault and the justice gap*. Hart.

Thompson, S. B. N., Merrifield, A. S., & Chinnery, H. (2011). Are Mock Jurors influenced by the defendants gender, socio-economic status and emotional state in forensic medicine? *Forensic Medicine, 2*(2), WMC001632.

Topping, A., & Barr, C. (2018). Revealed: Less than a third of young men prosecuted for rape are convicted. *Guardian.* https://www.theguardian.com/society/2018/sep/23/revealed-less-than-a-third-of-young-men-prosecuted-for-are-convicted. Accessed 3 April 2020.

Trocmé, N., & Bala, N. (2005). False allegations of abuse and neglect when parents separate. *Child Abuse & Neglect, 29*(12), 1333–1345.

Ussher, J. M. (2011). *The madness of women*. Routledge.

Ussher, J. M. (2013). Diagnosing difficult women and pathologising femininity: Gender bias in psychiatric nosology. *Feminism & Psychology, 23*(1), 63–69.

Webb, L. (2015). Shame transfigured: Slut-Shaming from Rome to Cyberspace. *First Monday, 20*(4), 41.

Weiser, D. A. (2017). Confronting myths about sexual assault: A feminist analysis of the false report literature. *Family Relations, 66*(1), 46–60.

Wessel, E. M., Bollingmo, G. C., Sonsteby, C., Nielsen, L. M., Eilertsen, D. E., & Magnussen, S. (2012). The emotional witness effect: Story content, emotional valence and credibility of a male suspect. *Psychology Crime & Law, 18*(5), 417–430.

Wilkinson-Ryan, T. (2005). Admitting mental health evidence to impeach the credibility of a sexual assault complainant. *University of Pennsylvania Law Review, 153*(4), 1373–1397.

Wingfield, A. H. (2010). Are some emotions marked 'whites only'? Racialized feeling rules in professional workplaces. *Social Problems, 57*(2), 251–268.

Zaccour, S. (2018). Crazy women and hysterical mothers: The gendered use of medical-health labels in custody disputes. *Canadian Journal of Family Law, 31*(1), 57.

CHAPTER 5

What Needs to Change?

Abstract This chapter first summarises the main argument of the book and then explores the implications for some key areas of criminal justice policy and practice as well as key areas for future research.

Keywords Rape myths · Cultural narratives · Court · Rape trials · Rape justice

This book has set out that rape myths continue to be mutably deployed by barristers in sexual offences trials and that broader cultural narratives are also drawn upon as a tool for bolstering the arguments and characterisations they put forth. The re/production of rape myths through oppressive cultural narratives exemplifies how Gavey's (2005) concept of cultural scaffolding operates in the courtroom. Whilst rape myths and cultural narratives were sometimes explicitly drawn upon, they were more often seeded through micro-examinations, demonstrating that it is not about questions or arguments in isolation. Rather, it is about the pattern of questions and the overall pictures these help to build, which culminate in character assassination in closing arguments. Crucially, this means that inaccurate assumptions about, or characterisations of, a witness's background or identity, such as their social class, go unchallenged. The credibility of victim-survivors and other witnesses is therefore undermined

© The Author(s), under exclusive license to Springer Nature   147
Switzerland AG 2022
E. Daly, *Rape, Gender and Class*,
https://doi.org/10.1007/978-3-030-93925-0_5

in relation to how they are perceived and portrayed regardless of any incongruence with who they are in reality.

It is well established within the rape myth literature that the function of rape myths is to blame women, undermine their stories, and excuse or minimise perpetrators (Eyssel & Bohner, 2008). This was clear in my observations, most especially in the interaction of rape myths with broader cultural narratives. The scrutiny of women's behaviour in the observed trials, including the sexual behaviour of both victim-survivors and their mothers, was clearly linked to the historic and continued tendency of our patriarchal society to police women's behaviour in ways in which men's behaviour is not. As such, rape myths were reinforced by portrayals of victim-survivors as irrational, unstable, and untrustworthy, and these portrayals were further transformed through classed, ageist, and ableist narratives. This suggests there are limitations to focusing research and policy and practice reforms on 'rape myths' alone and that it is therefore crucial to consider more nuanced understandings and approaches that take into account broader social contexts. The remainder of this chapter therefore explores the wider policy, practice, and research implications of this court observation study.

Ineffective Policy and Practice

The incredibly low prosecution and conviction rates for rape make clear that current CJS responses are inadequate for providing justice to the victim-survivors who choose to report sexual violence to the police (and those who want to report but choose not to because they do not have trust or confidence in the system). As has been pointed out elsewhere (Jordan, 2011; Walker et al., 2021), the standard Government response to public criticism of CJS responses to sexual violence seems to be to conduct a review. This gives the illusion of being seen to be taking action, when in fact decades of reviews, recommendations, and reforms have changed very little in practice (Jordan, 2011; Walker et al., 2021).

Most recently, Her Majesty's Inspectorate of Constabulary and Fire and Rescue Services (HMICFRS) 2021 inspection into how effectively police respond to violence against women and girls found failings and inconsistencies across all levels of policing and ultimately called for a fundamental overhaul of responses across the whole justice system (HMICFRS, 2021). It remains to be seen whether any real action will be taken or, crucially, whether any proposed actions are backed-up with appropriate funding and resources. Similarly, the Government's 2021 Rape Review (HM Government, 2021a) noted the need for urgent and sustained change and the importance of transparency and accountability, yet failed to tackle the systemic failings at the heart of the problems nor take up any radical suggestions for change (see EVAW, 2021b).

There are also significant omissions within both the HMICFRS report (2021) and the Rape Review report (HM Government, 2021a) specifically in relation to minoritised and marginalised victim-survivors (EVAW, 2021a, 2021b), which is especially disappointing given that campaigners have repeatedly signalled the importance of intersectional analysis in responding to violence against women (e.g. EVAW, 2020; Thiara & Roy, 2020). The Rape Review's accompanying Equality Statement (HM Government, 2021b), for instance, acknowledges that victim-survivors from minoritised and marginalised groups often have low confidence in the criminal justice process and that there is not enough specialist support available to victim-survivors within these groups. The statement talks of 'seeking' to record disaggregated data and states that they will undertake

> targeted research with rape victims to better understand their experiences, what they want from support services and how those services can best meet the needs of those disproportionately impacted by rape. (HM Government, 2021b, p. 5)

Whilst such research is without a doubt of critical importance, it talks only of support services and thus fails to commit to exploring systemic issues within criminal justice institutions that undoubtedly impact on decision-making throughout the justice process. As long as criminal justice institutions and policymakers fail to acknowledge *and* address the differing needs of victim-survivors from minoritised and marginalised groups and the differing ways they are impacted throughout the CJS, they will continue to fail to provide fair and adequate access to justice.

Changes to Prosecution Guidance

Following a public consultation, the CPS made changes to their rape and serious sexual offences (RASSO) guidance in 2021 in an attempt to improve their practice (the guidance can be found at CPS, 2021c). These changes included the introduction of a rape myth toolkit for prosecutors, with fresh guidance on digital evidence and online dating, as well as recognising the impact trauma can have on victim-survivors' memory and behaviour and the way they narrate their experiences. Importantly, the guidance states that:

> A person's experience of rape is unique and might be impacted by how it intersects with inequalities they may face in relation to aspects such as sex, age, disability, gender identity, race, ethnicity, religion or belief and class. (CPS, 2021c, Chapter 4, unpaginated)

This is an encouraging statement that is addressed in some detail throughout the guidance (see Chapter 5 and Annex A of the guidance). Whilst this acknowledgement of the complexities of victim-survivors' experiences of rape and its impacts is a step in the right direction, there needs to be accompanying transparency and accountability. Better recording and publishing of data disaggregated in accordance with that statement is crucial in achieving this. Without such data, it is difficult to understand the effectiveness of the guidance with regard to minoritised and marginalised victim-survivors. Indeed, accountability is distinctly lacking within the updated guidance as a whole, yet it is crucial for meaningful and long-lasting change. This is important because it cannot be assumed that a change in policy will automatically translate to a change in practice.

Indeed, this has been observed previously in relation to CJS policy and practice around requesting access to victim-survivors' digital data. Court of Appeal judges ruled in 2018 and 2019 that digital devices are not of automatic relevance to sexual offences investigations (*R v E* [2018] EWCA Crim 2426; *R v McPartland and another* [2019] EWCA Crim 1782), yet the routine download of victim-survivors' mobile phones continued to persist in investigations (see Smith & Daly, 2020). A later Court of Appeal ruling in *Bater-James & Mohammed v R* [2020] EWCA Crim 790 ruled that:

> It is not a 'reasonable' line of inquiry if the investigator pursues fanciful or inherently speculative researches...There is no presumption that a complainant's mobile telephone or other devices should be inspected, retained or downloaded (paras. 70, 78).

Accordingly, the CPS has reflected the *Bater-James* ruling in its updated guidance on digital materials, clearly stating that speculative searches are not permitted. In theory, this should mean that digital data is only accessed according to very limited parameters that are justifiable on the basis of the specific case, which in some cases may be not at all. This is crucial because what might on the surface seem to be an innocuous comment contained within a digital conversation can be made damaging for victim-survivors through the narration of that conversation at trial. This was the case for the victim-survivor in T1 whose diagnosis of depression was adduced through digital communications evidence and used to bolster the defendant's characterisation of her as 'crazy' (see Chapter 4). Relatedly, the CPS (2021b) has also said that it recognises the changing nature of contemporary dating and relationships and the ever-growing role of digital platforms within them. Prosecutors are therefore now able to access information on dating platforms, how they are used, and common terminology used. Whilst this seems positive, it does not appear in the formal RASSO guidance, which raises questions as to how much scrutiny will in reality be given to case decisions relating to online dating. This again speaks to a lack of accountability.

Another important change to the CPS RASSO guidance is a shift towards an offender-centric approach (see Chapter 3 of the guidance), as opposed to giving undue focus on whether or not the victim-survivor makes a 'credible' witness. The Rape Review also recommended a shift to an offender-centric approach (HM Government, 2021a), and it is currently being piloted in the South West of England (CPS, 2021a). Whilst on the surface this shift seems positive, there is not yet enough known about its usefulness and effectiveness in sexual offences investigations and so it certainly should not be seen as a panacea for the inadequacies of CJS responses to sexual violence. Rumney and McPhee (2021) conducted an analysis of police investigation case files for 11 sexual offences cases that included elements of the offender-centric approach, finding that there are indeed great benefits to the approach but that there are also significant challenges that must be understood and taken into account. For instance, they found that the offender-centric approach can be particularly useful in cases involving suspects whose sense of entitlement led to them failing to take any steps to ascertain consent. It can also identify patterns of predatory or problematic behaviour (Rumney & McPhee, 2021; see also Angiolini, 2015). A significant challenge noted by Rumney and McPhee was the potential for the offender-centric approach to become self-confirming if investigators and prosecutors do not keep an open mind. It was therefore suggested that proper analytical techniques should be employed in order to mitigate potential for such biases, just as they should be conversely employed to mitigate the influence of rape myths and other problematic cultural narratives regarding victim-survivors (Rumney & McPhee, 2021). Proper evaluation of the CPS pilot scheme is therefore of crucial importance in order to examine the effectiveness of the implementation of an offender-centric approach and the extent to which such an approach may achieve a fairer balance in the long term. Such an evaluation should include an examination of what impacts, if any, an offender-centric investigation approach has on what happens inside the courtroom. It may be that the approach limits opportunities for defence counsel to rely on rape myths and cultural narratives to reinforce ideas of what counts as 'reasonable belief' in consent, and this is best established through court observation research. It may also be that an offender-centric approach increases guilty pleas (see Rumney & McPhee, 2021) and thus saves victim-survivors from the added trauma of a trial, and this is again something that should be explored in an evaluation of the pilot scheme.

The Use of Sexual History Evidence

Section 41 of the *Youth Justice and Criminal Evidence Act 1999* prohibits the use of victim-survivors' sexual history evidence except in exceptional circumstances. The findings set out in Chapter 2 have several implications in relation to this because despite clear instances of good practice, my observations support a growing body of evidence that shows that s.41 is not working effectively. My observations notably came after procedural changes introduced by *Criminal Practice Directions 2015 (Amendment No. 6)* [2018] EWCA Crim 516 which came into force in April 2018 with the aim to ensure compliance regarding sexual history evidence restrictions and that rules are applied consistently and not circumvented (Brewis, 2018). This means my observations reflect practice governed by the latest procedural rules.

There have long been calls to tighten the remit of s.41 (McGlynn, 2017, 2018; Smith, 2018; see also Burman, 2009; Cowan, 2020 for similar calls in Scotland). My observations demonstrate that despite the tightening of procedures in 2018, victim-survivors were still questioned about irrelevant aspects of their sexual history, suggesting that a renewed look at reforming s.41 is therefore justified. Sexual history evidence is subject to stricter restrictions in some other adversarial jurisdictions, including Canada, New South Wales (Australia), and Michigan (United States), which demonstrates that there is room for workable reform in England and Wales (McGlynn, 2018). The view from the legal profession, however, seems to be that the legislation itself is adequate and does not need to be made stricter (Gillen, 2019; Hoyano, 2019). Smith (2018) suggested introducing a requirement for the prosecution to make applications to adduce sexual history evidence as well as the defence. This would aim to encourage more careful consideration of the contents of prosecution evidence, for example the collection of digital data and the editing of ABEs, to remove erroneous references to sexual history that inevitably arise from proper police investigation (Smith, 2018).

Scotland introduced this approach in 2002; however, an evaluation study highlighted a number of lessons that can be learnt from this change. For example, the evaluation found that the measure actually increased the number of applications and that they cannot be attributed solely to a change in procedure (Burman et al., 2007). Burman (2009) detailed a 'scatter gun' approach being taken to applications in Scotland, whereby defence counsel included applications on multiple aspects of sexual history and expanded greatly on them during questioning. Again, lessons can be learnt from this regarding the scrutiny given to s.41 applications and the adherence to them at trial.

Finally, the findings outlined in Chapter 2 demonstrated that it was not only victim-survivors' sexual behaviour that was scrutinised, but also, in some cases, that of their mothers. Whilst the sexual history of victim-survivors may be relevant in some circumstances, the sexual history of their mothers is rarely likely to be relevant and only serves to attack their character and credibility, and by extension that of the victim-survivor. Further research is needed to determine whether this is a widespread problem and if so, discussions should be had about extending the prohibition of sexual history evidence to all witnesses. Victim-survivors should not be able to be undermined based on character assassination of their parents.

'Myth-Busting' Judicial Directions

My observations, alongside previous observation studies (Lees, 2002; Smith, 2018; Temkin et al., 2018), make clear that rape myths persistently permeate sexual offences trials despite a variety of measures put in place. Judicial directions are one such measure that were put in place in an attempt to mitigate the impact of rape myths on jury deliberations (see Chapter 20 of the Crown Court Compendium; Judicial College, 2020a). Whilst the introduction of 'myth-busting' directions marked a positive step forward, it is clear that they are not enough to tackle the problem. For example, research has consistently shown that juries frequently misunderstand or fail to apply judicial directions (Chalmers & Leverick, 2018; Darbyshire et al., 2002; Ellison & Munro, 2009).

Furthermore, reflecting findings from previous court observations from 2012 (Smith, 2018), my observations saw that it remains easy for defence barristers to subvert these directions through, for example, acknowledging that a rape myth exists but then going on to explain why the case in question is an exception to it. This can be particularly effective where judges have delivered a split summing-up, whereby the judicial directions are delivered *before* the closing speeches and the summing-up of the evidence given afterwards. This means that the specific 'myth-busting' directions given by the judge can be addressed by the defence in their closing arguments and this would be the final thing the jurors heard about it. Whilst judges are free to repeat myth-busting directions at any point in the trial, in my observations, where split summing-up was given the 'myth-busting' directions were not repeated after the closing speeches. Furthermore, as my observations have shown, rape myths are often deployed with subtlety and reinforced through further subtle reference to embedded cultural narratives that reflect structural inequalities and systems of oppression. This interaction of rape myths with broader cultural narratives suggests that myth-busting measures may be unlikely to have the desired effect without taking account of broader structural inequalities and systems of oppression because rape myths become disguised and distorted in trial narratives, and thus unrecognisable when cast against the plainly worded myths in judicial directions. For instance, variations of the following standard direction were given in every trial I observed:

> From experience we know that there is no typical rape, typical rapist or typical person that is raped. Rape can take place in almost any circumstance. It can happen between all different kinds of people. And people who are raped react in a variety of different ways. So you must put aside any assumptions you have about rape. All of you on this jury must make your judgement based only on the evidence you hear from the witnesses and the law as I explain that to you. (Judicial College, 2020a, 20–25)

Such a direction does not address, for example, underlying cultural narratives that cast young working-class women as sexually provocative. Whilst judges are encouraged to adapt the example directions to fit the case in which they are being used, no guidance is given as to how they might be adapted. It could, for example, be noted within the guidance that for some cases it may be necessary to address problematic cultural narratives that assume sexual violence is considered permissible in some minoritised communities (see Thiara & Roy, 2020). Whilst a list of potential circumstances in which directions could be adapted could never be exhaustive, noting specifically that the perceived race, ethnicity, age, (dis)ability, or social class of those involved in the trial, and the way they have been portrayed during the trial, may warrant adaptations of directions would be a useful starting point. Notably, in *Andreous* [2014] EWCA Crim 1578 the Court of Appeal endorsed directions that address the culture, age, class, and occupation of a defendant. It seems, therefore, that including similar guidance within the Compendium (Judicial College, 2020a) should not be problematic.

Judicial directions alone, however, cannot solve the problem. There must be more accountability for juries because research has repeatedly and consistently found that rape myths do impact on jury deliberations (Leverick, 2020) even when judicial directions have been given (Ellison & Munro, 2009). Whilst Thomas (2020) claims that her research proves that jurors do not believe rape myths and therefore undermines the mock jury research that says otherwise, there are significant problems with this claim which are addressed in Daly et al. (2021). Thus, the ongoing problem with juries remains. Looking to other jurisdictions illuminates alternative ways of doing things that could provide a useful basis for discussion of reform. For example, in Spain and Russia, juries are required to provide judges with a written justification for their verdicts (Martín & Kaplan, 2013). Though this system is not unproblematic, it may offer insights as to how better to ensure that fair verdicts based on facts and correct application of the law are returned. This is particularly pertinent when considered in conjunction with the continued pervasiveness and reliance upon rape myths and pejorative cultural narratives.

Consideration should also be given as to how to reduce the prevalence of rape myths and oppressive cultural narratives at trial in the first place, rather than attempts to mediate their impact. Whilst elements of rape myths do in some circumstances have legitimate relevance, they very often have no relevance and are used simply as a means of impugning the character of victim-survivors. Barristers who draw on rape myths to bolster their cases should be required to justify why and how their argument is relevant. This could help to ensure fairness for victim-survivors and the upholding of public interests whilst still protecting the defendant's right to a fair trial.

Improving Access to Justice: Independent Legal Representation

There have been growing calls for the introduction of independent legal representation for victim-survivors in England and Wales (Smith, 2018). Whilst it is commonly argued that this is incompatible with an adversarial legal system, the majority of justice systems with adversarial elements do have models of representation for victim-survivors (Daly & Smith, 2020). These models vary and rarely reach levels comparable with representation and participation available in the majority of European jurisdictions, which are based largely on inquisitorial principles rather than adversarial principles. Nevertheless, adversarial systems are moving towards providing some sort of representation for victim-survivors, particularly in our closest jurisdictions. For example, in the Republic of Ireland, victim-survivors are entitled to legal representation regarding applications to introduce sexual history evidence and counselling records, although there are a number of problems in the structure and delivery of this model (Iliadis, 2019). A rape review in the Republic of Ireland recently recommended a move to a more extensive model (O'Malley, 2020) and the Gillen Review in Northern Ireland (Gillen, 2019) recommended the introduction of independent legal representation and this was due to be piloted in 2021 (Daly & Smith, 2020).

In Scotland, there have long been calls for the introduction of legal representation (Raitt, 2010), most recently with a fresh report recommending the introduction of legal representation for victim-survivors in relation to sexual history and bad character evidence (Keane & Convery, 2020). Furthermore, a pilot scheme of independent legal representation for rape victim-survivors was evaluated in Northumbria, England (Smith & Daly, 2020) and found that it increased victim-survivors' confidence in the CJS, gave better protection of their rights, and resulted in improved practice within the police and the CPS in relation to the collection of victim-survivors' private data. Following this pilot, the Labour Party backed calls for independent legal representation with their

Survivors' Support Plan (Reeves, 2021). It is clear then that legal representation for victim-survivors is seen as a necessary and important element in achieving fair justice in the majority of jurisdictions, and that there is renewed appetite in England and Wales.

Whilst the introduction of independent legal representation for victim-survivors of sexual offences may seem like a radical departure from adversarial principles, the above discussion demonstrates that this is not necessarily the case. Indeed, Iliadis et al. (2021) explored this issue in depth, robustly addressing critiques and offering an alternative model that goes beyond those that exist or are proposed in our neighbouring jurisdictions. Specifically, they argue that the inclusion of victim-survivor legal representatives can and should be extended beyond the pre-trial stage and that their parameters should go further to include *any* form of sensitive material, such as digital evidence, and in instances where permission to adduce 'bad character' evidence is sought. As my observations highlighted, digital communications evidence provided a key mechanism for rape myths and oppressive cultural narratives to be introduced and bolstered and, consistent with findings elsewhere (Smith & Daly, 2020), it appeared that not enough scrutiny had been given to the records adduced to the court. Under the model proposed by Iliadis et al. (2021), independent legal representation could have helped ensure that only relevant and proportionate data from those digital communications was adduced. This in turn would improve access to justice by removing or mitigating some of the all-too-common barriers victim-survivors face in the criminal justice process.

FUTURE RESEARCH DIRECTIONS

My observations have highlighted several areas for further research. Firstly, court observation research in general is crucial for uncovering what is happening in practice and ensuring a level of public accountability. As noted in the previous section, court observation research will be especially important in assessing impacts of changes in criminal justice policy and practice. Further court observation research is also needed to explore other crucial intersections, including but not limited to race, ethnicity, nationality, sexual orientation, gender from an adult male victim-survivor perspective, as well further exploration of class, age, and ableism. Such studies, including the present study, must be triangulated with research directly with victim-survivors as well as criminal justice professionals. Whilst the existing literature does address this, it is important that research also specifically addresses oppressive cultural narratives in the courtroom, rather than solely rape myths.

Damaging stereotypes and cultural narratives abound across our society, especially for minoritised and marginalised groups. Black women, for example, are routinely positioned hypersexualised, 'promiscuous', and sexually manipulative (Collins, 2000). This image can be used to give the illusion of consent by presenting Black women as always sexually available and thus 'unrapeable' and to imply victim-survivors' perceived hypersexuality provoked sexual violence (West, 2004). Similarly, in Western cultures South Asian women are often perceived as "passive victims of their cultures, communities and menfolk" (Thiara & Gill, 2010, p. 40). This can lead to problematic narratives excusing sexual violence through misguided assumptions of cultural or religious acceptance; indeed, this was observed in the courtroom by Smith (2018). Such narratives may also be formed around victim-survivors of Irish heritage and those from Gypsy, Roma, and Traveller communities (Jensen & Ringrose, 2014; Tosh, 2015).

The rape myths that presented in my observations related to female victim-survivors, which leaves the interaction between male rape myths (see Javaid, 2015) and cultural narratives unexplored in court observations. For example, gay male victim-survivors are often attributed more blame than heterosexual male victim-survivors (Rumney, 2009) and historically tracing cultural narratives demonstrates that some forms of sexual violence are assumed to be less traumatic for men (Bourke, 2007; Rumney, 2009). Furthermore, cultural narratives of heteronormative masculinity that position men as having uncontrollable sexual urges and being sexually insatiable could have strong undermining power for some male victim-survivors (Weare, 2021).

The above examples are by no means exhaustive but do demonstrate the importance of developing nuanced understandings of courtroom narratives that go beyond rape myths.

My findings relating to cultural narratives around victim-survivors' mothers highlight the need for an exploration of the role of parent-witnesses in sexual offences trials as there does not appear to be any existing research that addresses this. Such an exploration could provide crucial insights with regard to child sex offences in particular because of the protections offered to child witnesses during cross-examination (Judicial College, 2020b). Future research should investigate whether parent-witnesses of child victim-survivors are routinely used as a proxy for the character assassination often faced by adult victim-survivors in the courtroom.

The observations also highlighted that digital communications evidence plays a key role in reinforcing rape myths and problematic cultural narratives. Research is therefore needed to further explore how digital communications evidence is used in practice in the courtroom, particularly with a focus on private and sensitive data such as sexual and medical histories. This is particularly important given the changes to CPS RASSO guidelines and the piloting of offender-centric policing outlined earlier in this chapter.

Finally, research with 'real' jurors would prove incredibly useful in exploring the impact of oppressive cultural narratives and rape myths in the ways they are deployed in practice by barristers, as opposed to through questions from a rape myth acceptance scale. This would enable an opportunity to build on the one study that has been allowed to undertake rape myth research with real jurors (Thomas, 2020). As well as this, mock jury research should be carried out with these specific aims in mind. Though mock jury research has its detractors, it is incredibly valuable, and methods have advanced to enable a very realistic substitute to real jurors (Willmott et al., 2021).

FINAL THOUGHTS

This book has demonstrated that rape myths remain pervasive in sexual offences trials and that there is a re/producing relationship between rape myths and broader oppressive cultural narratives that strengthens their narrative power in the courtroom. Historically tracing rape myths (e.g. Edwards et al., 2011) demonstrates how they are formed from centuries-old classed and gendered narratives that remain embedded in today's society. Notions of who was considered respectable and trustworthy dictated who could be seen as a victim of rape and who was seen as 'unrapeable', who was worthy of belief and who was not (Bourke, 2007; Clark, 1987; Jordan, 2004). This was unmistakably borne out in the trials I observed. Whilst these trials took place in England, throughout the book I have sought to point the reader to consider how similar cultural narratives, particularly at the intersection of gender and class, may impact on the portrayals of victim-survivors in other Westernised jurisdictions. The established gendered narratives expressed through rape myths are undoubtedly common across nations, but the articulations of intersecting narratives would of course vary to those illuminated in this book but would invariably play a role in the courtroom narratives constructed by lawyers in sexual violence trials, as has been demonstrated by Powell et al. (2017) in the specific context of Milwaukee in the US state of Wisconsin.

Reforms are a sticking plaster on a system that is not fit for purpose and much more thought is needed on what justice means to victim-survivors and how this can be accomplished in a meaningful way without processes that retraumatise and cause or reinforce further injustices. Radical change is needed, but of course such changes do not happen quickly. There are, however, changes that can be made for victim-survivors that choose to report in the current system, some of which have been outlined in this chapter. Policymakers and criminal justice institutions must commit to making real changes and follow that up with tangible plans and actions, and genuine transparency and accountability. What is clear is that the current system and its rules and procedures do not go far enough to protect victim-survivors' interests. The continued reliance on rape myths and broader cultural narratives with no probative value other than to impugn the character of victim-survivors (and their mothers) is shameful.

Understanding the subtlety and nuance presented in this book is a key part in understanding what is going wrong; that is, why so few victim-survivors get the justice they seek through the CJS and why it dispro-portionately affects victim-survivors from minoritised and marginalised groups. This is not a radical idea; it arguably states the obvious. Yet it is something that policymakers and criminal justice institutions have failed to grapple with time and time again.

References

Angiolini, E. (2015). *Report of the independent review into the investigation and prosecution of rape in London.*

Bourke, J. (2007). *Rape: A history from 1860 to the present day.* Virago Press.

Brewis, B. (2018). Procedural Amendments for Adducing Sexual Behaviour Evidence Under s. 41 of the Youth Justice and Criminal Evidence Act 1999. *The Journal of Criminal Law, 82*(5), 378–380.

Burman, M. (2009). Evidencing sexual assault: Women in the witness box. *Probation Journal, 56*(4), 379–398.

Burman, M., Jamieson, L., Nicholson, J., & Brooks, O. (2007). *Impact of aspects of the law of evidence in sexual offence trials: An evaluation study.* Scottish Government.

Chalmers, J., & Leverick, F. (2018). *Methods of conveying information to jurors: An evidence review*. Scottish Government.

Clark, A. (1987). *Women's silence, men's violence: Sexual assault in England, 1770-1845*. Pandora.

Collins, P. H. (2000). *Black feminist thought* (2nd ed.). Routledge.

Cowan, S. (2020). *The use of sexual history and bad character evidence in Scottish sexual offences trials*. Equality and Human Rights Commission.

Crown Prosecution Service. (2021a). *Police-CPS Joint National RASSO (Rape and Serious Sexual Offences) Action Plan 2021*. https://www.cps.gov.uk/publication/police-cps-joint-national-rasso-rape-and-serious-sexual-offences-action-plan-2021. Accessed 23 September 2021.

Crown Prosecution Service. (2021b). *Prosecutors given additional tools to tackle harmful myths about online dating*. https://www.cps.gov.uk/cps/news/prosecutors-given-additional-tools-tackle-harmful-myths-about-online-dating. Accessed 23 September 2021.

Crown Prosecution Service. (2021c). *Rape and sexual offences—Overview and index of 2021 updated guidance*. https://www.cps.gov.uk/legal-guidance/rape-and-sexual-offences-overview-and-index-2021-updated-guidance. Accessed 23 September 2021.

Daly, E., & Smith, O. (2020). *Scoping review: Legal & non-legal advocacy for rape complainants in adversarial jurisdictions*. Loughborough University.

Daly, E., Smith, O., Bows, H., Brown, J., Chalmers, J., Cowan, S., et al. (2021). Myths about myths? A commentary on Thomas (2020) and the question of jury rape myth acceptance. *Journal of Gender-Based Violence* [online first]. https://doi.org/10.1332/239868021X16371459419254

Darbyshire, P., Maughan, A., & Stewart, A. (2002). *What can the English legal system learn from jury research*. Kingston Law School.

Edwards, K., Turchik, J., Dardis, C., Reynolds, N., & Gidycz, C. (2011). Rape myths: History, individual and institutional-level presence, and implications for change. *Sex Roles, 65*(11), 761–773.

Ellison, L., & Munro, V. (2009). Turning mirrors into windows? *The British Journal of Criminology, 49*(3), 363–383.

End Violence Against Women Coalition. (2020). *Briefing for second reading of the Domestic Abuse Bill*. https://www.endviolenceagainstwomen.org.uk/wp-content/uploads/EVAW-2nd-Reading-DA-Bill-Briefing-April-20-5-1.pdf. Accessed 1 October 2021.

End Violence Against Women Coalition. (2021a). *EVAW welcomes call by police inspectorate for whole system change to tackle violence against women and girls*. https://www.endviolenceagainstwomen.org.uk/evaw-welcomes-call-by-police-inspectorate-for-whole-system-change-to-tackle-violence-against-women-and-girls/. Accessed 10 January 2021.

End Violence Against Women Coalition. (2021b). *Leading women's groups deeply disappointed with lack of ambition in government's rape review.* https://www.endviolenceagainstwomen.org.uk/leading-womens-groups-deeply-disappointed-with-lack-of-ambition-in-governments-rape-review-2/. Accessed 1 October 2021.

Eyssel, F., & Bohner, G. (2008). Modern rape myths: The Acceptance of Modern Myths about Sexual Aggression (AMMSA) Scale. In M. A. Morrison & T. G. Morrison (Eds.), *The psychology of modern prejudice* (pp. 261–276). Nova Science Publishers.

Gavey, N. (2005). *Just sex?* Psychology Press.

Gillen, J. (2019). *Gillen review: Report into the law and procedures in serious sexual offences in Northern Ireland.*

Her Majesty's Inspectorate of Constabulary and Fire and Rescue Services. (2021). *Police response to violence against women and girls: Final inspection report.* https://www.justiceinspectorates.gov.uk/hmicfrs/wp-content/uploads/police-response-to-violence-against-women-and-girls-final-inspection-report.pdf. Accessed 01 October 2021.

HM Government. (2021a). *The end-to-end rape review report on findings and actions.* https://assets.publishing.service.gov.uk/government/uploads/system/uploads/attachment_data/file/1001417/end-to-end-rape-review-report-with-correction-slip.pdf. Accessed 1 October 2021.

HM Government. (2021b). *The end-to-end review of rape: Equalities statement May 2021.* https://assets.publishing.service.gov.uk/government/uploads/system/uploads/attachment_data/file/994169/rape-review-equality-statement.pdf. Accessed 01 October 2021.

Hoyano, L. (2019). Cross-examination of sexual assault complainants on previous sexual behaviour: Views from the barristers' row. *Criminal Law Review, 2,* 75–111.

Iliadis, M. (2019). Victim representation for sexual history evidence in Ireland: A step towards or away from meeting victims' procedural justice needs? *Criminology & Criminal Justice, 20*(4), 416–432.

Iliadis, M., Smith, O., & Doak, J. (2021). Independent separate legal representation for rape complainants in adversarial systems: Lessons from Northern Ireland. *Journal of Law and Society, 48*(2), 250–272.

Javaid, A. (2015). Male rape myths: Understanding and explaining social attitudes surrounding male rape. *Masculinities & Social Change, 4*(3), 270.

Jensen, T., & Ringrose, J. (2014). Sluts that Choose Vs Doormat Gypsies: Exploring affect in the postfeminist, visual moral economy of *My Big Fat Gypsy Wedding. Feminist Media Studies, 14*(3), 369–387.

Jordan, J. (2004). *The word of a woman?* Palgrave.

Jordan, J. (2011). Here we go round the review-go-round: Rape investigation and prosecution—Are things getting worse not better? *Journal of Sexual Aggression, 17*(3), 234–249.

Judicial College. (2020a). *Crown Court Compendium Part I*. https://www.judiciary.uk/wp-content/uploads/2020/07/Crown-Court-Compendium-Part-I-December-2020.pdf. Accessed 15 September 2021.

Judicial College. (2020b). *Equal Treatment Bench Book*. https://www.judiciary.uk/wp-content/uploads/2020/05/ETBB-February-2018-amended-March-2020-17.09.20-1.pdf. Accessed 15 September 2021.

Keane, E. P. H., & Convery, T. (2020). *Proposal for independent legal representation for complainers where an application is made to lead evidence of their sexual history or character*. University of Edinburgh.

Lees, S. (2002). *Carnal knowledge: Rape on trial* (2nd ed.). Women's Press.

Leverick, F. (2020). What do we know about rape myths and juror decision making? *International Journal of Evidence & Proof, 24*(3), 255–279.

Martín, A. M., & Kaplan, M. F. (2013). *Understanding world jury systems through social psychological research*. Taylor and Francis.

McGlynn, C. (2017). Rape trials and sexual history evidence: Reforming the law on third-party evidence. *The Journal of Criminal Law, 81*(5), 367–392.

McGlynn, C. (2018). Challenging the law on sexual history evidence: A response to Dent and Paul. *Criminal Law Review, 3*, 216–228.

O'Malley, T. (2020). *Review of protections for vulnerable witnesses in the investigation and prosecution of sexual offences*. Department of Justice and Equality (Ireland).

Powell, A. J., Hlavka, H. R., & Mulla, S. (2017). Intersectionality and credibility in child sexual assault trials. *Gender & Society, 31*(4), 457–480.

Raitt, F. (2010). *Independent legal representation for complainers in sexual offence trials: Research report for Rape Crisis Scotland*. Rape Crisis Scotland. http://discovery.dundee.ac.uk/portal/en/research/independent-legal-representation-for-complainers-in-sexual-offence-trials-research-report-for-rape-crisis-scotland(e23075e9-f117-4dab-ac57-b0daa9e82c68).html. Accessed 15 September 2020.

Reeves, E. (2021). *Labour unveils Survivors' Support Plan for victims of rape*. https://labour.org.uk/press/labour-unveils-survivors-support-plan-for-victims-of-rape/. Accessed 23 September 2021.

Rumney, P. (2009). Gay male rape victims: Law enforcement, social attitudes and barriers to recognition. *The International Journal of Human Rights, 13*(2–3), 233–250.

Rumney, P., & McPhee, D. (2021). Offender-centric policing in cases of rape. *The Journal of Criminal Law, 1*–16.

Smith, O. (2018). *Rape trials in England and Wales: Observing justice and rethinking rape myths*. Palgrave Macmillan.

Smith, O., & Daly, E. (2020). *Evaluation of the sexual violence complainants' advocate scheme.* Loughborough University.

Temkin, J., Gray, J. M., & Barrett, J. (2018). Different functions of rape myth use in court: Findings from a trial observation study. *Feminist Criminology, 13*(2), 205–226.

Thiara, R., & Gill, A. K. (2010). Understanding violence against South Asian women. In R. Thiara & A. K. Gill (Eds.), *Violence against women in South Asian communities* (pp. 29–54). Jessica Kingsley Publishers.

Thiara, R., & Roy, S. (2020). *Reclaiming voice: Minoritised women and sexual violence.* Imkaan. https://829ef90d-0745-49b2-b404-cbea85f15fda.fil esusr.com/ugd/f98049_a0f11db6395a48fbbac0e40da899dcb8.pdf. Accessed 10 January 2021.

Thomas, C. (2020). The 21st century jury: Contempt, bias and the impact of jury service. *Criminal Law Review, 11,* 987–1011.

Tosh, J. (2015). "Rape Me, I'm Irish": An analysis of the intersecting discourses of anti-irish racism and sexual violence. *Intersectionalities: A Global Journal of Social Work Analysis, Research, Polity, and Practice, 4*(1), 59–81.

Walker, T., Foster, A., Majeed-Ariss, R., & Horvath, M. (2021). The justice system is failing victims and survivors of sexual violence. *The Psychologist, 34,* 42–45.

Weare, S. (2021). "I feel permanently traumatized by it": Physical and emotional impacts reported by men forced to penetrate women in the United Kingdom. *Journal of Interpersonal Violence, 36*(13–14), 6621–6646.

West, C. M. (2004). Mammy, Jezebel, and Sapphire: Developing an 'oppositional gaze' toward the images of Black women. In J. C. Chrisler, C. Golden, & P. D. Rozee (Eds.), *Lectures on the psychology of women* (3rd ed., pp. 237–252). McGraw-Hill.

Willmott, D., Boduszek, D., & Hudspith, L. (2021). Jury decision making in rape trials: An attitude problem? In G. Towl & D. Crighton (Eds.), *Forensic psychology* (3rd ed., pp. 94–119). Wiley.

References

Abrams, D., Viki, G. T., Masser, B., & Bohner, G. (2003). Perceptions of stranger and acquaintance rape. *Journal of Personality and Social Psychology, 84*(1), 111–125.

Adler, Z. (1987). *Rape on trial.* Routledge & Paul.

Aiken, M. M. (1993). False allegation: A concept in the context of rape. *Journal of Psychosocial Nursing and Mental Health Services, 31*(11), 15–20.

Ainsworth, J. (2015). Legal discourse and legal narratives: Adversarial versus inquisitorial models. *Language and Law, 2*(1), 1–11.

Akrami, N., Ekehammar, B., & Araya, T. (2000). Classical and modern racial prejudice: A study of attitudes toward immigrants in Sweden. *European Journal of Social Psychology, 30*(4), 521–532.

Allen, K., & Mendick, H. (2013). Keeping it real? Social class, young people and 'authenticity' in reality TV. *Sociology, 47*(3), 460–476.

Angiolini, E. (2015). Report of the Independent Review into the Investigation and Prosecution of Rape in London.

Anthias, F. (2014). The intersections of class, gender, sexuality and 'race': The political economy of gendered violence. *International Journal of Politics, Culture, and Society, 27*(2), 153–171.

Associated Press. (2016). California passes mandatory sentences for sexual assault after Stanford scandal. *The Guardian.* https://www.theguardian.com/us-news/2016/sep/30/stanford-sexual-assault-case-california-rape-law. Accessed 25 March 2019.

Astor, M. (2018). California voters remove Judge Aaron Persky, who gave a 6-month sentence for sexual assault. *New York Times.* https://search.proquest.com/docview/2050328542. Accessed 25 March 2019.

© The Editor(s) (if applicable) and The Author(s), under exclusive license to Springer Nature Switzerland AG 2022
E. Daly, *Rape, Gender and Class,*
https://doi.org/10.1007/978-3-030-93925-0

Atkinson, K., Oerton, S., & Burns, D. (1998). 'Happy families?': Single mothers, the press and the politicians. *Capital & Class, 22*(1), 1–11.

Bailey, L., Griffin, C., & Shankar, A. (2015). "Not a good look": Impossible dilemmas for young women negotiating the culture of intoxication in the United Kingdom. *Substance Use & Misuse, 50*(6), 747–758.

Baird, V., & Newlove, H. (2018). *Article by Dame Vera Baird and Baroness Newlove on why disclosure must put victims first!* http://www.northumbria-pcc.gov.uk/article-dame-vera-baird-baroness-newlove-disclosure-must-put-vic tims-first/. Accessed 15 October 2020.

Baldwin, J. (2008). Research on the criminal courts. In R. D. King & E. Wincup (Eds.), *Doing research on crime and justice* (2nd ed., pp. 375–398). Oxford University Press.

Bar Standards Board. (2020). *The BSB Handbook.* https://www.barstandards board.org.uk/the-bsb-handbook.html. Accessed 5 January 2021.

Barker, A. B., Britton, J., Thomson, E., Hunter, A., Breton, M. O., & Murray, R. L. (2019). A content analysis of tobacco and alcohol audio-visual content in a sample of UK reality TV programmes. *Journal of Public Health, 42*(3), 561–569.

Barry, K. (1979). *Female sexual slavery.* Prentice-Hall.

Benedet, J. (2010). The age of innocence: A cautious defense of raising the age of consent in Canadian sexual assault law. *New Criminal Law Review: An International and Interdisciplinary Journal, 13*(4), 665–687.

Blackman, L., & Walkerdine, V. (2001). *Mass Hysteria.* Macmillan Education UK.

Blume, S. B. (1991). Sexuality and stigma: The alcoholic woman. *Alcohol Health and Research World, 15*(2), 139.

Bohner, G., Eyssel, F., Pina, A., Siebler, F., & Viki, G. T. (2009). Rape myth acceptance: Cognitive, affective and behavioural effects of beliefs that blame the victim and exonerate the perpetrator. In M. Horvath & J. Brown (Eds.), *Rape: Challenging contemporary thinking* (pp. 17–45). Willan.

Bourke, J. (2007). *Rape: A history from 1860 to the present day.* Virago Press.

Boux, H. J., & Daum, C. W. (2015). At the intersection of social media and rape culture. *University of Illinois Journal of Law, Technology & Policy, 2015*(1), 149–186.

Bowcott, O. (2018). CPS and police 'routinely failing' to disclose evidence. *The Guardian.* https://www.theguardian.com/law/2018/nov/15/cps-and-police-routinely-failing-to-disclose-evidence. Accessed 15 November 2019.

Boyle, K. (2018). What's in a name? Theorising the inter-relationships of gender and violence. *Feminist Theory, 20*(1), 19–36.

Brereton, D. (1997). How different are rape trials? A comparison of the cross-examination of complainants in rape and assault trial. *British Journal of Criminology, Delinquency and Deviant Social Behaviour, 37*, 242.

Brewis, B. (2018). Procedural Amendments for Adducing Sexual Behaviour Evidence Under s. 41 of the Youth Justice and Criminal Evidence Act 1999. *The Journal of Criminal Law, 82*(5), 378–380.

Brewis, B., & Stockdale, M. (2014). Interpretation of S.41 of the Youth Justice and Criminal Evidence Act 1999: Meaning of 'Sexual Behaviour of the Complainant': R v RP [2013] EWCA Crim 2331. *The Journal of Criminal Law, 78*(2), 106–109.

Bronitt, S. (1998). The rules of recent complaint: Rape myths and the legal construction of the "reasonable" rape victim. In P. Easteal (Ed.), *Balancing the scales: Rape, law reform and Australian culture* (pp. 41–59). Federation Press.

Brooks-Hay, O. (2019). Doing the "right thing"? Understanding why rape victim-survivors report to the police. *Feminist Criminology, 15*(2), 174–195.

Brooks, P. (2002). Narrativity of the Law. *Law & Literature, 14*(1), 1–10.

Brown, C. (2013). Women's narratives of trauma: (Re)storying uncertainty, minimization and self-blame. *Narrative Works, 3*(1), 1.

Brown, J., Horvath, M., Kelly, L., & Westmarland, N. (2010a). *Connections and disconnections: Assessing evidence, knowledge and practice in responses to rape* (Project Report). Government Equalities Office.

Brown, J., Horvath, M., Kelly, L., & Westmarland, N. (2010b). *Has anything changed? Results of a comparative study (1977–2010) on opinions on rape.* Government Equalities Office.

Brown, R., & Gregg, M. (2012). The pedagogy of regret: Facebook, binge drinking and young women. *Continuum, 26*(3), 357–369.

Browning, J. G. (2011). Digging for the digital dirt: Discovery and use of evidence from social media sites. *SMU Science and Technology Law Review, 14*(3), 465–496.

Brownmiller, S. (1975). *Against our will.* Secker.

Buchwald, E., Fletcher, P. R., & Roth, M. (1993). *Transforming a rape culture.* Milkweed Editions.

Bullock, H. E., Fraser Wyche, K., & Williams, W. R. (2001). Media images of the poor. *Journal of Social Issues, 57*(2), 229–246.

Burgin, R. (2019). Persistent narratives of force and resistance: Affirmative consent as law reform. *The British Journal of Criminology, 59*(2), 296–314.

Burgin, R., & Flynn, A. (2019). Women's behavior as implied consent: Male "reasonableness" in Australian rape law. *Criminology & Criminal Justice, 23*(1), 334–352.

Burman, M. (2009). Evidencing sexual assault: Women in the witness box. *Probation Journal, 56*(4), 379–398.

Burman, M., Jamieson, L., Nicholson, J., & Brooks, O. (2007). *Impact of aspects of the law of evidence in sexual offence trials: An evaluation study.* Scottish Government.

Burrowes, N. (2013). *Responding to the challenge of rape myths in court: A guide for prosecutors.* NB Research.

Burt, M. R. (1980). Cultural myths and supports for rape. *Journal of Personality and Social Psychology, 38*(2), 217–230.

Busby, K. (1997). Discriminatory uses of personal records in sexual violence cases. *Canadian Journal of Women and the Law, 9*(1), 148.

Busfield, J. (1996). *Men, women and madness.* Palgrave Macmillan.

Button, M., & Tunley, M. (2015). Explaining fraud deviancy attenuation in the United Kingdom. *Crime, Law and Social Change, 63,* 49–64.

Byrne, B. (2006). *White lives: Gender, 'race' and class in contemporary London.* Routledge.

Carabine, J. (1992). 'Constructing women': Women's sexuality and social policy. *Critical Social Policy, 12*(34), 23–37.

Carabine, J. (2001). Constituting sexuality through social policy: The case of lone motherhood 1834 and today. *Social & Legal Studies, 10*(3), 291–314.

Carimico, G., Huynh, T., & Wells, S. (2016). Rape and sexual assault. *The Georgetown Journal of Gender and the Law, 17*(1), 359–410.

Carline, A., & Gunby, C. (2011). "How an ordinary jury makes sense of it is a mystery": Barristers' perspectives on rape, consent and the Sexual Offences Act 2003. *The Liverpool Law Review, 32*(3), 237–250.

Carrabine, E. (2014). *Criminology: A sociological introduction* (3rd ed.). Routledge.

Centre for Women's Justice. (2020). *Evidence of CPS Failure on Rape.* https://www.centreforwomensjustice.org.uk/news/2020/6/29/1pti6p5e19unqgl o7wd9mm68d621b7. Accessed 12 April 2021.

Centre for Women's Justice, End Violence Against Women Coalition, Imkaan, & Rape Crisis England & Wales. (2020). *The Decriminalisation of Rape.* https://rapecrisis.org.uk/media/2396/c-decriminalisation-of-rape-rep ort-cwj-evaw-imkaan-rcew-nov-2020.pdf. Accessed 12 April 2021.

Chalmers, J., & Leverick, F. (2018). *Methods of conveying information to jurors: An evidence review.* Scottish Government.

Chalmers, J., Leverick, F., & Munro, V. E. (2021). Why the jury is, and should still be, out on rape deliberation. *Criminal Law Review, 2021*(9), 753–771.

Christie, N. (1986). The ideal victim. In E. A. Fattah (Ed.), *From crime policy to victim policy* (pp. 17–30). Palgrave Macmillan.

Clark, A. (1987). *Women's silence, men's violence: Sexual assault in England, 1770–1845.* Pandora.

Coates, L., Bavelas, J. B., & Gibson, J. (1994). Anomalous language in sexual assault trial judgments. *Discourse & Society, 5*(2), 189–206.

Collins, P. H. (2000). *Black feminist thought* (2nd ed.). Routledge.

Coltrane, S. (1996). *Family man.* Oxford University Press.

Conaghan, J., & Russell, Y. (2014). Rape myths, law, and feminist research: 'Myths about myths'? *Feminist Legal Studies, 22*(1), 48.

Conner, T. J. (2001). What you may not say to the jury. *Litigation, 27*(3), 36–67.

Cossins, A. (2020). *Closing the justice gap for adult and child sexual assault.* Palgrave Macmillan.

Cowan, S. (2020). *The use of sexual history and bad character evidence in Scottish sexual offences trials.* Equality and Human Rights Commission.

Cozzarelli, C., Tagler, M., & Wilkinson, A. (2002). Do middle-class students perceive poor women and poor men differently? *Sex Roles, 47*(11), 519–529.

Crown Prosecution Service. (2013). *Charging perverting the course of justice and wasting police time in cases involving allegedly false rape and domestic violence allegations.* CPS.

Crown Prosecution Service. (2020). *Crown Prosecution Service invites the public to comment on revised pre-trial therapy guidance.* https://www.cps.gov.uk/cps/news/crown-prosecution-service-invites-public-comment-revised-pre-trial-therapy-guidance. Accessed 16 May 2021.

Crown Prosecution Service. (2021a). *Police-CPS Joint National RASSO (Rape and Serious Sexual Offences) Action Plan 2021.* https://www.cps.gov.uk/pub lication/police-cps-joint-national-rasso-rape-and-serious-sexual-offences-act ion-plan-2021. Accessed 23 September 2021.

Crown Prosecution Service. (2021b). *Prosecutors given additional tools to tackle harmful myths about online dating.* https://www.cps.gov.uk/cps/news/prosecutors-given-additional-tools-tackle-harmful-myths-about-online-dating. Accessed 23 September 2021.

Crown Prosecution Service. (2021c). *Rape and Sexual Offences—Overview and index of 2021 updated guidance.* https://www.cps.gov.uk/legal-gui dance/rape-and-sexual-offences-overview-and-index-2021-updated-guidance. Accessed 23 September 2021.

Crown Prosecution Service. (n.d.). *Rape and Sexual Offences—Chapter 9: Forensic, Scientific and Medical Evidence.* https://www.cps.gov.uk/legal-gui dance/rape-and-sexual-offences-chapter-9-forensic-scientific-and-medical-evi dence. Accessed 14 August 2020.

Daily Mail. (2019). *Ava Max's Sweet But Psycho music video draws backlash from mental health advocates.* https://www.dailymail.co.uk/tvshowbiz/article-661 8161/Ava-Maxs-Sweet-Psycho-music-video-draws-backlash-mental-health-advocates.html. Accessed 21 June 2020.

Daly, E. (2021). Making new meanings: The entextualisation of digital commu-nications evidence in English sexual offences trials. *Crime, Media, Culture* [online first]. https://doi.org/10.1177/17416590211048251

Daly, E., & Smith, O. (2020). *Scoping review: Legal & non-legal advocacy for rape complainants in adversarial jurisdictions.* Loughborough University.

Daly, E., Smith, O., Bows, H., Brown, J., Chalmers, J., Cowan, S., et al. (2021). Myths about Myths? A Commentary on Thomas (2020) and the Question of Jury Rape Myth Acceptance. *Journal of Gender-Based Violence* [online first]. https://doi.org/10.1332/239868021X16371459419254

Daly, K., & Bouhours, B. (2010). Rape and attrition in the legal process: A comparative analysis of five countries. *Crime and Justice, 39*(1), 565–650.

Darbyshire, P., Maughan, A., & Stewart, A. (2002). *What can the English legal system learn from jury research.* Kingston Law School.

Davies, G. (2019). Men falsely accused of rape are victims too, says wrongly-charged student as he backs disclosure move. *Telegraph.* https://www.tel egraph.co.uk/news/2019/04/29/men-falsely-accused-rape-victims-says-wrongly-charged-student/. Accessed 14 August 2020.

Day, K., Rickett, B., & Woolhouse, M. (2020). *Class discourse and the media.* Springer.

Degler, C. N. (1974). What ought to be and what was: Women's sexuality in the nineteenth century. *The American Historical Review, 79*(5), 1467.

DeGroot, J. M., & Vik, T. A. (2019). "The weight of our household rests on my shoulders": Inequity in family work. *Journal of Family Issues, 41*(8), 1258–1281.

Department for Communities and Local Government. (2015). *The English Indices of Deprivation 2015. Statistical Release.* Department for Communities and Local Government.

Dermott, E., & Pomati, M. (2016). The parenting and economising practices of lone parents: Policy and evidence. *Critical Social Policy, 36*(1), 62–81.

Derzakarian, A. (2017). The dark side of social media romance: Civil recourse for catfish victims. *Loyola of Los Angeles Law Review, 50*(4), 741–764.

DiBennardo, R. A. (2018). Ideal victims and monstrous offenders: How the news media represent sexual predators. *Socius, 4.*

Dinos, S., Burrowes, N., Hammond, K., & Cunliffe, C. (2015). A systematic review of juries' assessment of rape victims: Do rape myths impact on juror decision-making? *International Journal of Law, Crime and Justice, 43*(1), 36–49.

Diss, L. E. (2013). Whether you 'like' it or not: The inclusion of social media evidence in sexual harassment cases and how courts can effectively control it. *Boston College Law Review, 54*(4), 1841.

Dodge, A. (2018). The digital witness: The role of digital evidence in criminal justice responses to sexual violence. *Feminist Theory, 19*(3), 303–321.

Dowds, E. (2020). Towards a contextual definition of rape: Consent, coercion and constructive force. *The Modern Law Review, 83*(1), 35–63.

Duggan, M. (2018). *Revisiting the 'ideal victim': Developments in critical victimology.* Policy Press.

Duke, L. A., Allen, D. N., Rozee, P. D., & Bommaritto, M. (2007). The sensitivity and specificity of flashbacks and nightmares to trauma. *Journal of Anxiety Disorders, 22*(2), 319–327.

Dunn, J. L. (2005). Victims' and 'survivors': Emerging vocabularies of motive for 'battered women who stay'. *Sociological Inquiry, 75*(1), 1–30.

Dunn, J. L., & Creek, S. J. (2015). Identity dilemmas: Toward a more situated understanding. *Symbolic Interaction, 38*(2), 261–284.

Durham, R., Lawson, R., Lord, A., & Baird, V. (2017). *Seeing is Believing The Northumbria Court Observers Panel. Report on 30 rape trials 2015–16.* Vera Baird Police & Crime Commissioner.

Dush, C. M. K., Yavorsky, J. E., & Schoppe-Sullivan, S. J. (2018). What are men doing while women perform extra unpaid labor? Leisure and specialization at the transition to parenthood. *Sex Roles, 78*(11–12), 715–730.

Edwards, K., Turchik, J., Dardis, C., Reynolds, N., & Gidycz, C. (2011). Rape myths: History, individual and institutional-level presence, and implications for change. *Sex Roles, 65*(11), 761–773.

Edwards, S. (1981). *Female sexuality and the law: A study of constructs of female sexuality as they inform statute and legal procedure.* M. Robertson.

Edwards, S. (2016). *California Passes Mandatory Minimum Bill in Response to Brock Turner Controversy.* https://jezebel.com/california-passes-mandatory-minimum-bill-in-response-to-1787289987. Accessed 19 October 2020.

Effron, D. A. (2012). Hero or hypocrite: A psychological perspective on the risks and benefits of positive character evidence. *Jury Expert, 24*(4), 46–51.

Ehrlich, S. (1998). The discursive reconstruction of sexual consent. *Discourse & Society, 9*(2), 149–171.

Ehrlich, S. (2001). *Representing rape.* Routledge.

Ehrlich, S. (2015). *'Inferring' consent in the context of rape and sexual assault* (p. 141). Oxford University Press.

Einon, D., & Potegal, M. (1994). Temper Tantrums in young children. In M. Potegal & J. F. Knutson (Eds.), *The dynamics of aggression* (pp. 175–212). Psychology Press.

Ellemers, N., & Barreto, M. (2009). Collective action in modern times: How modern expressions of prejudice prevent collective action. *Journal of Social Issues, 65*(4), 749–768.

Ellison, L. (2002). *The adversarial process and the vulnerable witness.* Oxford University Press.

Ellison, L. (2009). The use and abuse of psychiatric evidence in rape trials. *The International Journal of Evidence & Proof, 13*(1), 28–49.

Ellison, L., & Munro, V. (2009a). Reacting to rape. *The British Journal of Criminology, 49*(2), 202–219.

Ellison, L., & Munro, V. (2009b). Turning mirrors into windows? *The British Journal of Criminology, 49*(3), 363–383.

Ellison, L., & Munro, V. (2010). A stranger in the bushes, or an elephant in the room? Critical reflections upon received rape myth wisdom in the context of a Mock Jury study. *New Criminal Law Review, 13*(4), 781–801.

Ellison, L., & Munro, V. (2016). Taking trauma seriously: Critical reflections on the criminal justice process. *International Journal of Evidence and Proof, 21*(3), 183–208.

Ellison, L., Munro, V., Hohl, K., & Wallang, P. (2015). Challenging criminal justice? Psychosocial disability and rape victimization. *Criminology & Criminal Justice, 15*(2), 225–244.

End Violence Against Women Coalition. (2018). *Attitudes to Sexual Consent.* https://www.endviolenceagainstwomen.org.uk/wp-content/uploads/1-Attitudes-to-sexual-consent-Research-findings-FINAL.pdf. Accessed 12 November 2020.

End Violence Against Women Coalition. (2020). *Briefing for Second Reading of the Domestic Abuse Bill.* https://www.endviolenceagainstwomen.org.uk/wp-content/uploads/EVAW-2nd-Reading-DA-Bill-Briefing-April-20-5-1.pdf. Accessed 01 October 2021.

End Violence Against Women Coalition. (2021a). *EVAW welcomes call by police inspectorate for whole system change to tackle violence against women and girls.* https://www.endviolenceagainstwomen.org.uk/evaw-welcomes-call-by-police-inspectorate-for-whole-system-change-to-tackle-violence-against-women-and-girls/. Accessed 10 January 2021.

End Violence Against Women Coalition. (2021b). *Leading women's groups deeply disappointed with lack of ambition in Government's Rape Review.* https://www.endviolenceagainstwomen.org.uk/leading-womens-groups-deeply-disappointed-with-lack-of-ambition-in-governments-rape-review-2/. Accessed 01 October 2021.

Epting, L. K., & Burchett, J. (2019). Buzzwords: Identifying the language of gender and mental health status. *North American Journal of Psychology, 21*(3), 661–674.

Estrich, S. (1987). *Real rape.* Harvard University Press.

Evans, M. (2018). Rape evidence flaws may have put hundreds of innocents in jail. *Telegraph.* https://www.telegraph.co.uk/news/2018/06/05/hundreds-miscarriages-justice-feared-cps-apologises-disclosure/. Accessed 19 October 2020.

Evans-Lacko, S., Henderson, C., & Thornicroft, G. (2013). Public knowledge, attitudes and behaviour regarding people with mental illness in England 2009–2012. *The British Journal of Psychiatry. Supplement, 55*(Supplement 55), s51–s57.

Eyssel, F., & Bohner, G. (2008). Modern rape myths: The Acceptance of Modern Myths about Sexual Aggression (AMMSA) Scale. In M. A. Morrison & T.

G. Morrison (Eds.), *The psychology of modern prejudice* (pp. 261–276). Nova Science Publishers.

Fanghanel, A. (2020). *Disrupting rape culture*. Bristol University Press.

Feagin, J. R. (2020). *The white racial frame* (3rd ed.). Routledge.

Feist, A., Ashe, J., Lawrence, J., McPhee, D., & Wilson, R. (2007). *Investigating and Detecting Recorded Offences of Rape*. http://webarchive.nationalarchives. gov.uk/20110218140524/http://rds.homeoffice.gov.uk/rds/pdfs07/rdsolr 1807.pdf. Accessed 12 February 2019.

Fisher, R. J. (1993). Social desirability bias and the validity of indirect questioning. *The Journal of Consumer Research, 20*(2), 303–315.

Fivush, R. (2010). Speaking silence: The social construction of silence in autobiographical and cultural narratives. *Memory, 18*(2), 88–98.

Fouzder, M. (2019). *We will not be silenced: Liam Allan joined by protesters outside RCJ*. https://www.lawgazette.co.uk/news/we-will-not-be-silenced-liam-allan-joined-by-protesters-outside-rcj/5070731.article. Accessed 19 October 2020.

Franiuk, R., Seefelt, J., & Vandello, J. (2008). Prevalence of rape myths in headlines and their effects on attitudes toward rape. *Sex Roles, 58*(11), 790–801.

Frankenberg, R. (1993). *White women, race matters*. Routledge.

Fraser, C. (2015). From 'ladies first' to 'asking for it': Benevolent sexism in the maintenance of rape culture. *California Law Review, 103*(1), 141–203.

Friedman, W. J. (1993). Memory for the time of past events. *Psychological Bulletin, 113*(1), 44–66.

Galliano, G., Noble, L. M., Travis, L. A., & Puechl, C. (1993). Victim reactions during rape/sexual assault. *Journal of Interpersonal Violence, 8*(1), 109.

Gathings, M. J., & Parrotta, K. (2013). The use of gendered narratives in the courtroom. *Journal of Contemporary Ethnography, 42*(6), 668–689.

Gavey, N. (2005). *Just sex?* Psychology Press.

Geiger, B. B., Reeves, A., & de Vries, R. (2017). Tax avoidance and benefit manipulation: Views on its morality and prevalence. *British Social Attitudes, 34*.

Gelsthorpe, L. (2010). Women, crime and control. *Criminology & Criminal Justice, 10*(4), 375–386.

Gerger, H., Kley, H., Bohner, G., & Siebler, F. (2007). The acceptance of modern myths about sexual aggression scale: Development and validation in German and English. *Aggressive Behavior, 33*(5), 422–440.

Gillen, J. (2019). *Gillen Review: Report into the law and procedures in serious sexual offences in Northern Ireland*.

Gillies, V. (2007). *Marginalised Mothers*. Routledge.

Gilmore, L. (2001). *The limits of autobiography: Trauma and testimony*. Cornell University Press.

Gilmore, L. (2017). *Tainted witness: Why we doubt what women say about their lives.* Columbia University Press.

Glover, T. D. (2003). The story of the Queen Anne Memorial Garden: Resisting a dominant cultural narrative. *Journal of Leisure Research, 35*(2), 190–212.

Gowing, L. (1996). Women, status and the popular culture of dishonour. *Transactions of the Royal Historical Society, 6,* 225–234.

Gravelin, C. R., Biernat, M., & Bucher, C. E. (2019). Blaming the victim of acquaintance rape: Individual, situational, and sociocultural factors. *Frontiers in Psychology, 9,* 2422.

Gregory, J., & Lees, S. (1996). Attrition in rape and sexual assault cases. *British Journal of Criminology, 36*(1), 1–17.

Griffin, C., Szmigin, I., Bengry-Howell, A., Hackley, C., & Mistral, W. (2013). Inhabiting the contradictions: Hypersexual femininity and the culture of intoxication among young women in the UK. *Feminism & Psychology, 23*(2), 184–206.

Grubb, A., & Turner, E. (2012). Attribution of blame in rape cases: A review of the impact of rape myth acceptance, gender role conformity and substance use on victim blaming. *Aggression and Violent Behavior, 17*(5), 443–452.

Gunby, C., Carline, A., & Beynon, C. (2012). Regretting it after? Focus group perspectives on alcohol consumption, nonconsensual sex and false allegations of rape. *Social & Legal Studies, 22*(1), 87–106.

Gurnham, D. (2016). A critique of carceral feminist arguments on rape myths and sexual scripts. *New Criminal Law Review, 19*(2), 141–170.

Hamby, S. L., & Koss, M. P. (2003). Shades of gray: A qualitative study of terms used in the measurement of sexual victimization. *Psychology of Women Quarterly, 27*(3), 243–255.

Hammack, P. L., & Toolis, E. E. (2016). Putting the social into personal identity: The master narrative as root metaphor for psychological and developmental science. *Human Development, 58*(6), 350–364.

Hancock, L., & Mooney, G. (2011). 'Saints and scroungers': Constructing the poverty and crime myth. *Criminal Justice Matters, 83*(1), 26–27.

Harell, A., Soroka, S., & Ladner, K. (2014). Public opinion, prejudice and the racialization of welfare in Canada. *Ethnic and Racial Studies, 37*(14), 2580–2597.

Harper, J. (2021). Jury trials: A cornerstone of the rule of law? *New Law Journal,* 7924.

Harris, A., Carney, S., & Fine, M. (2001). Counter work: Introduction. In M. Fine & A. Harris (Eds.), *Under the covers: Theorising the politics of counter stories* (pp. 6–18). Lawrence & Wishart.

Harris, J., & Grace, S. (1999). *A question of evidence? Investigating and prosecuting rape in the 1990s* (No. 196). Home Office.

Harte, L. (2020). PPS report 'shows rape victims are being let down' by justice system in Northern Ireland. *Belfast Telegraph*. https://www.belfasttelegraph. co.uk/news/northern-ireland/pps-report-shows-rape-victims-are-being-let-down-by-justice-system-in-northern-ireland-39712516.html. Accessed   22 July 2021.

Harvey, D. (2005). *A brief history of neoliberalism*. Oxford University Press.

Haygarth, N. (2018). *UK press discourses surrounding representations of rape in film and the subject of male violence against women* (PhD thesis). http:// ethos.bl.uk/OrderDetails.do?uin=uk.bl.ethos.753920

Haylett, C. (2003). Culture, class and urban policy: Reconsidering equality. *Antipode, 35*(1), 55–73.

Heidt, J. M., Marx, B. P., & Forsyth, J. P. (2005). Tonic immobility and childhood sexual abuse: A preliminary report evaluating the sequela of rape-induced paralysis. *Behaviour Research And Therapy, 43*(9), 1157–1171.

Her Majesty's Inspectorate of Constabulary and Fire and Rescue Services. (2021). *Police response to violence against women and girls: Final inspection report.* https://www.justiceinspectorates.gov.uk/hmicfrs/wp-content/upl oads/police-response-to-violence-against-women-and-girls-final-inspection-report.pdf. Accessed 01 October 2021.

Herman, D. (1984). The rape culture. In J. Freeman (Ed.), *Women: A feminist perspective* (pp. 45–53). Mayfield.

Hester, M. (2013). *From Report to Court: Rape cases and the criminal justice system in the Northeast*. University of Bristol in association with the Northern Rock Foundation.

Hlavka, H. R., & Mulla, S. (2018). "That's how she talks": Animating text message evidence in the sexual assault trial. *Law & Society Review, 52*(2), 401–435.

HM Government. (2018). *Victims strategy*. Stationery Office.

HM Government. (2021a). *The end-to-end rape review report on findings and actions.* https://assets.publishing.service.gov.uk/government/uploads/sys tem/uploads/attachment_data/file/1001417/end-to-end-rape-review-rep ort-with-correction-slip.pdf. Accessed 1 October 2021.

HM Government. (2021b). *The end-to-end review of rape: Equalities statement May 2021.* https://assets.publishing.service.gov.uk/government/uploads/sys tem/uploads/attachment_data/file/994169/rape-review-equality-statement. pdf. Accessed 01 October 2021.

Hohl, K., & Conway, M. A. (2017). Memory as evidence: How normal features of victim memory lead to the attrition of rape complaints. *Criminology & Criminal Justice, 17*(3), 248–265.

Hohl, K., & Stanko, E. A. (2015). Complaints of rape and the criminal justice system: Fresh evidence on the attrition problem in England and Wales. *European Journal of Criminology, 12*(3), 324–341.

Horn, M. (1993). Inventing the problem child: "At risk" children in the child guidance. In R. Wollons (Ed.), *Children at risk in America: History, concepts, and public policy* (pp. 141–153). State University of New York Press.

Horvath, M., & Brown, J. (2006). The role of drugs and alcohol in rape. *Medicine, Science and the Law, 46*(3), 219–228.

Horvath, M., & Giner-Sorolla, R. (2007). Below the age of consent: Influences on moral and legal judgments of adult-adolescent sexual relationships. *Journal of Applied Social Psychology, 37*(12), 2980–3009.

Hovdestad, W., & Renner, E. (2021). *What does it mean to use a "real rape" myth in a sexual assault trial?* Social & Legal Studies Blog. https://socialandlegalstudies.wordpress.com/2021/02/08/what-does-it-mean-to-use-a-real-rape-myth-in-a-sexual-assault-trial/. Accessed 21 March 2021.

Howell, B. A., & Herberlig, B. M. (2007). The Lamar Owens case: How digital evidence contributed to an acquittal in an explosive rape case. *The Computer & Internet Lawyer, 24*(12), 1–4.

Hoyano, L. (2019). Cross-examination of sexual assault complainants on previous sexual behaviour: Views from the barristers' row. *Criminal Law Review, 2*, 75–111.

Hsu, R. (1996). 'Will the model minority please identify itself?': American ethnic identity and its discontents. *Diaspora, 5*(1), 37–63.

Humphreys, C., Mullender, A., Thiara, R., & Skamballis, A. (2006). Talking to My Mum. *Journal of Social Work, 6*(1), 53–63.

Hunt, J. S., & Budesheim, T. L. (2004). How jurors use and misuse character evidence. *Journal of Applied Psychology, 89*(2), 347–361.

Hutton, F., Griffin, C., Lyons, A., Niland, P., & McCreanor, T. (2016). "Tragic girls" and "crack whores": Alcohol, femininity and Facebook. *Feminism & Psychology, 26*(1), 73–93.

ICM. (2005). *Sexual Assault Research Report*. Prepared for Amnesty International. https://web.archive.org/web/20060207094708/https://www.amnesty.org.uk/images/ul/s/sexual_assault_summary_report_2.doc. Accessed 15 April 2019.

Iliadis, M. (2019). Victim representation for sexual history evidence in Ireland: A step towards or away from meeting victims' procedural justice needs? *Criminology & Criminal Justice, 20*(4), 416–432.

Iliadis, M., Smith, O., & Doak, J. (2021). Independent separate legal representation for rape complainants in adversarial systems: Lessons from Northern Ireland. *Journal of Law and Society, 48*(2), 250–272.

Janssen, S. M. J., Chessa, A. G., & Murre, J. M. J. (2006). Memory for time: How people date events. *Memory & Cognition, 34*(1), 138–147.

Javaid, A. (2015). Male rape myths: Understanding and explaining social attitudes surrounding male rape. *Masculinities & Social Change, 4*(3), 270.

Jensen, T. (2014). Welfare commonsense, poverty porn and doxosophy. *Sociological Research Online, 19*(3), 1–7.

Jensen, T., & Ringrose, J. (2014). Sluts that Choose Vs Doormat Gypsies: Exploring affect in the postfeminist, visual moral economy of *My Big Fat Gypsy Wedding*. *Feminist Media Studies, 14*(3), 369–387.

Jordan, J. (2004). *The word of a woman?* Palgrave.

Jordan, J. (2011). Here we go round the review-go-round: Rape investigation and prosecution—Are things getting worse not better? *Journal of Sexual Aggression, 17*(3), 234–249.

Jordan, J. (2013). From victim to survivor—And from survivor to victim: Reconceptualising the survivor journey. *Sexual Abuse in Australia and New Zealand, 5*(2), 48–56.

Jozkowski, K. N. (2016). Why does rape seem like a myth? In J. Manning & C. Noland (Eds.), *Contemporary studies of sexuality & communication: Theoretical and applied perspectives* (pp. 239–262). Kendall/Hunt Publishing.

Judicial College. (2020a). *Crown Court Compendium Part I*. https://www.judiciary.uk/wp-content/uploads/2020/07/Crown-Court-Compendium-Part-I-December-2020.pdf. Accessed 15 September 2021.

Judicial College. (2020b). *Equal Treatment Bench Book*. https://www.judiciary.uk/wp-content/uploads/2020/05/ETBB-February-2018-amended-March-2020-17.09.20-1.pdf. Accessed 15 September 2021.

Jun, M. (2019). Stigma and shame attached to claiming social assistance benefits: Understanding the detrimental impact on UK lone mothers' social relationships. *Journal of Family Studies* [online first].

Kahn, A. S., Jackson, J., Kully, C., Badger, K., & Halvorsen, J. (2003). Calling it rape: Differences in experiences of women who do or Do not label their sexual assault as rape. *Psychology of Women Quarterly, 27*, 233–242.

Keane, E. P. H., & Convery, T. (2020). *Proposal for independent legal representation for complainers where an application is made to lead evidence of their sexual history or character*. University of Edinburgh.

Kelly, L. (1987). The continuum of sexual violence. In J. Hanmer & M. Maynard (Eds.), *Women, violence and social control* (pp. 46–60). Macmillan.

Kelly, L. (1988). *Surviving sexual violence*. Polity Press.

Kelly, L. (2010). The (in)credible words of women: False allegations in European rape research. *Violence against Women, 16*(12), 1345–1355.

Kelly, L., Lovett, J., & Regan, L. (2005). *A gap or a chasm? Attrition in reported rape cases*. Home Office.

Kelly, L., Temkin, J., & Griffiths, S. (2006). *Section 41: An evaluation of new legislation limiting sexual history evidence in rape trials*. Home Office.

Kendall, D. E. (2005). *Framing class: Media representations of wealth and poverty in America*. Rowman & Littlefield Publishers.

Kitzinger, J. (2009). Rape in the media. In M. Horvath & J. Brown (Eds.), *Rape: Challenging contemporary thinking* (pp. 74–98). Willan.

Koss, M. P., & Harvey, M. R. (1987). *The rape victim: Clinical and community interventions*. Lexington.

Kovac, L. D., & Trussell, D. E. (2015). 'Classy and never trashy': Young women's experiences of nightclubs and the construction of gender and sexuality. *Leisure Sciences, 37*(3), 195–209.

Krahé, B., Temkin, J., & Bieneck, S. (2007). Schema-driven information processing in judgements about rape. *Applied Cognitive Psychology, 21*(5), 601–619.

Lafrance, M. N., & McKenzie-Mohr, S. (2014). Women counter-storying their lives. In S. McKenzie-Mohr & M. N. Lafrance (Eds.), *Women voicing resistance* (pp. 1–15). Routledge.

Larcombe, W. (2005). *Compelling engagements*. Federation Press.

Lawler, S. (2005). Disgusted subjects: The making of middle-class identities. *The Sociological Review, 53*(3), 429–446.

Lawler, S. (2012). White like them: Whiteness and anachronistic space in representations of the English white working class. *Ethnicities, 12*(4), 409–426.

Lea, S. J., Lanvers, U., & Shaw, S. (2003). Attrition in rape cases. Developing a profile and identifying relevant factors. *The British Journal of Criminology, 43*(3), 583–599.

Leahy, S. (2014). The corroboration warning in sexual offence trials: Final vestige of the historic suspicion of sexual offence complainants or a necessary protection for defendants? *International Journal of Evidence & Proof, 18*(1), 41–64.

Lees, S. (2002). *Carnal knowledge: Rape on trial* (2nd ed.). Women's Press.

Lehtonen, A. (2018, July). *The sexual and intimate life of UK austerity politics* (PhD thesis). http://etheses.lse.ac.uk/3800/

Leisenring, A. (2006). Confronting 'victim' discourses: The identity work of battered women. *Symbolic Interaction, 29*(3), 307–330.

Lennox, J., Emslie, C., Sweeting, H., & Lyons, A. (2018). The role of alcohol in constructing gender & class identities among young women in the age of social media. *International Journal of Drug Policy, 58*, 13–21.

Leverick, F. (2020). What do we know about rape myths and juror decision making? *International Journal of Evidence & Proof, 24*(3), 255–279.

Levin, S. (2016). Stanford sexual assault: Read the full text of the judge's controversial decision. *The Guardian.* https://www.theguardian.com/us-news/2016/jun/14/stanford-sexual-assault-read-sentence-judge-aaron-persky. Accessed 21 August 2020.

Lewis, T. E., Klettke, B., & Day, A. (2014). The influence of medical and behavioral evidence on conviction rates in cases of child sexual abuse. *Journal of Child Sexual Abuse, 23*(4), 431–441.

Limmer, M. (2016). "I don't shag dirty girls": Marginalized masculinities and the use of partner selection as a sexual health risk reduction strategy in heterosexual young men. *American Journal of Men's Health, 10*(2), 128–140.

Lodrick, Z. (2007). Psychological trauma: What every trauma worker should know. *British Journal of Psychotherapy Integration, 4*(2), 18–29.

London, K., Bruck, M., Wright, D. B., & Ceci, S. J. (2008). Review of the contemporary literature on how children report sexual abuse to others: Findings, methodological issues, and implications for forensic interviewers. *Memory, 16*(1), 29–47.

Lonsway, K. A., & Fitzgerald, L. F. (1994). Rape myths. *Psychology of Women Quarterly, 18*(2), 133–164.

Loseke, D. R. (2001). Lived realities and formula stories of 'battered women.' In J. F. Gubrium & J. A. Holstein (Eds.), *Institutional selves: Troubled identities in a postmodern world* (pp. 107–126). Oxford University Press.

Loseke, D. R. (2007). The study of identity as cultural, institutional, organizational, and personal narratives: Theoretical and empirical integrations. *The Sociological Quarterly, 48*(4), 661–688.

Lovett, J., & Horvath, M. A. H. (2009). Alcohol and drugs in rape and sexual assault. In M. Horvath & J. Brown (Eds.), *Rape: Challenging contemporary thinking* (pp. 125–160). Willan.

Lovett, J., Uzelac, G., Horvath, M., & Kelly, L. (2007). *Rape in the 21st Century: Old behaviours, new contexts and emerging patterns.* Economic and Social Research Council.

Lowe, E., Britton, J., & Cranwell, J. (2018). Alcohol content in the 'hyper-reality' MTV Show 'Geordie Shore.' *Alcohol and Alcoholism, 53*(3), 337–343.

Lundström, R. (2013). Framing fraud: Discourse on benefit cheating in Sweden and the UK. *European Journal of Communication, 28*(6), 630–645.

Lynch, K., Golding, J., Jewell, J., Lippert, A., & Wasarhaley, N. (2019). "She is his girlfriend—I believe this is a different situation": Gender differences in perceptions of the legality of intimate partner rape. *Journal of Family Violence, 34*(3), 213–230.

MacDonald, R., Shildrick, T., & Furlong, A. (2020). 'Cycles of disadvantage' revisited: Young people, families and poverty across generations. *Journal of Youth Studies, 23*(1), 12–27.

Mackiewicz, A. (2015). *Alcohol, young women's culture and gender hierarchies.* Policy Press.

MacLin, M. K., Downs, C., MacLin, O. H., & Caspers, H. M. (2009). The effect of defendant facial expression on mock juror decision-making: The power of remorse. *North American Journal of Psychology, 11*(2), 323.

Maeder, E. M., & Hunt, J. S. (2011). Talking about a Black Man: The influence of defendant and character witness race on jurors' use of character evidence. *Behavioral Sciences & the Law, 29*(4), 608–620.

Mangrum, R. C. (2015). I believe, the Golden Rule, send a message, and other improper closing arguments. *Creighton Law Review, 48*(3), 521.

Mannay, D. (2015). Achieving respectable motherhood? Exploring the impossibility of feminist and egalitarian ideologies against the everyday realities of lived Welsh working-class femininities. *Women's Studies International Forum, 53*, 159–166.

Manne, K. (2020). *Entitled how male privilege hurts women*. Allen Lane.

Mantyla, K. (2018). *Dave Daubenmire: It's 'sexual abuse' for women to lead men on*. https://www.rightwingwatch.org/post/dave-daubenmire-its-sexual-abuse-for-women-to-lead-men-on/. Accessed 09 February 2020.

Martín, A. M., & Kaplan, M. F. (2013a). *Understanding world jury systems through social psychological research*. Taylor and Francis.

Martín, A. M., & Kaplan, M. F. (2013b). Psychological perspectives on Spanish and Russian Juries. In M. F. Kaplan & A. M. Martín (Eds.), *Understanding world jury systems through social psychological research* (pp. 71–88). Psychology Press.

Martinez, T., Wiersma-Mosley, J. D., Jozkowski, K. N., & Becnel, J. (2018). 'Good guys don't rape': Greek and Non-Greek College student perpetrator rape myths. *Behavioral Sciences, 8*(7), 60.

McCormick, K. T., MacArthur, H. J., Shields, S. A., & Dicicco, E. C. (2016). New perspectives on gender and emotion. In T. A. Roberts, N. Curtin, L. E. Duncan, & L. M. Cortina (Eds.), *Feminist perspectives on building a better psychological science of gender* (pp. 213–230). Springer.

McGlynn, C. (2017). Rape trials and sexual history evidence: Reforming the law on third-party evidence. *The Journal of Criminal Law, 81*(5), 367–392.

McGlynn, C. (2018). Challenging the law on sexual history evidence: A response to Dent and Paul. *Criminal Law Review, 3*, 216–228.

McKenzie-Mohr, S., & Lafrance, M. N. (2011). Telling stories without the words: 'Tightrope talk' in women's accounts of coming to live well after rape or depression. *Feminism & Psychology, 21*(1), 49.

McKinney, C. J. (2019). *Durham Uni law academic sparks furious Twitter debate after claiming high-profile rape allegation wasn't necessarily 'false'*. https://www.legalcheek.com/2019/04/durham-uni-law-academic-sparks-furious-twitter-debate-after-claiming-high-profile-rape-allegation-wasnt-necessarily-false/. Accessed 19 October 2020.

McLean, K. C., Lilgendahl, J. P., Fordham, C., Alpert, E., Marsden, E., Szymanowski, K., & McAdams, D. P. (2018). Identity development in cultural context: The role of deviating from master narratives. *Journal of Personality, 86*(4), 631–651.

McLean, K. C., & Syed, M. (2016). Personal, master, and alternative narratives: An integrative framework for understanding identity development in context. *Human Development, 58*(6), 318–349.

McMahon, S., & Farmer, L. G. (2011). An updated measure for assessing subtle rape myths. *Social Work Research, 35*(2), 71–81.

McMillan, L. (2007). *Feminists organising against gendered violence*. Palgrave Macmillan.

McMillan, L. (2018). Police officers' perceptions of false allegations of rape. *Journal of Gender Studies, 27*(1), 9–21.

McMillan, L., & Thomas, M. (2009). Police interviews of rape victims: Tensions and contradictions. In M. Horvath & J. Brown (Eds.), *Rape: Challenging contemporary thinking* (pp. 255–280). Willan.

McRobbie, A. (2013). Feminism, the family and the new 'mediated' maternalism. *New Formations, 80*(80), 119–137.

Meaney, C. (2018). *Sweet but Problematic | Is Ava Max stigmatising mental illness?* https://www.headstuff.org/topical/opinion/ava-max-sweet-psycho/. Accessed 21 June 2020.

Meeussen, L., Laar, C. V., & Verbruggen, M. (2019). Looking for a family man? Norms for men are toppling in heterosexual relationships. *Sex Roles, 80*(7), 429–442.

Mehta, N., Kassam, A., Leese, M., Butler, G., & Thornicroft, G. (2009). Public attitudes towards people with mental illness in England and Scotland, 1994–2003. *The British Journal of Psychiatry, 194*(3), 278–284.

Messner, M. A. (2016). Bad men, good men, bystanders: Who is the rapist? *Gender and Society, 30*(1), 57–66.

Minch, C., & Linden, R. (1987). Attrition in the processing of rape cases. *Canadian Journal of Criminology, 29*(4), 389.

Ministry of Justice. (2011). *Achieving Best Evidence in Criminal Proceedings*. https://www.cps.gov.uk/sites/default/files/documents/legal_guidance/best_evidence_in_criminal_proceedings.pdf. Accessed 16 July 2020.

Ministry of Justice. (2018). *Criminal court statistics quarterly, England and Wales,* January to March 2018 (annual 2017). https://assets.publishing.service.gov.uk/government/uploads/system/uploads/attachment_data/file/720026/ccsq-bulletin-jan-mar-2018.pdf. Accessed 16 March 2019.

Ministry of Justice, Home Office, & Office for National Statistics. (2013). *An overview of sexual offending in England and Wales.* https://www.gov.uk/government/uploads/system/uploads/attachment_data/file/214970/sexual-offending-overview-jan-2013.pdf. Accessed 16 March 2019.

Molina, J., & Poppleton, S. (2020). *Rape survivors and the criminal justice system.* Victims' Commissioner.

Moran, P., Ghate, D., & van der Merwe, A. (2004). *What works in parenting support?: A review of the international evidence*. Department for Education and Skills.

Morris, C., & Munt, S. R. (2019). Classed formations of shame in white, British single mothers. *Feminism & Psychology, 29*(2), 231–249.

Morrison, J. (2019). *Scroungers: Moral panics and media myths*. Zed Books.

Morrison, M. A., Morrison, T. G., Harriman, R. L., & Jewell, L. M. (2008). Old-fashioned and modern prejudice toward aboriginals in Canada. In M. A. Morrison & T. G. Morrison (Eds.), *The psychology of modern prejudice* (pp. 277–305). Nova Science Publishers.

Moulding, N. T., Buchanan, F., & Wendt, S. (2015). Untangling self-blame and mother-blame in women's and children's perspectives on maternal protectiveness in domestic violence: Implications for practice. *Child Abuse Review, 24*(4), 249–260.

Muehlenhard, C. L. (1988). Misinterpreted dating behaviors and the risk of date rape. *Journal of Social and Clinical Psychology, 6*(1), 20–37.

Muehlenhard, C. L., & Linton, M. A. (1987). Date rape and sexual aggression in dating situations. *Journal of Counseling Psychology, 34*(2), 186–196.

Muehlenhard, C. L., & MacNaughton, J. S. (1988). Women's beliefs about women who "lead men on." *Journal of Social and Clinical Psychology, 7*(1), 65–79.

Munro, V. (2010). An unholy trinity? Non-consent, coercion and exploitation in contemporary legal responses to sexual violence in England and Wales. *Current Legal Problems, 63*(1), 45–71.

Munro, V., & Kelly, L. (2009). A vicious cycle?: Attrition and conviction patterns in contemporary rape cases in England and Wales. In M. Horvath & J. Brown (Eds.), *Rape: Challenging contemporary thinking* (pp. 281–300). Willan.

Murphy, A., Hine, B., Yesberg, J. A., Wunsch, D., & Charleton, B. (2021). Lessons from London: A contemporary examination of the factors affecting attrition among rape complaints. *Psychology, Crime & Law* [online first].

Murray, C. (1990). The British underclass. *Public Interest*, 4–28.

Murray, C. (1994). *Underclass: The crisis deepens*. IEA Health and Welfare Unit.

Murray, C. (2001). The British underclass: Ten years later. *Public Interest*, 25.

Nelson, H. L. (2001). *Damaged identities, narrative repair*. Cornell University Press.

Nilsson, G. (2019). Rape in the news: On rape genres in Swedish news coverage. *Feminist Media Studies, 19*(8), 1178–1194.

Nunn, H., & Biressi, A. (2010). Shameless?: Picturing the "underclass" after Thatcherism. In L. Hadley & E. Ho (Eds.), *Thatcher & After* (pp. 137–157). Palgrave Macmillan.

Nunn, H., & Biressi, A. (2013). Class, gender, and the docusoap: The only way is Essex. In C. Carter, L. Steiner, & L. McLaughlin (Eds.), *The Routledge Companion to Media and Gender* (pp. 269–279). Routledge.

Nurius, P. S., Norris, J., Macy, R. J., & Huang, B. (2004). Women's situational coping with acquaintance sexual assault. *Violence against Women, 10*(5), 450–478.

O'Hara, S. (2012). Monsters, playboys, virgins and whores: Rape myths in the news media's coverage of sexual violence. *Language and Literature: Journal of the Poetics and Linguistics Association, 21*(3), 247.

O'Malley, T. (2020). *Review of protections for vulnerable witnesses in the investigation and prosecution of sexual offences.* Department of Justice and Equality (Ireland).

O'Neal, E. N., Tellis, K., & Spohn, C. (2015). Prosecuting intimate partner sexual assault: Legal and extra-legal factors that influence charging decisions. *Violence Against Women, 21*(10), 1237–1258.

Official Charts. (n.d.). *Search the Official Charts.* https://www.officialcharts.com/search/singles/sweet-but-psycho/. Accessed 21 June 2020.

Osborne, S. (2018, January 30). Liam Allan: Met Police apologise to 22-year-old man falsely accused of rape after failing to disclose crucial text messages. *The Independent.* https://www.independent.co.uk/news/uk/crime/liam-allan-met-police-rape-accusation-false-evidence-disclosure-arrest-mistake-detectives-a8184916.html. Accessed 19 October 2020.

Owen, D. (2016). "Hillbillies", "welfare queens", and "teen moms": American media's class distinctions. In S. Lemke & W. Schniedermann (Eds.), *Class divisions in serial television* (pp. 47–63). Palgrave Macmillan.

Papendick, M., & Bohner, G. (2017). 'Passive victim—Strong survivor'? Perceived meaning of labels applied to women who were raped. *PLoS One, 12*(5), e0177550.

Parmar, A. (2017). Intersectionality, British criminology and race: Are we there yet? *Theoretical Criminology, 21*(1), 35–45.

Pascoe, C. J., & Hollander, J. A. (2016). Good guys don't rape. *Gender & Society, 30*(1), 67–79.

Patrick, R. (2016). Living with and responding to the 'scrounger' narrative in the UK: Exploring everyday strategies of acceptance, resistance and deflection. *Journal of Poverty and Social Justice, 24*(3), 245–259.

Payne, D., & Wermeling, L. (2009). Domestic violence and the female victim: The real reason women stay! *Journal of Multicultural, Gender and Minority Studies, 3*(1), 1–6.

Payne, G. (2013). Models of contemporary social class: The Great British class survey. *Methodological Innovations, 8*(1), 3–17.

Payne, H. M. (2016). *'Really damn sexist': A discourse analysis of the language used to portray gender inequality within reality television.* http://e-space.mmu.ac.uk/617867/. Accessed 23 April 2020.

Peat, J. (2020). *Amber Heard was booed and dubbed a 'liar' as crowds threw flowers at Depp's car.* https://www.thelondoneconomic.com/opinion/amber-heard-was-booed-and-dubbed-a-liar-as-crowds-threw-flowers-at-depps-car/02/11/. Accessed 5 February 2021.

Penfold, P. S. (1995). Mendacious moms or devious dads? Some perplexing issues in child custody/sexual abuse allegation disputes. *The Canadian Journal of Psychiatry, 40*(6), 337–341.

Peterson, Z. D., & Muehlenhard, C. L. (2011). A match-and-motivation model of how women label their nonconsensual sexual experiences. *Psychology of Women Quarterly, 35*(4), 558–570.

Phipps, A. (2009). Rape and respectability: Ideas about sexual violence and social class. *Sociology, 43*(4), 667–683.

Pierre, J. (2004). Black immigrants in the United States and the 'cultural narratives' of ethnicity. *Identities (yverdon, Switzerland), 11*(2), 141–170.

Powell, A, Henry, N., & Flynn, A. (2015). *Rape justice*. Palgrave Macmillan.

Powell, A. J., Hlavka, H. R., & Mulla, S. (2017). Intersectionality and credibility in child sexual assault trials. *Gender & Society, 31*(4), 457–480.

Profitt, N. J. (1996). 'Battered women' as 'victims' and 'survivors': Creating space for resistance. *Canadian Social Work Review, 13*(1), 23–38.

Raitt, F. (2004). Expert evidence as context: Historical patterns and contemporary attitudes in the prosecution of sexual offences. *Feminist Legal Studies, 12*(2), 233–244.

Raitt, F. (2010). *Independent legal representation for complainers in sexual offence trials: Research report for Rape Crisis Scotland*. Rape Crisis Scotland. http://discovery.dundee.ac.uk/portal/en/research/independent-legal-rep resentation-for-complainers-in-sexual-offence-trials-research-report-for-rape-crisis-scotland(e23075e9-f117-4dab-ac57-b0daa9e82c68).html. Accessed 15 September 2020.

Raitt, F. E., & Zeedyk, M. S. (2003). False memory syndrome: Undermining the credibility of complainants in sexual offences. *International Journal of Law and Psychiatry, 26*(5), 453–471.

Ramirez, F. A., & Denault, V. (2019). *Facebook, female victims, and social media evidence in sexual assault trials*. Presented at the 10th International Conference on Social Media & Society, Toronto, Canada.

Rasmussen, B. B., Klinenberg, E., Nexica, I. J., & Wray, M. (2001). *The making and unmaking of whiteness*. Duke University Press.

Reece, H. (2013). Rape myths: Is elite opinion right and popular opinion wrong? *Oxford Journal of Legal Studies, 33*(3), 445–473.

Reeves, E. (2021). *Labour unveils Survivors' Support Plan for victims of rape*. https://labour.org.uk/press/labour-unveils-survivors-support-plan-for-victims-of-rape/. Accessed 23 September 2021.

Reid, J. A., Haskell, R. A., Dillahunt-Aspillaga, C., & Thor, J. A. (2013). Contemporary review of empirical and clinical studies of trauma bonding in violent or exploitative relationships. *International Journal of Psychology Research, 8*(1), 37.

Rhodes, N. R., & McKenzie, E. B. (1998). Why do battered women stay? *Aggression and Violent Behavior, 3*(4), 391–406.

Richardson, L. (1997). *Fields of play*. Rutgers University Press.

Riemer, A. R., Gervais, S. J., Skorinko, J. L. M., Douglas, S. M., Spencer, H., Nugai, K., et al. (2018). She looks like she'd be an animal in bed: Dehumanization of drinking women in social contexts. *Sex Roles, 80*(9–10), 617–629.

RNZ. (2021). Low rape conviction rate shows system is failing—Women's Refuge. *RNZ*. https://www.rnz.co.nz/news/national/439802/low-rape-conviction-rate-shows-system-is-failing-women-s-refuge. Accessed 22 July 2021.

Roberts, K. (2011). *Class in Contemporary Britain* (2nd ed.). Palgrave.

Robinson, D. T., Smith-Lovin, L., & Tsoudis, O. (1994). Heinous crime or unfortunate accident? The effects of remorse on responses to mock criminal confessions. *Social Forces, 73*(1), 175–190.

Robinson, P. M. (1984). The historical repression of women's sexuality. In C. S. Vance (Ed.), *Pleasure and danger: Exploring female sexuality* (pp. 251–266). Routledge.

Robson, C., & McCartan, K. (2016). *Real world research: A resource for users of social research methods in applied settings* (4th ed.). Wiley.

Romano, S. (2017). *Moralising poverty: The 'undeserving' poor in the public gaze*. Routledge.

Rose, M., Nadler, J., & Clark, J. (2006). Appropriately upset? emotion norms and perceptions of crime victims. *Law and Human Behavior, 30*(2), 203–219.

Ross, J. (2004). 'He looks guilty': Reforming good character evidence to undercut the presumption of guilt. *University of Pittsburgh Law Review, 65*, 227–279.

Rossetti, P., Mayes, A., & Moroz, A. (2017). *Victim of the system: The experiences, interests and rights of victims of crime in the criminal justice process*. Victim Support.

Rosulek, L. F. (2015). *Dueling discourses: The construction of reality in closing arguments*. Oxford University Press.

Rothschild, B. (2000). *The body remembers*. Norton.

Rumney, P. (2006). False allegations of rape. *Cambridge Law Journal, 65*(1), 128–158.

Rumney, P. (2009). Gay male rape victims: Law enforcement, social attitudes and barriers to recognition. *The International Journal of Human Rights, 13*(2–3), 233–250.

Rumney, P., & McPhee, D. (2020). The evidential value of electronic communications data in rape and sexual offence cases. *Criminal Law Review*, 1–16.

Rumney, P., & McPhee, D. (2021). Offender-centric policing in cases of rape. *The Journal of Criminal Law*, 1–16.

Rumsey, M. C. (1976). Effects of defendant background and remorse on sentencing judgments. *Journal of Applied Social Psychology*, 6(1), 64–68.

Salter, E. (2018). A media discourse analysis of lone parents in the UK: Investigating the stereotype. In L. Bernardi & D. Mortelmans (Eds.), *Lone parenthood in the life course* (pp. 55–74). Springer.

Sanday, P. R. (1997). The socio-cultural context of rape: A cross-cultural study. In L. L. O'Toole & J. R. Schiffman (Eds.), *Gender violence: Interdisciplinary perspectives* (pp. 52–66). New York University Press.

Savage, J. (2016). *Mental health and housing*. Mental Health Foundation.

Savitsky, J. C., & Sim, M. E. (1974). Trading emotions equity theory of reward and punishment. *Journal of Communication*, 24(3), 140–147.

Schwark, S. (2017). Visual representations of sexual violence in online news outlets. *Frontiers in Psychology*, 8, 774.

Schwarz, K. (2021). Barriers to justice: 'We are still governed by the idea that women lie about sexual assault'. *The Guardian*. https://www.theguardian.com/society/2021/mar/20/barriers-to-justice-we-are-still-governed-by-the-idea-that-women-lie-about-sexual-assault. Accessed 22 July 2021.

Scottish Government. (2020). *Criminal proceedings in Scotland: 2018–2019*. Scottish Government. https://www.gov.scot/publications/criminal-proceedings-scotland-2018-19/pages/4/. Accessed 22 July 2021.

Seidman, S. (1991). *Romantic longings: Love in America, 1830–1980*. Routledge.

Selseng, L. B. (2017). Formula stories of the "substance-using client": Addicted, unreliable, deteriorating, and stigmatized. *Contemporary Drug Problems*, 44(2), 87–104.

Shields, S. A. (2013). Gender and emotion: What we think we know, what we need to know, and why it matters. *Psychology of Women Quarterly*, 37(4), 423–435.

Sholl, E. W. (2013). Exhibit facebook: The discoverability and admissibility of social media evidence. *Tulane Journal of Technology and Intellectual Property*, 16, 207–230.

Shorter, E. (1991). *Women's bodies*. Transaction Publishing.

Sims, C. M., Noel, N. E., & Maisto, S. A. (2007). Rape blame as a function of alcohol presence and resistance type. *Addictive Behaviors*, 32(12), 2766–2775.

Skeggs, B. (1997). *Formations of class & gender*. Sage.

Skeggs, B. (2004). *Class, self, culture*. Routledge.

Skeggs, B. (2005). The making of class and gender through visualizing moral subject formation. *Sociology*, 39(5), 965–982.

Skeggs, B. (2011). Imagining personhood differently: Person value and autonomist working-class value practices. *The Sociological Review*, 59(3), 496–513.

Skeggs, B., & Wood, H. (2012). *Reacting to reality television.* Routledge.

Smart, C. (1989). *Feminism and the power of law.* Routledge.

Smart, C. (1992). The woman of legal discourse. *Social & Legal Studies, 1*(1), 29–44.

Smart, C. (1995). *Law, crime and sexuality.* Sage.

Smith, O. (2018). *Rape trials in England and Wales: Observing justice and rethinking rape myths.* Palgrave Macmillan.

Smith, O. (2020). *Researching English sexual violence trials using court observation methods: Research methods cases Part 1.* Sage.

Smith, O. (2021). Cultural scaffolding and the long view of rape trials. In R. Killean, E. Dowds, & A. M. McAlinden (Eds.), *Sexual violence on trial* (pp. 241–253). Routledge.

Smith, O., & Daly, E. (2020). *Evaluation of the sexual violence complainants' advocate scheme.* Loughborough University.

Smith, O., & Skinner, T. (2017). How rape myths are used and challenged in rape and sexual assault trials. *Social & Legal Studies, 26*(4), 441–466.

Somer, E., & Szwarcberg, S. (2001). Variables in delayed disclosure of childhood sexual abuse. *American Journal of Orthopsychiatry, 71*(3), 332–341.

Spencer, B. (2016). The impact of class and sexuality-based stereotyping on rape blame. *Sexualization, Media, & Society, 2*(2), 1–8.

Stabile, B., Grant, A., Purohit, H., & Rama, M. (2019). "She Lied": Social construction, rape myth prevalence in social media, and sexual assault policy. *Sexuality, Gender & Policy, 2*(2), 80–96.

Stanko, B., & Williams, E. (2009). Reviewing rape and rape allegations in London: What are the vulnerabilities of the victims who report to the police? In M. Horvath & J. Brown (Eds.), *Rape: Challenging contemporary thinking* (pp. 207–225). Willan.

Stanko, E. (2013). *Intimate intrusions.* Taylor and Francis.

Stanley, C. A. (2007). When counter narratives meet master narratives in the journal editorial-review process. *Educational Researcher, 36*(1), 14–24.

Stepney, M. (2015). The challenge of hyper-sexual femininity and binge drinking: A feminist psychoanalytic response. *Subjectivity, 8*(1), 57–73.

Stevenson, K. (2000). Unequivocal victims: The historical roots of the mystification of the female complainant in rape cases. *Feminist Legal Studies, 8*(3), 343–366.

Stewart, J. (2016). *Child guidance in Britain, 1918–1955: The dangerous age of childhood.* Routledge.

Sue, D. W., Capodilupo, C. M., Torino, G. C., Bucceri, J. M., Holder, A. M. B., Nadal, K. L., & Esquilin, M. (2007). Racial microaggressions in everyday life. *The American Psychologist, 62*(4), 271–286.

Swain, S., & Howe, R. (1995). *Single mothers and their children: Disposal, punishment and survival in Australia.* Cambridge University Press.

Swim, J. K., Aikin, K. J., Hall, W. S., & Hunter, B. A. (1995). Sexism and racism: Old-fashioned and modern prejudices. *Journal of Personality and Social Psychology, 68*(2), 199–214.

Talwar, V., & Crossman, A. M. (2012). Children's lies and their detection: Implications for child witness testimony. *Developmental Review, 32*(4), 337–359.

Taylor, N., & Joudo, J. L. (2005). *The impact of pre-recorded video and closed-circuit television testimony by adult sexual assault complainants on jury decision-making: An experimental study*. Australian Institute of Criminology.

Temkin, J. (1984). Regulating sexual history evidence—The limits of discretionary legislation. *International and Comparative Law Quarterly, 33*(4), 942–978.

Temkin, J. (2000). Prosecuting and defending rape: Perspectives from the bar. *Journal of Law and Society, 27*(2), 219–248.

Temkin, J. (2002). Digging the dirt: Disclosure of records in sexual assault cases. *Cambridge Law Journal, 61*(1), 126.

Temkin, J. (2010). 'And always keep a-hold of nurse, for fear of finding something worse': Challenging rape myths in the courtroom. *New Criminal Law Review: An International and Interdisciplinary Journal, 13*(4), 710–734.

Temkin, J., Gray, J. M., & Barrett, J. (2018). Different functions of rape myth use in court: Findings from a trial observation study. *Feminist Criminology, 13*(2), 205–226.

Temkin, J., & Krahé, B. (2008). *Sexual assault and the justice gap*. Hart.

The Bible. (2000). *Contemporary English Version*. HarperCollins.

Thiara, R., & Gill, A. K. (2010). Understanding violence against South Asian women. In R. Thiara & A. K. Gill (Eds.), *Violence against women in South Asian communities* (pp. 29–54). Jessica Kingsley Publishers.

Thiara, R., & Roy, S. (2020). *Reclaiming voice: Minoritised women and sexual violence*. Imkaan. https://829ef90d-0745-49b2-b404-cbea85f15fda.fil esusr.com/ugd/f98049_a0f11db6395a48fbbac0e40da899dcb8.pdf. Accessed 10 January 2021.

Thomas, C. (2020). The 21st century jury: Contempt, bias and the impact of jury service. *Criminal Law Review, 11*, 987–1011.

Thompson, S. B. N., Merrifield, A. S., & Chinnery, H. (2011). Are Mock Jurors influenced by the defendants gender, socio-economic status and emotional state in forensic medicine? *Forensic Medicine, 2*(2), WMC001632.

Tihelková, A. (2015). Framing the 'scroungers': The re-emergence of the stereotype of the undeserving poor and its reflection in the British press. *Brno Studies in English, 41*(2), 121–139.

Topping, A. (2021). Rape prosecution review failed to engage with victims, say survivor groups. *The Guardian*. https://www.theguardian.com/society/

2021/may/27/rape-prosecution-review-failed-to-engage-with-victims-say-sur vivor-groups. Accessed 23 September 2021.

Topping, A., & Barr, C. (2018). Revealed: Less than a third of young men prosecuted for rape are convicted. *Guardian*. https://www.theguardian. com/society/2018/sep/23/revealed-less-than-a-third-of-young-men-prosec uted-for-are-convicted. Accessed 03 April 2020.

Tosh, J. (2015). "Rape Me, I'm Irish": An analysis of the intersecting discourses of anti-irish racism and sexual violence. *Intersectionalities: A Global Journal of Social Work Analysis, Research, Polity, and Practice, 4*(1), 59–81.

Trades Union Congress. (2017). *Mental health and employment*. Trades Union Congress.

Trocmé, N., & Bala, N. (2005). False allegations of abuse and neglect when parents separate. *Child Abuse & Neglect, 29*(12), 1333–1345.

Uncel, M. (2011). "Facebook is now friends with the court": Current federal rules and social media evidence. *Jurimetrics, 52*, 43–69.

Ussher, J. M. (2011). *The madness of women*. Routledge.

Ussher, J. M. (2013). Diagnosing difficult women and pathologising femininity: Gender bias in psychiatric nosology. *Feminism & Psychology, 23*(1), 63–69.

Vagni, G. (2019). Alone together: Gender inequalities in couple time. *Social Indicators Research, 146*(3), 487–509.

van Doorn, B., & Bos, A. (2017). Are visual depictions of poverty in the US gendered and racialized? In W. van Oorschot, F. Roosma, B. Meuleman, & T. Reeskens (Eds.), *The social legitimacy of targeted welfare* (pp. 113–126). Edward Elgar Publishing.

Vera-Gray, F. (2017). Outlook: Girlhood, agency, and embodied space for action. In B. Formark, H. Mulari, & M. Voipio (Eds.), *Nordic Girlhoods* (pp. 127–135). Palgrave Macmillan.

Waites, M. (2005). *The age of consent*. Palgrave Macmillan.

Walker, T., Foster, A., Majeed-Ariss, R., & Horvath, M. (2021). The justice system is failing victims and survivors of sexual violence. *The Psychologist, 34*, 42–45.

Walkerdine, V., & Lucey, H. (1989). *Democracy in the kitchen*. Virago.

Watt, P. (2006). Respectability, roughness and 'race': Neighbourhood place images and the making of working-class social distinctions in London. *International Journal of Urban and Regional Research, 30*(4), 776–797.

Weare, S. (2021). "I feel permanently traumatized by it": Physical and emotional impacts reported by men forced to penetrate women in the United Kingdom. *Journal of Interpersonal Violence, 36*(13–14), 6621–6646.

Webb, L. (2015). Shame transfigured: Slut-Shaming from Rome to Cyberspace. *First Monday, 20*(4), 41.

Weiser, D. A. (2017). Confronting myths about sexual assault: A feminist analysis of the false report literature. *Family Relations, 66*(1), 46–60.

Welshman, J. (2013). *Underclass: A history of the excluded since 1880* (2nd ed.). Bloomsbury.

Wessel, E. M., Bollingmo, G. C., Sonsteby, C., Nielsen, L. M., Eilertsen, D. E., & Magnussen, S. (2012). The emotional witness effect: Story content, emotional valence and credibility of a male suspect. *Psychology Crime & Law, 18*(5), 417–430.

West, C. M. (2004). Mammy, Jezebel, and Sapphire: Developing an 'oppositional gaze' toward the images of Black women. In J. C. Chrisler, C. Golden, & P. D. Rozee (Eds.), *Lectures on the psychology of women* (3rd ed., pp. 237–252). McGraw-Hill.

Wheatcroft, J. M., Wagstaff, G. F., & Moran, A. (2009). Revictimizing the victim? How rape victims experience the UK legal system. *Victims & Offenders, 4*(3), 265–284.

Wilkinson-Ryan, T. (2005). Admitting mental health evidence to impeach the credibility of a sexual assault complainant. *University of Pennsylvania Law Review, 153*(4), 1373–1397.

Willmott, D., Boduszek, D., & Booth, N. (2017). The English Jury on Trial. *Custodial Review, 82*, 12–14.

Willmott, D., Boduszek, D., & Hudspith, L. (2021). Jury decision making in rape trials: An attitude problem? In G. Towl & D. Crighton (Eds.), *Forensic psychology* (3rd ed., pp. 94–119). Wiley.

Wingfield, A. H. (2010). Are some emotions marked 'whites only'? Racialized feeling rules in professional workplaces. *Social Problems, 57*(2), 251–268.

Wolchover, D., & Heaton-Armstrong, A. (2008). Debunking rape myths. *New Law Journal, 158*(7305), 117.

Wolfinger, E. (2014). Australia's welfare discourse and news: Presenting single mothers. *Global Media Journal: Australian Edition, 8*(2), 1–16.

Wood, H. (2017). The politics of hyperbole on Geordie Shore: Class, gender, youth and excess. *European Journal of Cultural Studies, 20*(1), 39–55.

Wood, H., & Skeggs, B. (2008). Spectacular morality: Reality television, individualisation and the re-making of the working class. In D. Hesmondhalgh & J. Toynbee (Eds.), *The media and social theory* (pp.177–193). Routledge.

Yamamoto, E. K., Haia, M., & Kalama, D. (1994). Courts and the cultural performance: Native Hawaiians' Uncertain Federal and State Law Rights to Sue. *University of Hawai'i Law Review, 16*, 1–493.

Young, S. L., & Maguire, K. C. (2003). Talking about sexual violence. *Women and Language, 26*(2), 40.

Zaccour, S. (2018). Crazy women and hysterical mothers: The gendered use of medical-health labels in custody disputes. *Canadian Journal of Family Law, 31*(1), 57.

INDEX

Printed by Printforce, United Kingdom